Raving at Usurers

Raving at Usurers

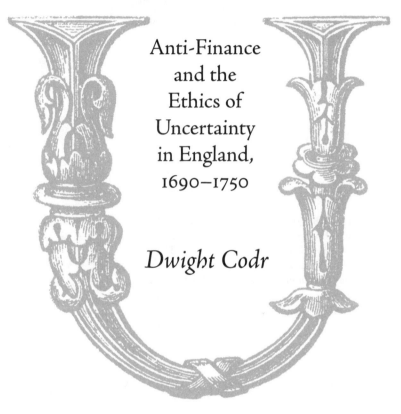

Anti-Finance
and the
Ethics of
Uncertainty
in England,
1690–1750

Dwight Codr

UNIVERSITY OF VIRGINIA PRESS

Charlottesville and London

University of Virginia Press
© 2016 by the Rector and Visitors of the University of Virginia
All rights reserved
Printed in the United States of America on acid-free paper

First published 2016

1 3 5 7 9 8 6 4 2

Library of Congress Cataloging-in-Publication Data
Codr, Dwight, 1975–
    Raving at usurers : anti-finance and the ethics of uncertainty in England, 1690–1750 /
Dwight Codr.
        pages   cm
    Includes bibliographical references and index.
    ISBN 978-0-8139-3780-9 (cloth : alk. paper) — ISBN 978-0-8139-3781-6 (e-book)
        1. Usury—Great Britain—History—18th century. 2. Usury in literature—History—18th
century. 3. Usury—Religious aspects—Christianity—History. 4. Finance—Great Britain—
History—18th century. 5. Economics—Great Britain—History—18th century. 6. Great
Britain—Economic conditions—18th century. I. Title.
    HG1623.G7C63 2016
    332.8'3094209033—dc23

                                                                                2015025725

To my parents
Josef and Pearl Codr

Contents

Acknowledgments

What began as an exploration of the rise of financial capitalism in the eighteenth century and ended as a book on the legacy of resistance to that rise would not have been possible without the inspiration, encouragement, advice, generosity, and patience of countless people. But since I've discovered that the seeds of books are planted long before the research and writing begins, I must thank, first and foremost, my many teachers: Francis McMann of George Washington High School, Cedar Rapids, Iowa; Cheryl Herr, Ruedi Kuenzli, and Robert Latham, all then at the University of Iowa; Barbara Correll, Reeve Parker, Harry Shaw, Gordon Teskey, and Rachel Weil, all then at Cornell University; and Vincent Pecora, whose seminar on modernity and religion at the School for Criticism and Theory at Cornell first introduced me to many of the topics and authors explored in this book. Most importantly, Laura Brown, Fredric Bogel, and Neil Saccamano provided essential guidance and advice as the earliest incarnations of this project took shape as a dissertation at Cornell, and I am deeply grateful for their further support since then.

At the opposite end of the spectrum were the institutions whose material assistance made the completion of this manuscript possible. Thank you to Elisabeth Fairman and Sarah Welcome, at the Yale Center for British Art, for their help in researching images relating to commerce and risk in the eighteenth century and to the Yale Center itself for permission to reprint both Christopher Wren's plan for London and the cover image for this book. Thanks as well to Rachel Cosgrave, at Lambeth Palace Library, London, for her assistance in tracking down materials pertaining to David Jones and St. Mary Woolnoth. Finally, I would like to thank the Office of the Dean of the College of Liberal Arts and Sciences and the CLAS Book Support Committee here at UConn for providing a subvention to underwrite the publication of this book. I consider myself fortunate to work with colleagues and administrators who express their commitment to humanistic research and publication in meaningful, tangible ways.

Between these two, I wish to acknowledge my former colleagues at Tulane University. Thomas Albrecht, Michelle Kohler, Felipe Smith, and Molly Travis provided moral support, wisdom, and encouragement during my time there. I owe special thanks to Scott Oldenberg, who patiently listened to me as the argument for this book came into focus and provided insight into the commercial and cultural worlds of early modern England.

When I arrived at the University of Connecticut in 2011, I was greeted with, and profoundly benefited by, the wisdom and friendship of the members of its faculty. Charles Mahoney, in particular, offered support, advice, and input from the beginning of my time at UConn to the finishing stages of this project, but many others contributed along the way, including Frederick Biggs, Tom Deans, Anna Mae Duane, Clare Eby, Albert "Hap" Fairbanks, Oliver Hiob, Clare Costley King'oo, Rachael Lynch, Jean Marsden, Shawn Salvant, Cathy Schlund-Vials, Gregory Colón Semenza, Fiona Somerset, Kathleen Tonry, Sarah Winter, and Chris Vials. I would also like to extend my gratitude to Wayne Franklin, Margaret Breen, and Robert Hasenfratz, whose value as colleagues and friends was often exceeded by their value as my advocates during their respective times as heads of the Department of English. In addition to generally providing tireless support of the intellectual community at UConn, Sherry Harris and Brendan Kane, in their respective capacities as director and associate director of the University of Connecticut Humanities Institute, supported a talk on the earliest versions of my research on David Jones (now chapter 1).

Many people in the wider community of eighteenth-century studies patiently endured my thoughts on the topics addressed in this book in formal or informal contexts or provided me with suggestions for improvement. I am particularly grateful to Ramesh Mallipeddi for his incisive and challenging but invariably supportive commentary on my work for several years but also for introducing me to Angie Hogan at the University of Virginia Press. Jesse Molesworth and Rebecca Spang kindly invited me to participate in the Center for Eighteenth-Century Studies annual workshop at Indiana University, Bloomington, where Fritz Breithaupt generously responded to an early version of chapter 4.

My gratitude also extends to Katherine Ellison, Kathleen "Kit" Kincaide, Andreas Mueller, Benjamin Pauley, Wolfram Schmidgen, Nicholas Seager, and other members of the Daniel Defoe Society for allowing me to share my work with them. Christine Desan, Chris Fauske, James Hartley, and Sean

Moore of the Money, Power, Print interdisciplinary study group helped me to refine what was once a rough conception of 1690s literature on projects into chapter 2. Concerning that work, I would also like to thank Brett McInelly and the AMS Press for permission to reprint parts of "Expectation and amendment maketh me to become an usurer: Usury, Providentialism, and the Age of Projects," from *Religion in the Age of Enlightenment* 1:1 (Spring 2010): 147–69, which now appear in chapters 1 and 2.

Many other individuals offered insight and encouragement along the way, and in a book that concerns itself with gifts and the unexpected returns they may yield the giver, one at once feels a particular obligation to note occasional contributions and simultaneously recognizes the inadequacy of doing so. Even so, a warm thank-you to David Alvarez, Srinivas Aravamudan, Joseph Bartolomeo, Gabriel Cervantes, Al Coppola, Andrew Curran, Kathryn Duncan, David Fairer, Michael Genovese, Evan Gottlieb, Eugenia Zuroski Jenkins, Betty Joseph, Suvir Kaul, Jess Keiser, Robert Markley, Andrew McKendry, Heather McKendry, James Mulholland, Daniel O'Quinn, Laura Rosenthal, Michael Rotenberg-Schwartz, Courtney Weiss Smith, Susan Spencer, Laura Stevens, Rajani Sudan, and Phyllis Thompson. I would like to single out David Mazella for particular thanks. No one who knows David can deny his extraordinary generosity, and I write with complete confidence that without it neither this book nor its author would be where they are today.

To my students over the years, I thank you for giving me the opportunity to turn my rarified thoughts into (mostly) sensible ideas. I am particularly grateful to the graduate students in my Culture of Money before the Science of Economics seminar at UConn in the spring of 2013: Brandon Benevento, Cory Charpentier, Matthew Jones, George Moore, Erick Piller, Eleanor Reeds, and Emily Slater. Christina Solomon and Melissa Rohrer have also provided invaluable contributions to the present work.

I would also like to give thanks for the incredible support and encouragement of the wonderful team at the University of Virginia Press. Angie Hogan's commitment of time, energy, and enthusiasm for this project came at precisely the right time in this project's development. I cannot imagine it possible to work with a more generous and rigorous editor. Morgan Myers and Joanne Allen provided essential editorial services and support, without which the current book would not live up to the name. I am also thankful to the anonymous readers of this manuscript, whose suggestions proved invaluable in the final course of revisions.

Friends and family provided laughter, love, and, most of all, perspective throughout the long process of bringing this project to completion. Gail

Braddock-Quagliata, LeBaron "Loyal Friend" Codr, David Coombs, Deborah and Timothy Freeman, Michelle Gerber, Susan Hall, Brandon Harvey, Raymond Malewitz, George McCormick, Sarah Mesle, Tom Moody, Paula Morris, Angela Naimou, Niko Poulakos, Justin Quagliata, "Sweet" Lou Rust, Joseph Skala, and Meredith and Stephen Wu provided hefty doses of all three. In addition to providing all of the above, my sister, Stacie Codr, and her husband, Jason Miller, provide me with living reminders of the ethics this book aims to promote. And without the love, kindness, and very material support of my parents, Josef and Pearl Codr, not only would I have been unable to write this book, which required support in all of these forms, but I would have had nothing to write about. For these and a thousand other reasons this book is dedicated to them.

Finally, thank-you to my loving and beloved wife, Meghan Freeman. My warmest advocate, closest confidant, wisest counselor, sharpest critic, and best friend, her spirit is woven into every page of this book. While I take responsibility for all of its failings, she deserves credit for any and all of its successes.

Raving at Usurers

Introduction

USURY HAS always suffered from problems of definition; usurers themselves, therefore, were long considered somewhat difficult to identify. As the Church of England clergyman Miles Mosse put it toward the end of the sixteenth century, "So many shapes he had, as no man can expresse. So may we say of usurers: sometimes they appear in one shape, sometimes in another, sometimes they take one course, sometimes another: yea they have many a quillitie, and many a subtiltie, which no writer that hath not been bounde twise seven yeares prentise to the trade, is able to disclose" (68). "Had I," Mosse goes on to lament, "an hundred tounges [*sic*], or a marble memorie, or an infatigable industry, I could no more utter, or record, or finde out, the innumerable devices which usurers have to oppresse the poore" (68). Appreciating the history that gave rise to Mosse's frustration in trying to delineate the scope of usurious practice, Eric Kerridge has convincingly shown that usury meant different things for different early modern writers and that its narrow meaning, the meaning we attribute to it most often today—that is, the taking of excessive interest on loans—was only one among many possible understandings of it.[1] In the larger context of economic history, usury's rich, nuanced, and nonlinear course—already anticipated in Mosse's recognition of usury's polymorphism, its inability to be uttered, recorded, or even fully discovered in an account of it—reaches, nevertheless, a rather sudden and definitive end. As the eminent modern historian of usury Norman Jones put it in a brief Internet postscript to his brilliant study *God and the Moneylenders:*

Usury and Law in Early Modern England (1989), "By the eighteenth century
the moral issue of usury was no longer of interest to most Protestant thinkers.
In practice lending at interest with collateral had become normal, as had deposit banking" ("Usury").[2] In its essence, this view keeps with the scholarship
of a previous generation, which likewise argued that by "the middle of the
seventeenth century, the traditionalist forces [against usury] had been thoroughly routed in Protestant lands" (Nelson 95).[3] Beyond Norman Jones and
Ben Nelson, historians of the modern economy largely agree that after nearly
two thousand years, the volatile history of usury had abruptly come to a close.
Coinciding with what P. G. M. Dickson has called "the financial revolution
in England," this conclusion also marked a new beginning: that of modern
financial capitalism.

This book aims to explore usury's oddly abrupt terminus in what amounts
to the decade of the 1690s, when Dickson's revolution was truly under way,
instances of raving rather than rational argument, an ethic grounded in risk
and uncertainty, the bedrock upon which the early modern critique of usury
had been based, continued in literary, intellectual, and cultural contexts of the
late seventeenth and eighteenth centuries. The reason this was possible—that
concerns about usury were obviated, while the ethic underlying usury's prohibition remained in force—was that usury meant not one but at least two
things. In terms of charging interest on loans, usury was legally prohibited,
a prohibition deriving from the Old Testament and from certain readings
of Aristotle's hypothesis regarding the innate barrenness of money. That is,
there were explicit biblical commands that prohibited the taking of interest
on money loans. But for early modern writers especially, usury also meant the
illicit attainment of certain future outcomes. This meaning was based principally on ethical principles of the New Testament, Luke 6:34–35 in particular:
"And if you lend only where you expect to be repaid, what credit is there in
that? Even sinners lend to each other to be repaid in full. But you must love
your enemies and do good, and lend without expecting any return; and you
will have a rich reward." These principles encouraged one to regard the narrow
goals of wealth as ultimately subordinate to a higher economy in which providence, not profit, was paramount. Appreciating that these two understandings of usury were not only distinct but often at odds with each other, I challenge the notion that the story of usury ends when the financial revolution
begins. I will argue that such a notion not only overlooks a complex of ethical
values—the ethics of uncertainty—that play an important but historiograph-
ically underdeveloped part in the financial-revolution story but also overlooks

the ways eighteenth-century writers such as Daniel Defoe and Henry Fielding maintained, mediated, and translated those values for a new era.

To access and explore the ethics of uncertainty, wherein it is the openness of the future and the resistance to closure that is privileged over and
against systems of power and meaning that aim at certainties, I have elected
to approach the intersection of money and culture from an anti-financial perspective. *Anti-finance*, a term that appears in the subtitle to this book, is thus
intended to refer to a way of reading or interpreting. For if *finance*, as the
OED informs us, quite literally means "to end" or "to settle a debt," a bringing
about of the end of things by settling debts, and making certain that assets
that are out come back in—a practice whose literary critical embodiment is
the reading of a text whose recompense and return is a meaning that the text
otherwise stingily withholds—*anti-financial* reading aims not only to discover
the positive existence in the time of financial revolution of a historically real
valorization of economic forms and goals at odds with such endings but also
to read literary texts with an eye to the way the texts open themselves up to
their readers and thereby relinquish control over their meanings. The neol-
ogism *anti-finance* is warranted, I argue, because it makes visible key ideas
about money and economic rationality that histories of finance or histories
structured by a financial motive or guided by financial assumptions tend
to overlook. This deliberately contrarian term, further, helps to recover and
reactivate an ethical position in history that narratives of financial progress
obscure or overwrite because of their exclusive focus on explicitly economic
texts and events. As David Hawkes crucially observes, because the critique of
capitalism in early modern England "was couched in the terms and concepts
of religion . . . it may not sound to twentieth century ears as though it has
anything to do with economic matters" (16). While Hawkes believes that the
period after the Reformation witnessed the emergence of a discrete economic
sphere (17, 191–92), I will suggest that because the early modern critique of
capitalism was couched in "the terms and concepts of religion," and because
those "terms and concepts" continued to give shape to eighteenth-century ethical thought, it is possible to see how that critique was extended and mediated
in eighteenth-century literature and culture.

Accordingly, anti-finance does not presuppose the nature of the archive
of economic history, even after the financial revolution, nor does it seek to
offer in any way a set of rules or prescriptions for the economic order. This
is because anti-finance, understood as a method for reading literature and
culture with an eye to openings and uncertainties, resists the temptation to
separate the economic order out from a more encompassing ethical order. By

contrast, I use the term *finance* (and its cognates) to refer not simply to the practical and theoretical developments in the movement, use, value, and organization of money in the late-seventeenth and eighteenth centuries but to a paradigm wherein these two orders—the economic and the ethical—are seen as in some way separate and distinct, which encourages one to make decisions with regard to one of these orders without having to refer to the other. Anti-finance seeks to recapture a moment that is prior, in both ontological and historical senses, to the existence of distinctively economic ways of knowing and being, before economics as such had become disembedded from a more capacious framework of experience. This requires a survey of texts not immediately recognizable as belonging to the category of economic literature. Which texts "belong" in the archive of economic history depends, in other words, on just what the disciplinary and discursive boundaries of economics are. As to its prescriptions, if anti-finance contains any positive suggestion at all, it is that the future ought to be allowed to arrive uncalculated, unscripted, unanticipated. In contrast, finance expressly aims to achieve the opposite in one manner or another, using an orthodox set of institutions and tools (banks, contracts, loans, etc.); or by employing strategies now more typically regarded as morally dubious or illegal (monopolization or engrossing, market manipulation, insider trading, etc.); and by encouraging the cultivation of habits of thought that conduce to what is often called "financial security," when the future ceases to be a matter of concern because it has become closed. That these tools, strategies, and ways of thinking today can be comfortably accommodated under the umbrella terms *finance, financial acts*, and *financial thinking* is perhaps some confirmation of Mosse's view that usury, which word I take to be an early modern approximation for *finance*, extended well beyond the clear-cut act of lending money for interest: "So many shapes he had, as no man can expresse" (68).

Notwithstanding the prominence of the ethic of uncertainty in early writings on usury, dominant models of economico-historical analysis can only treat such an ethic as aberration or delusion. This is because those models assume the naturalness and inevitability of a form of subjectivity that the ethic of uncertainty reveals to be a contingent product of historical circumstance; in particular, economics assumes that the subject wishes to minimize risk (the subject is rational), aims toward profit (the subject is self-maximizing), and therefore values expediency and efficiency (the subject must make haste to bring the future to him or her, wasting neither time nor resources). Consequently, I have found that poststructuralist ethical formulations, such as that of "the gift," are more useful in bringing this ethic to light than even the most oppositional political economies of the nineteenth and twentieth centuries, which often take for granted these or other economistic assumptions that theories of the gift expressly aim to critique.[4] What guides this study is a desire to approach the history of economics before these economistic assumptions— *economistic* rather than *economic* since they are specifically "of economists"— were allowed to drive the analysis, and to avoid presupposing the existence of the object that economic history aims to describe.[5] Chronologically speaking, the archive of anti-finance begins with early modern writings on the matter of usury, but not because such writings are part of the orthodox history of economics (though they certainly are). Rather, it is because such writings illustrate in vital ways—and arguably serve as the foundation for—an ethic that spreads itself across eighteenth-century literature and culture: the ethic of uncertainty.

Although it is my intention to interrogate the matter of finance using a rather different set of guidelines and goals, this study would not have been possible without the foundational work done on the eighteenth-century culture of credit by historians and literary critics, work that has grown from vital insights into the civic humanist tradition and the rise of credit, which J. G. A. Pocock defined as the fount from whence came both the radical Whiggism of the authors of *Cato's Letters*, John Trenchard (1668/69–1723) and Thomas Gordon (d. 1750), and the Country/Tory views of Henry St. John, 1st Viscount Bolingbroke (1678–1751). The frenzied post–South Sea Bubble attack by "Cato" on the fraudulence of stockjobbers and Bolingbroke's insistence upon the need for continued, vigilant resistance to the court and to oligarchy both entailed a fear that the moral basis of social order was being corrupted by privileged insiders. Insofar as civic humanists across the spectrum, in the name of justice, sought relief from the unequal and corrupt distribution of resources and power, they may be classed among the preoccupations of anti-finance. This study, however, departs from the Pocockian thesis that it was solely or even primarily the civic humanism of James Harrington (1611–1677) and his followers that provided an ideological basis for resistance to the financialization of England, arguing that an equally rich and more demotic basis for the antipathy to the idea that finance could or should be considered apart from other moral considerations can be located in a radical, Protestant, ethical claim that the merit of any practice, commercial or otherwise, consisted in the extent to which the subject exposed himself or herself to loss. In other words, anti-finance locates places where the very distinctions between commercial and noncommercial, economic and noneconomic, financial and nonfinancial are blurred or disputed, sometimes tacitly, sometimes explicitly. *Anti-finance* is meant to refer, therefore, not to a belief system adopted by individuals who were opposed to the interests of what we now might refer to as financiers; rather, anti-finance is a way of reading that seeks to bring into view a self-abnegating, often self-sacrificial ethic, one whose origins can be located in Protestant and especially Puritan traditions, an ethic that neither the openly anti-religious Bolingbroke nor the reformist "Cato," writing in the wake of the South Sea Bubble, would have been able to express, much less to commit to openly. It is not that Cato or Bolingbroke cannot be read anti-financially; the sorts of questions anti-finance asks and the forms of thought it seeks to recover are as relevant to them as they are to the texts and authors under consideration here. But because the ethic of uncertainty that anti-finance seeks to describe is more visible in texts of a spiritual nature, Bolingbroke and Cato factor less in this particular analysis.

It is perhaps because the archive studied by Pocock remains so distant from spiritual matters—if not religious ones, for his treatment of ecclesiastical politics is important to the story he unfolds—that he is able to proclaim changes in finance following the 1688 revolution as being "in a material and secular sense more revolutionary than anything to be detected in the generation of radical Puritanism."[6] But if, as Pocock argues, a "developing style of political economy" was "the dominant mode of Augustan political thought," it was also true that not all of those writing during the "Augustan half-century" would have understood "political economy" as Pocock does: roughly, as an embryonic form of the thoroughly "material and secular" political economy of Jeremy Bentham, Adam Smith, and David Ricardo (*MM* 426). For the assumptions and claims of anti-finance are less stably located than the civic humanist ideas charted by Pocock—who more or less finds their full articulation in Harrington—and their origins are scattered throughout ethical and spiritual discourses, rather than in political and ecclesiastical debates.[7] Indeed, even within "pro-finance" tracts that supported the *political* interests of monied men of the City, it is possible to discover support for an *ethics* of uncertainty. In due course, I will suggest that many of those developments toward a modern system of finance that Pocock's civic humanists expressly deemed ill-suited for a modern state—the development of a system of credit, most notably—can be read not as the overthrow of early modern anti-usury opinion but as its fulfillment and apotheosis; hence, the harmony between the ethic of uncertainty and neo-Harringtonianism is disrupted by the fact that the "financial revolution" happened not in spite of but because of the ethic of uncertainty. Thus, *anti-finance* is not simply meant to refer to a position adopted by writers, but to a way of thinking about the course of economic history in the transitional period charted by scholars such as Dickson and Pocock.

Since it would seem to contradict itself—that an ethic of uncertainty directed against finance gave rise to what we deem to be financial modernization—let me clarify that statement, since it also helps to account for the quotation marks I placed around the phrase *financial revolution* in the preceding paragraph. If we read the emergence of a market in credit and tradable paper securities, not as an expression of secular modernity, wherein religious belief and ethical scruples serve as so many hindrances to the triumphal emergence of modern capitalism, but rather as the logical outgrowth of the critique of the consolidation of wealth and the illegitimate circumvention of risk and uncertainty that made such consolidation possible, then what we have been calling a financial revolution could instead be described as an "anti-financial revolution," a revolution intended to counteract a growing tendency within the court to exercise power with and through the figure of money and to thus foreshorten, circumscribe, and delimit future possibility. Viewed from one perspective, the emergence of a national debt and the founding of the Bank of England seem to constitute breaks with history, new forms appropriate to a new, modern era. Viewed from another perspective, however, both of these developments created opportunities to break up the monopoly on finance by democratizing risk, by distributing risk opportunities to a wider swath of the English populace than had ever been known, and by institutionalizing what Craig Muldrew has called an "economy of obligation," wherein being "a creditor in an economic sense still had a strong social and ethical meaning" (3). This book aims to take those meanings seriously and to place them at the forefront of an analysis of financial culture in the later seventeenth and eighteenth centuries. Whereas most accounts of financial culture of this period suppose that the force driving these changes was a desire for greater wealth and for financial security, I will argue that another reason for "financial revolution" was the desire to subordinate economic security to higher ethical imperatives, which entailed the promotion of a system in which honest losses were preferable to dishonest gains. Individuals undoubtedly sought personal gain, but as the chapters that follow seek to show, new credit instruments and investment opportunities were capable of placating as well a deeply felt need to commit oneself, and to see others commit themselves, to forces beyond one's control and to thus satisfy an ethical demand that was at least as important as the desire for profit.[8]

Returning to Pocock, whereas he sees in the moralistic pro-credit writings of the mercantilist Charles Davenant (1656–1714) "the *beginnings* of a civic

morality of investment and exchange," arguing that Davenant aims to establish "an *equation* of the commercial ethic with the Christian" by frustrating
the selfish interests of "professional creditors" and promoting a "new morality"
of credit (*MM* 440, my emphasis), I would argue that far from the beginnings of such a morality, Davenant's belief in the vital role played by trust,
compassion, and dependency upon others in pecuniary affairs is little more
than a testament to the fact that an equation hardly needed to be made. It
had long been present in the early modern insistence upon the subordinacy
of the economic to the ethical.[9] For Pocock, Davenant's writings take on the
appearance of a "beginning" of commercial morality because the separation
of the "commercial ethic" from the "Christian" ethic is to a certain extent presupposed in the analysis.[10] I will argue that the equation of a commercial and
Christian ethic was a tacitly held view and that credit is important from a
historiographic standpoint not simply for the ways in which it signals modern
corruption but also for the ways in which it represents the extension of religious belief. And if it does represent such an extension, then the notion of the
emergence of a secular economic sphere at the end of the seventeenth century
must be reconsidered. This book aims to provide just such a reconsideration.

Lady Credit's Ancestors: Usury and Credit in the Financial Revolution

Among the most important historiographic indexes of scholarly belief in
a rupture between premodern and modern finance is the difference between
the chosen objects of study. Whereas early modern scholars tend to focus
on usury and appreciate its centrality to early economic thought, late-seven-
teenth- and eighteenth-century scholars tend to focus on the emergence of
a culture of credit because, it is argued or assumed, moral concerns about
lending and borrowing were dead. The modern era's central financial problem,
it is argued, is therefore not moral or religious but epistemological; the new
system of credit is challenging to writers of this later period not because of
its morality but because it calls into question what one knows, or thinks one
knows, about other people in that same system. This epistemological crisis
finds its rhetorical embodiment, it is argued, in the emergence of the trope
of Lady Credit. A rhetorical construct appearing most notably in the work of
Daniel Defoe (in the *Review*) and Joseph Addison (1672–1719) (in the *Spectator*), it was in the context of Pocock's argument regarding the emergence
of a distinction between land and paper values that he drew attention to the
figure, and scholars have tended to follow his lead in arguing that it is in this

context that Lady Credit takes on meaning.[11] I will read Lady Credit in a different context, but it is helpful to rehearse Pocock's argument to show how anti-finance provides a different way of seeing the decades of financial revolution. For if the "death of usury" argument depends upon an overly narrow conception of what usury was, so too has Lady Credit's signification been unduly limited by an insistence upon her function as a sign of epistemological crisis and upon her status as a unique by-product of financial revolution.

In the later decades of the seventeenth century, Pocock argues, faced with the rise of new institutions of credit, the landed interest formulated and promoted a revived civic humanist ideology that valorized, in Catherine Ingrassia's words, "the paternal, stable, and rational figure of the landed citizen" over and against the unstable, passionate, and chaotic figure of the financial speculator (3). The modern world of mobile property and credit "stood for fantasy, fiction, and social madness, the menace of a false consciousness which would engulf men in a sort of political Dunciad" (Pocock, *MM* 458). One of the more powerful strategies used to accomplish the goals of this ideology was feminizing the financial speculator, a figure described as being in thrall to Lady Credit. Adepts in the new world of credit became tainted by association; as a "feminized economic man" the speculator's "preoccupation with his own fantasies, desires, and imagination caused him to circulate as a vision of an undesirable socio-economic future" (Ingrassia 21). Credit, a fictional, fleeting, feminine source of value, associated with Fortuna and lunar variability, was widely repudiated by those who preferred instead the solid, masculine, feudal world of the past: "She contributed nothing beyond fantasy, opinion, and passion to making society virtuous in the first place. . . . Credit was irredeemably subjective and it would take all the authority of society to prevent her from breaking loose to submerge the world in a flood of fantasy" (Pocock, *MM* 457). In general, critics have followed Pocock's lead in arguing that Lady Credit portended a chaotic world of worthless paper in which signs would become detached from referents and everything that once was solid would melt into air.

More recently, however, Mary Poovey has observed that these difficulties notwithstanding, Lady Credit may have inadvertently served to enable the progress of finance insofar as she "drew the reader into an imaginary situation that built on, but then departed from, what the reader might personally have known and then enticed the reader to make another imaginative leap into a quasi-imaginary realm where the writer's own beliefs held sway" (98). Neither fact nor fiction, Lady Credit gave readers a tool to think with, an intellectual context wherein they could situate a certain experience or set of experi-

ences. In this respect, Lady Credit was not so much a figure for or against the
changing financial times, as Pocock and Ingrassia emphasize, but a moniker
to attach to those times so that their difference from earlier times might be
more clearly perceived. Because Lady Credit took on many of the attributes
of the figure of the virginal or coy "lass," eighteenth-century readers of Lady
Credit texts could situate their understanding of financial experience in terms
of prejudices regarding the characters of young women.

However, by stressing continuities, rather than ruptures, between the premodern and modern financial worlds, it is possible to see that readers would
have been able to understand Lady Credit not simply in terms of the coy
virgin featured in Restoration drama, the amatory novel, and the misogynist
poetry of the Augustan Age but also in terms of a longer history of allegorical
representations of wealth as a desirable woman, a history that extends back
to the time when attitudes toward usury determined one's relation to wealth
and commerce. While connections between Fortuna and Lady Credit, most
of which affirm the Pocockian image of credit's unpredictability and volatility,
have been duly noted, the history I write of here includes an entirely different
set of figures, including William Langland's Lady Meed (*Piers Plowman*, late
fourteenth century; *meed:* "something given in return for labour or service;
wages, hire; recompense, reward, deserts; a gift," but also, later, "corrupt gain;
bribery"), Thomas More's Lady Money (*Utopia*, 1516), Robert Wilson's Lady
Lucre (*Three Ladies of London*, 1584), Edmund Spenser's Lady Munera (*The
Faerie Queene*, 1596), Richard Barnfield's Lady Pecunia (*The Encomion of Lady
Pecunia*, 1598), Robert Burton's Queen Money (*Anatomy of Melancholy*, 1621),
Ben Jonson's Lady Argurion (*Cynthia's Revels*, 1601) and his Princess Pecunia
(*The Staple of News*, 1631), and the emblematic figure of Regina Pecunia, featured in Dutch paintings of the sixteenth and seventeenth centuries (Schama
327–29). In these texts and paintings, all featuring personified, female forms
of mobile property, it is often money's corruption by men, and not money
as such, that constitutes the problem. While some of the texts in this older
tradition—such as Spenser's—take an unequivocally negative stance on the
nature of material, earthly wealth, evoking all manner of stereotypes, most
contain the seeds of, or outright signs of, their authors' ambivalence on the
matter.[12] Much like the eighteenth-century Lady Credit, these earlier incarnations of mobile property often virtualize a commercial space or paradigm
that in itself is neither good nor bad but merely susceptible to abuse, exploitation, excess, and corruption. Often styled as a regent, these figures overlap and
intersect with the despotic figure of Fortuna. But unlike Fortuna, who raises
and destroys individuals irrespective of their actions, these personifications

are all meant to highlight the fact that the individuals who encounter or court them must make an ethical choice with respect to wealth. Clearly echoing Fortuna in certain respects, Lady Credit is connected as well to these other, moralistic figures in providing an opportunity for writers to comment on the ethical and spiritual life of those who pursue worldly goods.

Situating the figure of Lady Credit in this tradition, rather than regarding it as a unique by-product of financial revolution, raises the question whether Lady Credit, these older figures' eighteenth-century emblematic heir, ought also to be read as a figure for that which might be corrupted only under certain particular, abusive circumstances, and not as a fearful figure regarding the nature of credit per se. If so, if it is not credit but the abuse of credit that is at stake in the Lady Credit texts, then what is needed is a reassessment not only of the view that Lady Credit was uniquely responsible for a "lexicon of feminizing vocabulary that characterizes the commercial" (Sharpe and Zwicker 13), for Lady Pecunia was every bit as characteristically commercial as Lady Credit, but also, more broadly, of the "fantasy, fiction, and social madness" so often regarded as central to the forces that resisted financial revolution (Pocock, *MM* 458). Both Pocock and Carl Wennerlind, in their historical appraisals of the emergence of a credit economy, show that the instability of credit enabled its abuse, but neither notes the reverse of this formulation, that is, that if credit were treated in an ethical manner, so to speak, then presumably the economy would be healthy. Perhaps a better way of saying this would be that the deployment of Lady Credit in print culture signals the belief that a healthy economy is a reflection of an ethical citizenry. The misogynistic implications of connecting economic health and stability to feminine delicacy are still very much in evidence, but thinking about the connection in this way nevertheless shifts emphasis toward questions of commercial morality.

In reading Lady Credit in purely negative epistemological terms, as a modern form of whimsical Fortuna, Pocock reads the emergent moral discourse surrounding credit as a case of a more fundamentally amoral credit's need to be moralized (*MM* 439–41). Might Lady Credit have been developed for moral reasons in the first place? to signify a space of commerce more ethically sound than one in which a handful of privileged insiders hoarded the nation's wealth and tyrannically steered its commercial path? Wennerlind argues that credit's manipulability provided an opportunity for writers to promote their own, ultimately selfish political interests and agendas.[13] But insofar as many texts on credit, particularly Davenant's and Defoe's, present selfish interests as the great *threat* to credit, it is the selfishness, and not credit, that is under attack. I would not dispute that the manipulation of credit took place; I merely

wish to suggest that Lady Credit may also have signaled a utopian desire for
a more just commercial order, an order in which ethics, rather than interests,
would provide guiding principles. That credit was, or was capable of being,
selfishly manipulated does not, in other words, point to problems with credit
itself (this is not Wennerlind's argument, but it needs saying); rather, by per-
sonifying a system in which credit could possibly thrive, Lady Credit helped
to dramatize the potential impact of ethically unscrupulous financiers on such
a system. Neither Wennerlind nor Pocock addresses the fact that a world of
credit—which is to say, an interlocking system of faith and trust—might have
been seen as capable of reflecting, with greater accuracy, the ethical lives of the
people who participated in it and that Lady Credit therefore might have been
developed to help bring this ethical possibility into view.

Developed may not be the best term here, for to the extent that Lady
Credit did bring this ethical possibility into view, as a foil for the selfish agents
who concocted dubious plans for her, the figure was more a reproduction of
the tradition of Lady Pecunia, Lady Money, and so forth, than a reflection of
a unique, late-seventeenth-century "shift from a culture of honor and martial
prowess to a society of commerce and consumption" (Sharpe and Zwicker
13). On the contrary, as an iteration of this older tradition, Lady Credit suggests important continuities between the time when usury was a focal point
in the debate over commerce and the time after financial revolution, when the
discourse of usury is said to have lost its critical efficacy and the conceptual
foundations of usury's prohibition allegedly had crumbled under the force of
rationality and the decaying influence of secularization. I would not wish to
discount the fact that Lady Credit spoke to the particular instabilities and cultural forms of a new order of paper and belief, but it is important to note that
figure's ties to earlier, personified forms of fungible, mobile property. Marieke
de Goede has insightfully remarked that the eighteenth-century Lady Credit
is "neither essentially a virgin nor a whore, . . . she is what financial man will
make of her" (66). Likewise, for Richard Barnfield, writing at the end of the
sixteenth century, his Lady Pecunia "is, as shee is used; / Good of her selfe, but
bad if once abused" (160, lines 281–82).

While Barnfield's ironic encomium, in its dependence upon a dichotomy
of praise and blame, would seem to be criticizing Lady Pecunia and those in
thrall to her, his ultimate point is that these are two very different things and
that Lady Pecunia is, in fact, a force for good: "Good of her selfe, but bad if
once abused" (160, line 282). This is what further distinguishes her (and other
such female personifications of wealth) from Renaissance portrayals of Mammon as David Landreth has characterized that figure, with Mammon signify-

ing the coming of a time in which "gold will have erased all other values" (67). That is, unlike Mammon, whose filthy materiality makes money altogether sinful, Lady Pecunia and her kind signify a potentially salutary social arrangement of goods and resources. For Barnfield, it is, among other things, the illicit clipping of coins that constitutes an abuse of an otherwise unproblematic social phenomenon (money); in the case of Lady Pecunia's eighteenth-century heir, Lady Credit, it might similarly be said that the problem is less with her than it is with those who "abuse" her, who attempt to control or manipulate her for selfish reasons. It is an aspect of her character that is in evidence in both Whig and Tory representations. In Addison's *Spectator* allegory of Lady Credit, for instance, the forces of Tyranny, Anarchy, Bigotry, Atheism, and the Old Pretender cause Credit to flag, while the arrival of the forces of Liberty, Monarchy, Moderation, Religion, and Prince George enable her to flourish (190–91). For Defoe, yes, Lady Credit was elusive and fickle, bespeaking crises of representation and knowledge akin to the instabilities engendered by Fortuna, but she also served as an emblem for economic justice itself. As he put it in his characterization of Charles II's Stop of the Exchequer, "Thinking he had got her [Lady Credit] fast in his *Exchequer*, [Charles II] claps upon her, and shut up the Place; but she was too nimble for him: he got the Money indeed, *but he lost the* CREDIT; away she flew, and she never came near him again as long as he liv'd" (*Review* 3.5:18). For Defoe, who almost gleefully rehearses this Stuart misfortune, credit speaks the truth of commerce precisely because it is unstable, fickle, and fleeting, its volatility giving it power even over kings. Credit has a mind of its own, one that punishes those who seek to manipulate it. Speaking of Defoe's depiction of Lady Credit in the *Review*, Poovey rightly observes that Defoe "cast credit as the charming, enigmatic dominatrix," providing his readers with "an imaginative experience of the passivity and wonder Defoe says the tradesman felt" (100). Credit's instability was not a reason for its rejection, but the source of its strength and, I would add, its ethical appeal.

Lady Credit's distinguishing feature, therefore, was not instability but the implicit justice that instability guaranteed when individuals attempted to keep wealth all to themselves or to master the course of the nation's wealth. Insofar as she represented the decentralization of monetary and commercial power, Lady Credit did, as Pocock argues, threaten to destabilize traditional value, symbolized by land and incarnated as the civically minded landed aristocrat. But Lady Credit also pointed to the existence of strange motive powers beneath the surface of the "economy" that governed outcomes and ensured that those outcomes would reflect the moral and spiritual values of the people. It is true that under the spell of Lady Credit commerce might spin out of control, but the opposite of the loss of control was *not*, as some accounts of the period suggest, rational economic management or organization. The opposite of credit was financial chicanery, meddling, scheming, hoarding, conniving, jobbing, selfish pursuits, and crass materialism. Whereas Lady Credit is often read as an index of attitudes regarding the distinction between land and paper, where that figure's implied unpredictability and instability correspond to the uncertain realm of paper credit, Lady Credit also serves as an index of attitudes regarding the distinction between a world in which ethics constrains commercial practices and a world in which commerce—whether land- or paper-based matters not—seeks to break free from ethical constraints altogether. According to this alternative, structuring ideological divide, what some scholars have called the fickleness of Lady Credit might also be called the *fairness* of Lady Credit insofar as her existence beyond the control of individual humans meant that her decline would reflect the absence of fairness in an economic environment, while her increase would reflect the fact that that environment was healthy in an ethical sense.

The rise and fall of credit, as Addison puts it, results from exogenous factors, not from credit's inherent whimsy or arbitrariness. The Whig propagandist Abel Boyer (1667?–1729) similarly viewed credit as distinct from the people who made use of it and stressed how important moral virtues among the people were to its maintenance (Wennerlind 178–80). Charles Davenant made similar claims in his *Discourses on the Publick Revenues* (1.54, 2.273–76). In his *Essay upon Public Credit* (1710) Defoe expressed a related view: "[Credit is in] no way dependent upon Persons, Parliaments, or any particular Men, or Sett of Men, *as such*, in the World. . . .'Tis the Honour, the Justice, the Fair-Dealing, and the equal Conduct of *Men*, Bodies of Men, Nations, and People, that raise the thing call'd *Credit* among them; wheresoever this is found, CREDIT will live and thrive, grow and encrease" (53).[14] That he considered the forward and outward attempt to manage the economy pernicious to the health of his society is evidenced further in a companion essay to that on public credit, *An Essay upon Loans* (also 1710). There Defoe wrote that the establishment of the Bank of England in the 1690s "turn'd the whole City into a Corporation of Usury, and they appear'd not as a *Bank*, but rather one general Society of Bankers" who "Imposed upon and Opprest" the government until it could come to more favorable terms with subscribers to the bank (69). Defoe's emphasis, in other words, was not on the difference between land and paper but on the difference between oligarchic, oppressive systems of commerce and systems of commerce based, finally, upon honor, justice, fair dealing, and "the equal Conduct of *Men*," where credit had a vital, harmonizing purpose to play. Under such conditions, a bank could exist without turning into an oppressive "Corporation of Usury" (even in the eighteenth century we see that usury meant more than simply interest on loans). After the South Sea Bubble (1719), having borne witness to a crisis precipitated by the underhanded dealing of a few men who attempted to capitalize on their insider positions within the South Sea Company, Defoe could sincerely ask, "Do we ever think to restore Credit, and not restore Honesty?" (*Director* 276). The "mortal Stab to our Credit" that Defoe blamed on the company directors was not a sign of problems with the system of credit but a sign that England no longer deserved any credit (*Director* 276). As money had been for Barnfield, for Defoe credit was "Good of her selfe, but bad if once abused."

In terms of anti-finance, the version of Lady Credit I have described here is important because the figure reflects English culture's continuing commitment to an ethical foundation for the "economy." It is not simply that honesty is conducive, in an instrumental sense, to credit; for Defoe, they are two sides of the same coin. Credit was the institutional expression of the citizenry's ethical inner life, and not only was it impossible in practice to alter one without materially altering the other but it did not make theoretical sense. The interdependence of ethics and economics meant that it was more important to sustain an honest loss than to achieve a dishonest gain and that one needed to present himself or herself to the market as a vulnerable subject, constrained by higher ethical commitments, not as *homo economicus,* obedient only to the needs and desires of the self.

Situating Lady Credit in the history of female allegorical personifications of wealth—Money, Pecunia, and so on—further enables us to see how vitally connected credit is to the history of usury, understood in the broader ethical sense to which I alluded earlier, which chapters 1 and 2 explore in greater detail. I would like to focus briefly on one early modern anti-usury text in which an ethical economic arrangement of the nation comes to the reader in the form of a female figure. Unlike the more ambivalent portrayals of money by Langland, Spenser, More, Burton, Barnfield, Jonson, and others, that offered by Gerard de Malynes (fl. 1585–1641) in his 1601 allegory *Saint George for England* is an unabashed paean to a world in which commerce—figured in his text as the "faire & peereless daughter" rescued in the Saint George legend—is free from the vexations and terrors of a "Dragon" who flies on wings of "Usura palliata" and "Usura Explicata" (cloaked and open usury) and "devoureth and destroyeth daily the inhabitants of" the "flourishing Island" that the narrator of the allegory claims to be visiting (5).[15] We learn of this daughter and this dragon and the crimes of the dragon's many followers from an inhabitant of the island whom the narrator meets upon arrival. This inhabitant goes on to explain the island's dire need for rescue and the people's hopes "that God will be pleased to stirre up" a champion like Saint George who will be able to "destroy this hideous monster" (5).

Malynes's text is characterized by Wennerlind as part of the tradition of neo-Aristotelian political economy, but it is worth noting that while it is possible to view the tract as political economy, neo-Aristotelian or otherwise, casting it as such presents certain problems. Because the discourse of political economy as we understand it today largely eschews the treatment of Christian spiritual matters, viewing Malynes's work as political economy necessitates the elision of the very heart of his tract.[16] As Malynes puts it in the "Epistle Dedicatorie," "So ought all Christians alwaies to be ready to abandon all worldly goods & honours, for to follow their said generall Jesus Christ chearfully & with courage, for they do heare the note of battell daily preached unto them, under the most peaceable governement of her most excellent Majesty" ("Epistle Dedicatorie"). To presume that such professions of faith are adventitious to Malynes's more fundamentally "political economic" claims, neo-Aristotelian or otherwise, is to obscure the reasons why he wrote the tract and replace its spiritual grounding with a secular grounding that Malynes would have regarded as itself the very problem with the economic order.

For Malynes, an "economy" or a "political economy" without God and without the limiting conditions Christianity places on wealth and profit would be the very thing that he rails against: a culture of the dragon of usury. The fair and equal distribution of resources before the dragon had invaded the island (England) was

> manifest proofe, Justice to be ordained of God, as a measure amongst men on earth, to defend the feeble from the mighty, for the suppressing of injuries, and to roote out the wicked from among the good, prescribing how to live honestly, to hurt no man wilfully, and to render every man his due, carefully furthering what is right, and prohibiting what is wrong. . . . [Under such a regime] all things in the course of trafficke were caried on with an equalitie, free lending was used, hospitality maintained, commiseration towards the poore was exercised, and love which is the very summe and substance of the Law, did flourish to the generall comfort of a Christian society. (14–15)

Echoing Portia's mercy speech in William Shakespeare's *Merchant of Venice*, staged roughly two years prior to *Saint George's* publication, Malynes's claim that "Love . . . is the very summe and substance of the Law" reveals not only how important such a claim was in the fight against usury but also that Malynes and others defined usury as the absence of love and an abundance of "worldly cares" (16). A focus on these "worldly cares" leads one to turn "that which ought to be freely given" (a gift) into that which is sold (a commodity) (16). Under the influence of this "worldly" (by which Malynes means material and secular) influence of the dragon, all divine justice is banished: "I demaund where *Celestial* justice (which is the perfect consideration and dutie to God) is [to be] found" (27). Usury, for Malynes, encompassed a panoply of financial crimes, crimes, in fact, that political economy might consider virtues: husbanding one's resources, selling rather than giving, refusing charity, regarding one's wealth as a function of individual industry or wisdom (all wealth flows from God, Malynes insists), aspiring to new heights of wealth and accomplishment, indulging one's appetites, profiting in times of scarcity, working for wealth, and so forth. The usurer "maketh money to be the creede of the world, and perswade[s] men to seeke first money" (46); he will "not have men to depend upon the reward of God, but upon the reward of man" (46); the spirit of usury causes men to have their "harts set onely on worldly things" (48). The inhabitant goes on to enumerate the many crimes for which "usury" is responsible, but it should be clear that (a) usury is not understood as the *cause* of other crimes but is the category that subsumes all "economic" crimes; and (b) *usury* refers, for Malynes, not to interest on loans but to what we today call *economism*, the view that economics should be unimpeded by ethics, a view that enables all manner of crimes to take place under the guise of being simply amoral.

To return to the matter of female personifications of the economic sphere, Malynes's native inhabitant, having listed the dragon's various crimes, asks the narrator to compare the suffering of his "flourishing Island" to the suffering of the princess who was captured by the dragon and later rescued by Saint George. Compare, he asks, his beleaguered society to the "faire & peereles daughter" of the king of the realm in those legendary times, whose "bright splendent beames of angelicall beauty, do dim my sight, and, captivate my understanding" (49). This "Virgin and noble creature" on the one hand surely represents the then reigning "Virgin Queen" Elizabeth, but she also represents, in her innocence, mildness, and morality, a state of equality and fairness in the so-called economic sphere that the dragon Usury threatens to destroy.[17] The most sustained description in the text, Malynes's depiction of this "angellical beauty" comes in the form of a blazon enumerating her various noble attributes and serves as the pure image of which the preceding list of the dragon's myriad crimes can now be seen as a distorted and grotesque reflection. Her soft heart and eyes are juxtaposed to the hard-hearted usurers (52, 14); her companion "Lambe" stands against the dragon, who "feedeth most greedily" upon "the poorer sort" (52, 12); she submits to the dragon's cruelty with "perfect patience" (54), while those under the spell of the dragon anxiously labor to secure themselves against the loss of worldly goods (29–30, 35).

If she is a figure for a moral economy, however, she is also subject to variability and abuse in ways that anticipate, or perhaps prefigure, many of those attributes that would come to be associated with Lady Credit: in addition to being virginal and beautiful, she is "shining as the Moone" (51); when faced with the dragon, her mind, not unlike that of Addison's Lady Credit on beholding the forces of Tyranny, Atheism, and so on, is in a state of "agony" and she is "perplexed" (53); she cannot rescue herself from the dragon any more than Addison's or Defoe's Lady Credit can rescue herself from abuse. The inhabitant's comparison of his country to this particular "Lady" is expressly intended to show that the crimes of the people are reflected in the health and happiness of the economic order. What is required to restore both, Malynes continues, is the figure of Saint George, a figure who remarkably resembles and perhaps serves as a source for Addison's "Prince George," who, equally knight-errant-like, and aided by Liberty, Monarchy, Moderation, and Religion, rescues the wilting Lady Credit of *Spectator* 3. Finally, in Malynes's text, Saint George, representing the collective body of England itself, enters to figure the administration of justice armed with "faith," "righteousness," "salvation," "verity," and "the Cross": thus armed, "with the sword of the Spirit [he did] destroy this monster, and delivered this *Indian Phenix* & this Island, of that contagion & abominable hell hound" (55). For Malynes, a legal prohibition on lending would not alone solve the problem; also needed was an affirmation of Christian ethical virtues to counteract the rapacious cultural tendencies of finance. For Addison, administrative and executive power had to have ethical supports for their actions of and relating to credit, since credit's vitality depended not on a policy action but on a continual and unpredictable unfolding of interpersonal relationships that extended into the future. Although Malynes's tract may at first seem far afield from the concerns of the post-financial-revolution system of credit, his vision of an imperiled maiden saved from economic injustice by an authority animated by ethical principles nevertheless brings us quite close to Lady Credit, if she is understood not in terms of the division between land and paper but in terms of the division between ethical commerce and commerce conceived of as separate from ethics.

Anti-Finance and the Economic Sphere

The insight that writers of the early eighteenth century could not have comprehended the idea of an autonomous economic sphere, much less one whose rules, aims, and processes were unhinged from ethical traditions, has afforded scholars a powerful analytical tool for the reevaluation of eighteenth-century subjectivity, literature, and philosophy.[18] Mary Poovey and Margaret Schabas have shown that in the eighteenth century, before the autonomy of the realm of goods and services was posited by political economy, finance was mediated by imaginative social and cultural forms that are today no longer recognizably economic in appearance.[19] In the course of her analysis, Poovey observes that because early-eighteenth-century writers were not yet being guided by the distinction between fact and fiction, writing about such matters as credit and finance was, strictly speaking, neither fact nor fiction and could thus in a sense take on the appearance of either (77–85, 99–101). Poovey does direct her attention to an array of texts that do, in retrospect, display financial characteristics of one sort or another, but as both her and Sandra Sherman's readings of Defoe's novel *Roxana* as a medium for the discussion of credit also demonstrate, some of the texts that bore financial lessons, instructions, or meanings are to modern readers less obviously exemplary of financial writing than others.[20] By widening our view as to what constitutes the field of economics and finance, Poovey and Sherman have revealed surprising, alternative origins and contexts for what we now call the economic domain.[21] Beginning her study with the recognition that "political economy was not viewed as a separate and coherent discipline until" the mid-eighteenth century, Schabas, to take another example, has been able to show that eighteenth-century writers' "strong allegiance to the deity" (10–11) was fundamental to Enlightenment economic thought. Although I wish to locate points of resistance to, rather than anticipations of, political economy, I concur with these and other such scholars' view that the use of the terms and concepts of political economy in the analysis of seventeenth- and early-eighteenth-century life and culture produces a misleading image of such times. So I would like to extend the boundaries of financial writing farther still, using an abstracted set of beliefs about risk and calculation of future returns as they were articulated in debates about usury—the ethic of uncertainty—to link together texts both recognizably and not so recognizably financial in nature and to chart a historical dynamic that does not rise or fall so much as percolate and recur in new forms for ever-changing contexts.

Before the distinction between fact and fiction became operative, before the autonomy of economics as a discipline was fully established in the later eighteenth and nineteenth centuries, and before political economists, in their dreamy visions, had disembedded financial experience from the total lifeworld of individuals, writers also communicated lessons and ideas about the ethics of finance in realms far afield from what we today would regard as commercial or economic discourse.[22] But what is just as important, terms such as *credit*, *projects*, and *prudence*, which in their time were conceptually bound up with less obviously economic aspects of life (such as travel, religion, gift giving, love, and moral judgment), would eventually be wrenched from their original contexts and then conscripted into the service of a big-*E* Economics that needed to find traces of itself before it was disciplinarily manifest in order to establish the universality and eternality of its claims, in order to make it seem as though Economics was always there, waiting for systematization, latent in such tracts as those concerning credit, projects, and prudence. To be clear, the narrative of financial revolution has contributed immensely to our understanding of the ways in which England became modern, but it is only one narrative. And owing to the fact that the archive on which that narrative is founded depends upon a version of economic life that is itself a rhetorically constituted rather than real entity, deeply rooted and long-standing ethical reservations concerning what sixteenth-, seventeenth-, and eighteenth-century Protestants simply considered (and called) "worldliness"—under which banner the links between the economic and, say, the amorous become more apparent—have not been sufficiently factored into the narrative of financial history. It is not that religious tracts go unheeded by historians of economics, of course; rather, the ethical concerns such tracts raise—concerns typically couched in religious terms—are often regarded as being of secondary importance to a more primary economic meaning. To create a more complete picture of the historical culture of economics, it is critical to restore those elements that do not conform to or fit easily within a secular history of economics in the West.[23]

Appearing prominently in discourses concerning money and usury, these ethical reservations touched upon such matters as moneylending, profiteering, and fairness in commerce, but they also touched upon the calculative rationality and selfishness that modern financial regimes demand of their participants. Such matters appear to be strictly economic or financial, but only by virtue of narratives of modernization and secularization that posit separations of the economic and financial from earlier, relative totalities.[24] In fact, as I will argue, the narrative of financial revolution depends in part upon the view that those older reservations were in a state of decline or had become altogether obsolete. I will argue that an ethical embrace of risk and uncertainty—wherein it was one's vulnerability, rather than one's security, that constituted the ethical position—was pitted not so much against the *events* narrated in the history of the financial revolution but against the idea of a history in which economic life could be regarded as distinct from a natural, providential, and moral order. What I aim to illustrate is that while financial and economic systems did change in the seventeenth and eighteenth centuries in ways that rendered the terminology of usury ineffectual, the core values espoused in debates on usury persist in modified forms and were diffused into culture at large. What is at stake in recovering the history of ethical challenges to the regime of modern finance from these alternative contexts, from this wider archive, is the production of an awareness that while our present time is marked by an urgent need for reform, there is a rich tradition of thinking and writing *anti-financially* that can guide us in that process.

If we begin the story of modern finance from the standpoint of its ideological and institutional *triumph*, to use the term preferred by Albert O. Hirschman in his seminal book *The Passions and the Interests: Political Arguments for Capitalism before Its Triumph*, then a gradual conquering of religious belief by a newly moralized category of interests, the erosion of premodern values, and the adoption of forms of rationality suited to the world of interests are revealed. But in the midst of—or in the wake of? or in the face of?—yet another global economic crisis it is worth considering whether the linear story of triumph is not itself somehow vital to the maintenance of financial capitalism as it is currently understood and institutionally practiced. In the midst of crisis, that is, what does it mean to speak of triumph? It is better to think of it in terms of Raymond Williams's idea of hegemony.[25] In what does the hegemony of financial capitalism consist? Surely in the exploitation of labor, but also important is the iteration and reiteration of the narrative proclaiming its triumph over other patterns of thought and conduct. If we were to locate fundamental continuities between the premodern world of ethically regulated and restrained commercial practice and the events of the financial revolution, how would we evaluate the triumph of financial capitalism? Would that profession of triumph not itself come to seem one of the most potent ways for capitalism to insist upon its autonomy from ethics? This book does not attempt to offer a new history of finance so much as to reinterpret the meaning of finance at the end of the seventeenth century and

the beginning of the eighteenth, when economic and ethical life are often seen
to have been splitting apart. It argues that the financial revolution grew out
of, not in spite of, ethical beliefs promulgated in anti-usury literature. Altering
our perspective on financial revolution in this way reveals that the problem is
not so much the events of that revolution as the way in which those events
have been represented as discontinuous with the ethics of the past.

   Accordingly, this book attempts to go beyond a strictly economic paradigm when considering the risky decisions made by eighteenth-century writers and their characters. The economic paradigm dictates that taking risks
willfully is aberrant and irrational and, thus, decisions of consequence are
read and evaluated *economically*, that is, according to the degree to which they
satisfy need, maximize utility, or accommodate desire. What is left, I ask, of
decisions that are made without those goals—or any goals—in mind? The in-
terrogation of a certain modern understanding of political agency is thus also
an important objective of this book. While the chapters that follow illustrate
some of the benefits of reading the century from the standpoint of risk rather
than security, they do not aim to provide coverage of the ethic of uncertainty
so much as to define it and to show some of the principal ways in which its
remediation in the eighteenth century was also responsible for its apparent
decline.

   While I wish to retain something of what might be called human responsibility, and while I draw on an archive and history that is different from
hers, I share with Sandra Macpherson the sense that the contractual understanding of liberal agency is inadequate in addressing the complexities of the
eighteenth-century text or in accounting for self-canceling and ironic authorial
maneuvers that leave much of the work of understanding to the texts' future
readers, which I detect in both *Robinson Crusoe* and *Tom Jones* (3–4, 20–21).
To address this complexity, I have found useful David Hawkes's observation
that before the advent of political economy the most vibrant and challenging
perspectives on finance and capitalism are to be found not in economic texts
but in religious ones (16), though I wish to argue that the eighteenth century
continues the history he firmly places in the early modern period. Likewise,
while the focus of my study is somewhat different, I believe that Mark Valeri's
and Jennifer J. Baker's insights into the early transatlantic and American commercial worlds—where, in Baker's words, "financial outcomes" are intelligible
only as "providential dispensations" (28) and where, in Valeri's words, "systems
of exchange in the transatlantic market appeared to be means of society and
instruments of divine rule in the world" (*Heavenly Merchandize* 9)—can and
should be brought more fully to bear on the culture of eighteenth-century

England, where the force of religious conviction remained every bit as powerful as it was at its imperial periphery (Barnett 81–94). And finally, whereas Sean Moore has observed that the "Irish financial revolution" was the product of "an informal republic based on the shared risk of mutual investment, in which each lender depended on the others for protection of existing property and future interest payments," I would like to emphasize how this ethic of "shared risk" is made manifest as well within the "fiscal-military state" of England itself (3–4, 13). For if the Occupy Wall Street protests have taught us one thing, it is that financial societies are deeply divided ones. It is thus out of a posthumanist understanding of ethical possibility and a post-Weberian treatment of the relationship between economic and religious life that this book attempts to reconstruct the social logic of a culture under the sway of the ethics of uncertainty, bearing in mind throughout that not everything is reducible to a species of rationality that a much later liberal political economy invented and naturalized.

Relatedly, I argue that we must keep in mind that an economistic model of human motivations and desires influences most *accounts* of eighteenth-century literature and culture, even those that do not expressly aim to address economic history. Hence, while I aim to read certain familiar texts from the eighteenth century in new ways, I also discuss how twentieth- and twenty-first-century critical interpretations of writers such as Defoe and Fielding have embedded within them economistic assumptions that it is the aim of this book to reveal and critique. Jean Baudrillard provides some insight into the dangers of such an influence when he writes that economics exercises its power over other disciplines by forcing them to accept certain fundamental assumptions about rationality and need. Conceding that some disciplines have allowed for the cultural contingency of needs, Baudrillard goes on to remark that economism still haunts the analysis of social phenomena, pointedly observing that the admission of cultural contingency "is the zenith of liberal analysis, beyond which it is congenitally incapable of thinking" (73).

So much might be said of historical perspectives on eighteenth-century English culture that offer modern readers one of two alternatives: the needs of landed gentlemen or the needs of City merchants. Whose needs, it is asked, carried the day? How were these competing sets of needs negotiated in Parliament, for example, or in the coffeehouses? These are important questions, without a doubt, but the problem, ultimately, is that "the postulate of man endowed with needs and a natural inclination to satisfy them is never questioned. It is simply immersed in a historical and cultural dimension" (Baudrillard 73). Baudrillard's trenchant criticism of the sociology and psychology of

his day is perhaps even more valid as a criticism of economic historiography
of the seventeenth and eighteenth centuries, since the ethical constraints engendered by the usury prohibition were then still powerful enough to keep
economics fully embedded in the ethical lives of English men and women.
What would it mean to offer a history of economics, or to offer an economic
history of eighteenth-century literature, that does not use what amounts to
homo economicus—a need-satisfying, acquisitive, and rational individual—as
the elemental unit of its analysis? Anti-finance, I propose, enables one to approach such a history, as it attempts to call the naturalness and inevitability of
that unit into question.

   Chapters 1 and 2 aim to provide a history of the ethic of uncertainty and
illustrate that ethic's rootedness in the discourse concerning usury. Beginning on the threshold of financial revolution, in chapter 1 I reconstruct an
important but neglected pamphlet battle, precipitated by a sermon on usury
delivered in 1692 at a church on Lombard Street by a Welsh minister named
David Jones. The centrality—geographical and historical—of the Jones event
makes it one of considerable interest when trying to document the fate of
the anti-usury position in history, understood in the sense of both the facts
of history and the process of interpreting those facts.[26] Rereading the event
in both of these senses, I argue that not only does Jones evidence the persistence of an anti-usury position in a time and space presumably disposed to
exclude such a position, but his later elimination from the record shows how
the narrative of financial modernity's triumph produces a distorted and in
some ways inaccurate account of financial modernization. The chapter thus
serves two purposes. First, it shows that moral concerns about usury were
still very much alive at the end of the seventeenth century and that the belief
that ethics should constrain commerce, far from having been surmounted,
remained as intense as it had ever been. What must be accounted for, then, is
not why moral concerns about usury died but how they came to be thought
of as being dead. By tracing the decline of Jones's reputation in the eighteenth
century—in newspaper stories, occasional citations of the Jones affair in satires and essays, and in an oft-printed eighteenth-century poem written by
Christopher Pitt—and then situating that decline alongside a broader effort to discredit anti-usury discourse, I argue that the death of usury was
more a product of print culture than a historical reality. Jones could serve as a
handy reference point for highlighting the madness of being against finance,
while Jones's madness could be firmly established by a political economic perspective on history and subjectivity that could not accommodate the ethic
he promoted. Having confused the two distinct reasons behind resistance to

usury—or having conflated the two into one, namely, the taking of interest on loans, of which Jones himself was also somewhat guilty—both writers and their readers lost the one discourse that had long enabled ethical opposition to financialization.

In an attempt to show how different and often how incompatible these two reasons were, chapter 2 moves from Aristotle and the Bible to early modern commentary on usury—covering such authors as Martin Luther, John Calvin, and Francis Bacon, as well as lesser theological luminaries such as Miles Mosse, Andrew Willet, John Blaxton, Robert Bolton, and Christopher Jelinger—seeking to show that the real problem with usury was not interest but what early modern writers referred to as "certainties." Quite distinct from the Deuteronomic legal prohibition and the Aristotelian argument against the naturalness of interest, the critique of certainties, the assurance that one would profit or remain secure, was grounded on the notion that the future, the province of God, was to remain undetermined and radically open. The openness of the future, I show, was vitally connected to the question whether an economy could be said to exist at all. The reason certainties were decried was that they presupposed that the world could be understood as a field of objects and bodies that could be governed, directed, steered, controlled, and otherwise mastered by human beings. Against this view stood the providential order, which implied the impossibility of man's attaining such a position of mastery and in which the reduction of objects and people to mere economic entities was unthinkable. The crime of the financier was not his greed, so to speak, for morality could attach to bankers and lenders and stockbrokers and merchants just as easily as it could to the clergy or to nobles; the crime was the financier's tacitly atheistic attempt to avoid the real riskiness of the universe by retreating to a comparatively stable "economic" field. The problem of certainty, and thus the problem of usury, was, therefore, the very problem of economics *as such*. After establishing this intellectual tradition, I look more closely at certain key events in the history of financial revolution and show how they may be seen as proceeding from rather than contravening the prohibition on certainties and as affirmations of the concomitant ethical privileging of risk. Concluding with a discussion of the seventeenth-century merchant and astrologer Samuel Jeake, this chapter aims to illuminate the broader context in which so-called economic decisions were made and to explore seventeenth-century perspectives on commerce without the distorting influence of nineteenth- and twentieth-century political economic assumptions about the autonomy of economic life.

If chapter 1 shows how the discourse of usury became discredited, and

chapter 2 that the ethic of uncertainty nevertheless remained alive, chapters 3
and 4 focus on two eighteenth-century sites where that ethic might be said to
have migrated. Detecting traces of the ethic of uncertainty in the debate over
the moral legitimacy of projects and the moral status of prudence, chapters
3 and 4 look at the work of Daniel Defoe and Henry Fielding, respectively.
Chapter 3 is divided into two interlocking parts. Defoe's *Essay upon Projects*,
a more ostensibly "secular" component of 1690s economic culture than Jones's
sermon, nevertheless raises some of the same issues. I argue that in employing
the figure of Noah to resolve the tension between the controllable world implied by projects and the uncontrollable world implied by providence, Defoe
discovered the value of using formal solutions to address philosophically unre-
solvable conflicts. Extending and complicating Jay Fliegelman's "fortunate fall"
reading of Defoe's *Robinson Crusoe*—wherein Crusoe's departure is regarded
as essential to his salvation—I then go on to read *Crusoe* as a remediation
of the debate about risk and projects, arguing that Crusoe's decision to risk
himself on the high seas, far from being his "original sin," should instead be
read as a vital step on his path toward redemption. Critical to this reading is
a revaluation of the speech deemed central to Crusoe's later moral condition:
his father's advice that he stay in England. I see in this speech not the moral
voice of the author but a sinister attempt to lure Crusoe into a state of con-
tented relaxation, a state of rest that had been vigorously attacked by the seventeenth-century Puritan theologian Richard Baxter, with whom Defoe was
very familiar. Rest was to be avoided because it blunted one's sense of urgency
and dangerously diminished the vital ethical role of risk in one's life. Crusoe
must reject his father's advice because it aims to dissuade him from venturing,
while Crusoe's (and Defoe's) righteous concealment of the sinfulness of his
father's recommendation takes us back once again to Noah—not to the Noah
of the ark but to the other Noah, whose shameful, drunken nakedness was
first exposed by Ham and later concealed by Shem and Japheth. Providing
close analysis of Baxter enables this reading, but it also enables us to see how
and why Ian Watt's characterization of Crusoe as *homo economicus* depended
upon Max Weber's misinterpretation of Baxter. One of the additional implications of this chapter is thus a new perspective on the relationship between
the Protestant ethic and the spirit of capitalism.

Chapter 4 explores the century's complicated understanding of prudence
and situates the controversy surrounding it within the broader context of anxieties concerning the emergence of a distinctively economic realm. Today, the
term *prudence* most often presents itself to us in financial discourse and even
in the names of prominent financial services companies, such as Prudential

Financial, Inc.; Prudence Financial, Inc.; and Prudent Financial. This is no accident, I argue, and the ease with which now we—and the *Oxford English Dictionary*—connect the concept and word *prudence* to the concept and word *finance* is very much the product of changing eighteenth-century ideas about the autonomy of the economic sphere. I argue that the discourse on prudence was where the autonomy of economic life was being ethically investigated after the conversation about usury came to a close and that Henry Fielding's works on prudence and prudence's constant antithetical companion, gambling, explore the limits of a conception of reality understood as an economy. With this context in mind, I turn my attention to his early play *The Modern Husband* (1732) and his novel *The History of Tom Jones, a Foundling* (1749) to show how Fielding differentially approached the relation between ethics and economics. *The Modern Husband* bespeaks an allegiance to the early modern ethic of uncertainty, while the novel suggests that he had moved past it. Fielding's decision to bestow the tainted virtue of prudence upon the erstwhile relentlessly *good* Tom Jones—at the last possible moment—suggests his recognition of the tacit economism lurking even at the heart of the early modern ethic of uncertainty: the providential (and narrative) economy of rewards and punishments. Unmaking his hero's goodness in the interest of keeping ethics rooted in something human and something earthly, Fielding thus points to the possibility of an ethics without exchange.

In the conclusion, I build upon the previous chapters' claims that the events of the 1690s and the mediations of the ethic of uncertainty in the eighteenth century constituted an anti-financial revolution, articulations of rather than deviations from a tradition of ethical thought that emphasized the importance of distributing risk in commercial affairs. The view that England suddenly abandoned its ethical disposition toward finance in the seventeenth century depends upon a narrow historiography of usury, and while the majority of this book is concerned with correcting that history, here I point to some of the consequences of that error. Primarily, it is an error that continues to obscure, and increasingly obscures, the link between a "premodern" world in which economics is constrained by ethics and our "modern" world, in which advocates for economic justice plead for an ethical determination of and delimitation for the ravenously amoral beast of global capitalism, one not altogether unlike Malynes's dragon of usury. As a result of the obfuscation of the ethic of uncertainty—an ethic that I would argue premodern and modern worlds share—opponents of financial injustice have tended to present themselves in one of two ways: as being responsive to something never seen before (and thus unable to understand themselves as part of an ethical tradition) or

as reactionary, often religious utopians (not as participants in an ethical tradition but as spokespersons for a nonnegotiable and unchanging moral law).
Here, I leap forward into the nineteenth century, drawing particular attention
to John Ruskin's invocation of David Jones's sermon in one of the letters included in his magisterial *Fors Clavigera* (1871–84). I consider how the difficulties that Ruskin faced as a result of the way he aligned himself with the
antiquated prohibition of interest on loans might have been overcome had he
chosen instead to align himself with a living tradition of ethical uncertainty, a
tradition that Ruskin came very close to articulating in his political economic
tracts and that lives even to this day in theorizations regarding the aporia
constituted by the gift. For theorists such as Jacques Derrida, not only must
the gift not expect a return but it must not even be cognized or understood as
a gift when it is given. Such an aporia, writes Michael Anker, draws us "toward
the possibility of ethical becoming, the possibility of living an 'ethical' life in a
world without absolute measure—an ethics, in other words, of uncertainty"
(106).[27]

By providing an alternative genealogy of attitudes against usury, I aim to show
that what economists might label "irrational" was once the same thing as "ethical." To take risks, to avoid the lazy certainties of rolling money from place
to place, to escape the trap of finance and the perils of security—these are
the ethical mandates of a different eighteenth century than the one so often
described in narratives of the rise of finance and the triumph of capitalism
and too often uncritically relied upon in assessments of authors and texts
from the period. Privileging justice and blind sacrifice over and against what
is expedient and self-aggrandizing, the eighteenth century that anti-finance
aims to describe is one less concerned with security than with the dangers
that a maniacal fixation on personal securitization presents to the self. That
Security is the name of the villainous usurer of *Eastward Hoe*, Ben Jonson,
George Chapman, and John Marston's 1605 comedy, illustrates how deeply
intertwined usury, security, and sin were for early modern writers. Thus,
when it comes time to assess the lives of those who lived before the "modern"
era, such puzzling conceptions are taken into account, though only on the
condition that they mark a now unintelligible and intellectually discredited
premodernity. But, eighteenth-century literature also abounds with scenarios
in which the sacrificial tendencies and blind acts of giving and forgiving of
a hero or heroine are exploited by a villain whose defining trait is his or her
security, often his or her financial security. When it comes time to assess the
lives, motives, and commitments of the eighteenth-century *authors* of such

scenarios, however, such tendencies, adhering to an economistic understanding of subjectivity, are considered unviable or simply wrong. That this is so testifies to how narrowly defined the human has become for us and shows how rarely models of subjectivity openly defiant of economism inform the historical and cultural analysis of even the most ostentatiously devout writers and thinkers of the early modern period and the eighteenth century. What Emmanuel Levinas says of the human, for example, might be an alternative but equally productive place to begin: "The human is the . . . capacity to fear injustice more than death, to prefer to suffer than to commit injustice, and to prefer that which justifies being over that which assures it" (85). It is worth thinking about the value of death, suffering, and "that which justifies being over that which assures it" when considering eighteenth-century culture, if only because the eighteenth-century text seems far more preoccupied with these matters than with the bare assurance of life and the unchecked accumulation of worldly goods.

The chapters that follow encourage us to locate seventeenth- and eighteenth-century origins, parallels, and inspirations for theories of ethics predicated on the aporia that constitutes the gift and, as well, an anticipation of some very recent critiques of financial capitalism deriving from somewhere other than classical or neoclassical economic foundations. For instance, Franco Berardi and Maurizio Lazzarato have given voice to the idea that the problem with the current configuration of global finance capital lies in its tendency to foreclose the possibility of a future. Trapping everyone in debt both personal and public, and abetted by the power of the state, finance, they argue, removes the possibility of a truly radical and open future. I wish to suggest that while these arguments have taken on a new urgency, they are not exactly new. The discourse of ethical risking always moves in step with financialization, and the only real triumph of capital was to persuade the world that the ethic of uncertainty was a myth that needed to be (and had been) left behind. So I begin the story of anti-finance where the story of usury typically ends: in London in the 1690s.

CHAPTER I

Raving at Usurers

The Life and Death of David Jones

SOMETIME IN 1692, most probably in February or early March, David Jones (1662/63–1724) delivered a farewell sermon provocatively aimed at that increasingly prominent, eventually preeminent group of London citizens: the bankers.[1] An Anglican minister for the London church of St. Mary Woolnoth, Jones would soon after the sermon be dismissed from his post because his sermons had attracted throngs of Dissenters to his parish. Generally, Jones's farewell sermon took aim at the rapacious tendencies implicit in the new financial order of things; specifically, Jones railed at usury:

> Usury is forbid by the Word of God. . . . He that taketh *Any* Increase above the Principal, not Six in the Hundred; but let it be never so little, and never so moderate: He that taketh *Any* Increase, is an Usurer, and such a one, as shall surely Die for his Usury, and his Blood shall be upon his own Head. This is that Word of God, by which you shall all be Saved or Damned at the Last Day; and all those Trifling and Shuffling Distinctions, that Covetous Usures [*sic*] have invented, shall never be able to excuse your Damnation. (29)

Extreme as they are, demanding an outright cessation of lending money for interest and promising damnation for the transgression of this ancient Christian command, Jones's words largely repeat those of countless theologians who had come before him, since the time of St. Mary Woolnoth's establishment in

1438 and, indeed, for much of the course of Western civilization.[2] In fact, the bulk of Jones's comments on the sinfulness of usury were taken directly from the Anglican bishop Robert Sanderson (1587–1663), who had been dead for almost thirty years and who himself had been restating traditional Christian anti-usury doctrine rather than advancing a new line of thinking.

In this chapter I explore this sermon, Jones himself, the controversy surrounding the sermon's delivery and subsequent publication, and its aftermath in the popular imagination and in a poetic tradition that, perhaps surprisingly, intersected with and arguably lent fuel to the budding discourse of political economy toward the end of the eighteenth century. As fascinating as the episode is in its own right, my discussion of Jones serves two purposes in terms of the overall project of this book. First, the sermon and its aftermath serve as *evidence* for the claim that tales of the death of moral concern about usury have been somewhat exaggerated. While many individuals were in positions of power and had the opportunity to revel in and exploit new financial opportunities, what I aim to show is that Jones and his followers—who exist only at the margins of his text, allusively in his biography, and in the textual penumbra to which the sermon gave rise—suggest a popular resistance to finance that was grounded in ethics. Second, the story of Jones—in which his later disappearance from the historical record is perhaps the most important detail of all—serves to *symbolize* a form of ethical thinking that, though prevalent in the seventeenth and eighteenth centuries, has become all but invisible since then. Jones's movement from his position as spokesperson of popular morality to the lunatic fringe, later known less for his religious wisdom than for having, in the words of the poet Christopher Pitt (1699–1748), "rav[ed] at usurers in Lombard Street," mirrors the three larger transitions discussed in this book: a historiographic assertion of the triumph of financial modernity over and against an earlier, superstitious, irrational religious premodernity (chapter 2); a shift in the meaning of risk, from a precondition for ethics to that which must be avoided in the interest of personal security (chapter 3, in which I concentrate on Daniel Defoe); and a shift in the meaning of prudence from moral judgment to economic rationality (chapter 4, on Henry Fielding's approach to the debate on prudence). The way Jones was later regarded—disgraced, in a word—thus comes to serve as an emblem or symbol of the larger patterns this book seeks to trace. My recuperation of Jones within financial history could thus be regarded as the method whereby the readings of the ensuing texts are performed.

In its content, but more in its reception, the Jones affair, in other words, adumbrates an important but heretofore unexamined set of beliefs and values with respect to the changing culture of finance and economics in late-seventeenth- and eighteenth-century England, beliefs and values grounded in the ethics of uncertainty. Critics of the ethics of the new finance in the eighteenth century wrote and spoke of their opponents in terms of usury—much as Jones does in his sermon—which has led to numerous errors in assessing past attitudes toward financial progress at the close of the seventeenth century. In its narrow sense—lending money for interest—usury had by this time become acceptable, but in its broader and far more important sense—making certain profit—it continued to signify the dangers and evils that finance potentially entailed. Though Jones himself does not appear to appreciate the distinction, this dual meaning of *usury* is evident in Jones's use of the word *usurer* in the above passage to describe not only those who take interest specifically but, more generally, all individuals who seek to shift the burden of risk onto others in an attempt to secure themselves against loss. This second definition appears near the close of Jones's quotation from Sanderson: "In every *common Charge*, [the usurer] slippeth the Collar, and leaveth the Burden upon those that are less able" (David Jones 31–32). Owing to this overlooked, secondary meaning—usury as a shifting of burdens onto others and thus the avoidance of risk—critics of finance such as Jones, the traditions from which his opinions emerged, and the discourses to which critics of finance contributed in the long run have been omitted from histories that stress the origins, rise, and/or triumph of modern finance and capitalism. This omission is owing in part to seventeenth- and eighteenth-century writers themselves, whose problematical reliance upon an imprecise, unendingly contested, and pliant term for their critique (i.e., *usury*) made it difficult to perceive a difference between the two traditions out of which their anti-usury opinions grew: a legal prohibition, grounded in Deuteronomic and Aristotelian claims; and an ethical prioritization of gifts over loans, grounded in New Testament claims. It was out of the ethical prioritization that the risk criterion was developed.

A second reason for the omission from the historical record of the tradition that I describe here—which enables us to see figures like Jones as having been central rather than marginal actors—is that the efficacy of the story of financial modernization depends in part upon the idea that rigid, older views were superseded by more fluid and less confining categories for the interpretation, moralization, and legitimation of various financial practices. However, when Jones complains in his sermon of the "Trifling and Shuffling Distinctions" employed by usurers in the defense of their financial practices, he in fact anticipates this very narrative, or at least responds directly to the very attempt to manufacture new categories for interpretation and distinction. Jones's attack

on the making of distinctions itself demonstrates the existence of not simply
a tension between the superstitious past and the modern age (between Jones
and financiers, between the religious and the secular) but a tension between
those that believed such a tension to exist and those who believed that pos-
iting a tension or dichotomy between the spiritual and the secular was itself
criminal and corrupt.[3] That Jones's detractors eventually won is evidenced by,
among other things, the fact that the distinctions between the two reasons
for usury's rejection are frequently elided, making it possible to argue that the
legalization of interest spelled the end of usury as a matter of serious moral
concern. It is difficult to lay the blame on someone such as Jones, who, bereft
of a critical vocabulary sufficient to describe the transformations unfolding
before his eyes, could only relate to the new financial order in terms familiar
to him. The institutionalization of finance to which he bore witness—close
witness, as the ensuing discussion aims to show—was legible to him as nothing less than the institutionalization of sin, a monstrous crime that was for
him unparalleled in human history, prompting him to close his sermon with
an apocalyptic vision: "*Verily I say unto you, it shall be more tolerable for the
Land of* Sodom and Gomorah [*sic*], *in the day of Judgment, than for that City*
[of London] . . . From which dreadful judgment, good Lord deliver this Place
for Christ's sake" (35).

   This study takes David Jones's sermon, with its plea for change within the
geographical center of the financial revolution, as a symbol of the concurrency
of financial modernization and the resistance to aspects of that process. For if
the many violent, public, political acts of resistance to modern finance—such
as the outcry following the South Sea Bubble or the attack on the Bank of
England by the Gordon Rioters—are routinely tucked away in the closets of
an economic history that stresses the triumph of capitalism, the ethics of uncertainty are located in economic history's cellar. But long ago a part of daily
life, eventually put away for storage, and now forgotten, that ethic nevertheless *lingers*. Part of the very foundations of our economic history, it is where
David Jones has been hiding.

The David Jones Affair in Its Time and Place

   Given the many seventeenth-century statements concerning usury, what
makes Jones's in particular worth remembering? To begin, it was delivered in
the crucial decade of the 1690s, a decade that not only on its face appears to have
been particularly active in terms of developments in finance and economic
thought but has been regarded as such in virtually all historical accounts of it.

On the one hand, the decade began with the publication of John Locke's foundational work on the nature of property, his *Two Treatises of Government;* on the other, it has been regarded as a decade that bore witness to the beginnings of what the twentieth-century economic historian P. G. M. Dickson refers to as "the financial revolution in England" (15).[4] While other scholars set the precise dates of the beginning of this revolution earlier or later, the 1690s are of indisputable consequence in terms of both financial history and financial historiography. The neoinstitutionalist economic historians Douglass North and Barry Weingast, for example, find the decades immediately after the Glorious Revolution of particular importance because of the enhanced institutional support for a regime of private property.[5] J. G. A. Pocock, drawing upon Dickson's research, observes that among "the institutions of the new finance," the Bank of England and the national debt—both established in the 1690s— were "the most important" in terms of financial revolution (*MM* 425). It was the decade that saw William Lowndes (1652–1724) ask Isaac Newton, Master of the Royal Mint, to assist him, as well as Locke, in a general recoinage to address the clipped and shaved currency that was compromising the integrity of British commercial transactions, which Isaac Kramnick suggests helped to galvanize gentry opposition to the new finance and thus pave the way for Bolingbroke's eventual rise to power (63).

The 1690s, moreover, saw a Dutch monarch oversee England's transition to Dutch financial methods, an event that the economic historian Richard Sylla, along with countless others, points to as a necessary step in the march toward modern finance (301). That march was enabled by a supportive Parliament, which, in the same year as Jones's farewell sermon, "appointed a committee of ten to 'receive Proposals for raising a Sum of Money towards the carrying on the War against France upon a Fund of perpetual Interest'" (Dickson 50). Among these proposals was one advanced by William Paterson (1658–1719), who "believed, that himself, and some others, might come up to advance Five hundred thousand Pounds" ("House of Commons Journal" 632). Leading eventually to the founding of the Bank of England (1693–94), of which Paterson would be appointed the first director, the discussion of debt and perpetual interest in the Commons was part of a larger discussion that would also lead to the Million Lottery (1694). Echoing North and Weingast's emphasis on the importance of the security of private property to economic development, Craig Muldrew remarks that the Bank, the lottery, and the devolution of the control of money from the monarch to Parliament "created a new type of security which was based on the politics of taxation, and not the credit of individual bankers. The stop of the Exchequer in 1672 had caused

many of the goldsmith bankers to fail, and the creation of public funds and
the expansion of opportunities to invest in joint stock companies provided
a more secure form of investment" (116). I discuss this particular assessment
in greater detail in chapter 2, but the idea that the Bank of England and the
lottery culminated a process that had been unfolding since the Stop is by no
means unique to Muldrew.

Among the many notable works of political economy, the 1690s saw
Charles Davenant publish several important works on political economy
and saw Daniel Defoe publish his *Essay upon Projects* (1697), an exposition
and defense of new financial and political undertakings. Carl Wennerlind
highlights the significance of Defoe's *Essay* when remarking that the "1690s
[was] the epicenter of the Financial Revolution" (109).[6] Summarizing these
various developments in finance in the 1690s, though rather less observant
of the historiographic stasis that characterizes characterizations of that decade, Henry Roseveare observes that "one cannot fail to be impressed by the
remarkable fertility of the 1690s"; these developments "unquestionably add
up to a revolution" (47). Thus, given the epochal transformations under way
in financial theory and practice, David Jones could not have selected a better
time to launch his assault on finance; given the historical *narrative* of those
transformations, however, he could not have selected a worse time. An irritat-
ing reminder of the past and of different ways of seeing, Jones does not fit into
modern finance's origin story.

There are additional reasons for revisiting Jones's words. If the historical
coincidence of Jones's sermon and the financial revolution is worth noting, the
site of its delivery warrants equal attention. Fronting Lombard Street, near
the intersection of Cornhill and Threadneedle Streets (the site of the Bank
of England after its move from Grocers' Hall), St. Mary Woolnoth Church
could be fairly described as also situated at the *geographical* epicenter of the
financial revolution. This is just as true today as it was in the 1690s. One can
stand at the street-level entrance to the Bank subway, or "tube," station and
see the Bank of England—designed and developed by Sir John Soane (1753–
1837) in the last decades of the eighteenth century—as well as the Royal Exchange. Turning around, one is presented with a view of St. Mary's. Greeted
daily with precisely this view on his way to work, the Lloyds Bank employee
T. S. Eliot would record in *The Wasteland* the image of its projecting clock, a
later addition to the structure but one in keeping with the culture of City business (66). Going back in time, the edifice's very existence was dependent upon
the benefactions of one of England's principal financiers: when the church
was badly damaged in the Great Fire of 1666, Sir Robert Viner (1631–88)

gave Christopher Wren (1632–1723) the funds necessary to keep the church in operation.[7] In the church itself, further, is a memorial penned by Samuel Pepys (1633–1703) to the merchant and future Bank of England co-director, James Houblon (1629–1700).[8] Stepping outside the church, a few blocks to the northwest was Grocers' Hall, which less than two years after Jones's sermon would be leased to James's brother, John Houblon (1632–1712), for the operations of the newly established Bank. Just to the northeast lay the Royal Exchange, recently rebuilt after its destruction by fire. The destination for foreign imports, aspiring entrepôt for all of Europe, the haunt of shopkeepers, merchants, jobbers, slave traders, and consumers, the Exchange was the commercial center of England. A scant hundred feet from the Lombard Street entrance to St. Mary's were the south ends of Pope's Head Alley and Exchange Alley, the primary zones for the incipient London trade in securities, insurance, information, and lottery tickets. Just south of St. Mary's, on St. Swithin Lane, lived Sir Gilbert Heathcote (1652–1733), another founding member of the Bank, an agent to Jamaica, a principal early Whig voice, and the richest commoner of the eighteenth century, dying with the astonishing sum of seven hundred thousand pounds (Price). Surrounding the church were the important coffeehouses John's and Garraway's, as well as Lloyd's Coffee House, the epicenter of maritime insurance contracts, which had relocated to Lombard Street in 1691. On his death, Edward Lloyd (1648–1713) would be interred in St. Mary's. Nearby were a host of liveried companies and the addresses of other notable financiers of the era, many of whom would have passed the church on their way to the Exchange or to Exchange Alley to do business.

Or perhaps even *through* it. In an unsigned note contained among the papers of Archbishop of Canterbury Thomas Tenison (1636–1715) Viner is reported to have contrived the installation of a door allowing direct access into the church from his adjoining house to avoid having to "goe a great way Round in the dirt and wett before they can get to the Church."[9] While the note suggests that the door was meant to provide Viner with easy access to the church for worship purposes, it is tempting to speculate whether Viner may have used the church as an extended foyer, allowing him to approach the entrance to the Exchange while avoiding the inclement weather and those dangers of the busy streets eventually detailed by John Gay (1685–1732) in *Trivia; or, The Art of Walking the Streets of London* (1716).[10] Capitalizing on St. Mary's unique location, Viner might well have found his own way, as Gay put it, "to walk clean by day, and safe by night" (5). To illustrate how savvy Viner was in recognizing the importance of the church's location, it is worth noting that had Wren's plan for the rebuilding of London after the Great Fire been

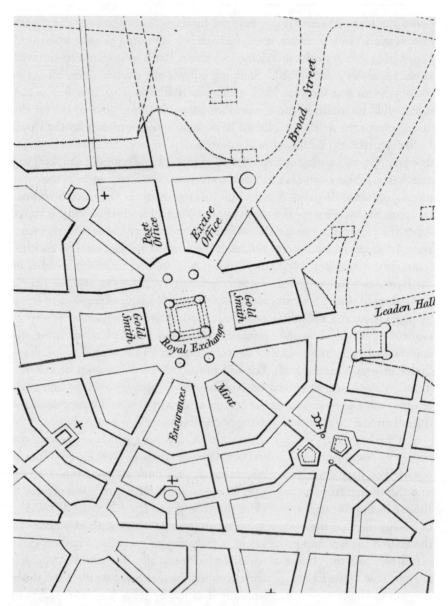

Detail from Christopher Wren's design for rebuilding the city of London after the Great Fire in 1666. (Yale Center for British Art, Paul Mellon Collection)

adopted, St. Mary Woolnoth likely would have been squeezed—had it not been altogether demolished to make space—somewhere between the Mint, the offices of the goldsmith bankers, the Royal Exchange, the Excise Office, and "Ensurance" building (fig. 1).

In light of this unique topographic and temporal convergence of a sermon devoted to attacking the new finance and the revolution in finance that was under way, it comes as something of a surprise that Jones's words have been almost entirely forgotten. The sermon was a loud, public, and much-discussed oppositional one. It rang from a pulpit that was literally surrounded by "financial revolution," in a church that the most important figures of that revolution entered for worship, passed through for safety, or were buried in for eternity. The sermon would become a lightening rod for discussion of the ethics of finance in the press; as such, it presents an invaluable opportunity to take the temperature of Londoners' attitudes about finance during a time of immense change.

If Jones was forgotten, it was not because he was unimportant; rather, the exclusion of Jones from the historical record and, more importantly, what Jones represents validate a certain triumphalist version of financial history, one that stresses the decline of ethical anxieties about finance and the emergence of something that would eventually be described as a modern, secular, economic order. An anti-usury sermon in the heart of the London financial district in 1692 did, does, and always will present complications for the narrative of that modernity. There were only two ways to treat Jones in the narrative of financial revolution: he could be ignored, or he could be treated as a lunatic. Nearly everyone who has written on the changing economic climate of this period—including both Dickson and Pocock—has elected to ignore Jones entirely, while the lunacy treatment, a feature of eighteenth-century writings upon him, may have helped to encourage our modern ignorance of him and of the controversy he provoked.

Judging from the few comments that *have* been made on Jones's sermon, it would seem to have been a trifling affair. This dismissive attitude, however, is the product of a naïve understanding of Jones and symptomatic of a broader cultural tendency to approach usury anachronistically, as signifying nothing more than interest on loans. For the early-twentieth-century historian William Cunningham, the sermon missed the point entirely. By 1692, Cunningham remarks, "the [usury] controversy was practically over, and though Mr. David Jones . . . roused passing excitement, it was treated with contemptuous ridicule" (154n3). R. H. Tawney attributes a bit more significance to it, asserting that Jones's dismissal from St. Mary's was owing to the sermon, but fails to notice that the sermon was *delivered* as a "farewell"; that is, Jones was already on his way out when the sermon was delivered (246–47).[11] Manfred Brod, in his entry on Jones in the *Oxford Dictionary of National Biography*, is less dismissive than Tawney, briefly noting the sermon in an entry centering on Jones's "inability to accept people or affairs on any terms other than his own."[12] This characterization, true as it may be given Jones's other moral and professional failings, nevertheless completes the process of historical forgetting by emphasizing Jones's singularity and obstinacy, isolating him from a historical milieu by highlighting his aberrant personality or psyche. Emphasis on Jones's bad behavior—which, in Brod's defense, seems to have been very bad at times—delinks him from a larger community of potentially like-minded skeptics who may have been as implacable and idealistic as he was. If Jones would not "accept people or affairs" other than his own, then History—as written by Cunningham, Tawney, and others—has no particular obligation to accept Jones.

These commentators can hardly be blamed, however, as the historiographic omission of the Jones controversy is in keeping with the general tendency to think of the usury issue as resolved by 1700, making the sermon seem both belated and futile. Indeed, usury itself was of relatively minor importance to economic theorization and debate in the eighteenth century when compared with its place in the financial debates of the period covered by Norman Jones in *God and the Moneylenders, 1571–1624*, "when Parliament finally legitimized loans with no more than the specified rate of interest" (Oldham 169). By the eighteenth century, it is often averred, the necessity of moneylending was well established, its excesses curtailed, and its practice legitimated, most notably by the 1694 founding of the Bank of England. Gone were the days, it would seem, of paying serious attention to writers like Miles Mosse (fl. 1580–1614), whom I quoted at the beginning of the introduction and whose unequivocally condemnatory *Arraignment and Conviction of Usurie* (1595) was so hyperbolically titled, the author tells us, merely to distinguish it from the countless other anti-usury tracts of his time ("To the Reader," n.p.). By 1700, historians inform us, the usury problem had been solved, rendering the plaints of someone like David Jones eccentric (Tawney) or even mildly psychopathic (Brod).[13]

But while historians have overlooked Jones's sermon, his contemporaries took it quite seriously and responded to it with a degree of energy that is surprising only if we believe that by the end of the seventeenth century the usury "controversy was practically over," as Cunningham put it. Was it? Insofar as lending for interest had become legal and common, it was. But the record of commercial transactions and laws concerning lending tell us only one side of the story of finance, one that does not appreciate the force the term *usury* continued to carry into and through the financial revolution. If we allow the term its broader signification, as a catchall for villainous financial chicanery that aimed at circumventing risk, and if we situate Jones in terms of the ethics of uncertainty rather than in the history of anti-usury—which, because anti-usury contains a wide array of grounds for rejecting usury and an equally wide array of definitions of what is being rejected, is multiple, contradictory, and inconsistent—we discover a very different 1690s than the one we have become accustomed to rehearsing and see that Jones and what he represents have more important roles to play in the history of finance than has been acknowledged. Jones's sermon, printed in 1692, was followed by a lengthy reply, dated 5 March 1692, by John Dunton (1659–1733) in his *Athenian Mercury* (and the *Mercury* revisited the Jones controversy less than three weeks later, on 26 March). A counter to Dunton came shortly thereafter: the anonymously penned *Mr. David Jones's Vindication Against the Athenian Mercury*. Two longer pamphlets were still to come that year: the printer Samuel Crouch's (1674–1717) *A Discourse upon Usury . . . (Occasioned by Mr. David Jones's late Farewel Sermon)* and *The Lombard-Street Lecturer's Late Farewell Sermon, Answer'd. . . .* In response to the latter of these two, another anonymous writer composed *Innocense clear'd: or, a short defence of Mr. Jones's farewel-sermon. . . .* These statements collectively reveal that both the sermon and Jones were treated with a great deal more than "contemptuous ridicule" (Cunningham).

Jones is not explicitly mentioned in the 1695 tract *Usury Explain'd*, but the author, Philopenes—the pseudonym of the Jesuit priest John Huddleston (1636–1700)—is nevertheless responding to a widely held anti-usury sentiment that Jones proclaimed more loudly than anyone else in his time. Huddleston remarks in the preface to his tract that it was written to counterbalance the writings of individuals who out of "Zeal" had attacked a steady and legitimate practice. "To make a Sin, of no Sin," writes Huddleston, "is as irregular, as to make no Sin, of a Sin." This was a common retort against writers such as Jones, who advocates of lending saw as blowing the matter out of proportion, of taking a minor sin and turning it into a mortal one. Wishing to establish the irrational, overblown, and zealous qualities of the anti-usury position through the language of Christian hamartiology, Huddleston in some ways prefigures a financial historiography that posits that Jones's views are, for their period, irregular, raving, and eccentric rather than reasonably skeptical or critical of the transformations he perceived in St. Mary Woolnoth and the City in general.

Thompson Cooper, who authored the *Dictionary of National Biography* entry on Huddleston, speculates that the tract was written against Bishop James Smith's treatise on usury, but this is almost certainly incorrect, no such treatise having ever existed.[14] And so it is highly likely that his tract too was aimed at Jones. What is important is that while Jones's sermon served as an occasion for debate and public discussion, there were numerous writers who in the 1690s asserted the moral bankruptcy of usury. It is probable that even so notable a divine as William Sherlock (ca. 1641–1707) was provoked by Jones's words to deliver a sermon on usury roughly one month after Jones's (the title page for Sherlock's sermon tells us that it was delivered "Tuesday of Easter-Week," or 6 April 1692). Sherlock does not name Jones, but he would appear to gesture toward him and his followers when he refers to "those who so universally condemn all Usury" (8). Sherlock, who allowed for the lending of money for moderate interest and even argued that charging interest to the poor would make them more industrious, nevertheless stated in his sermon that extracting wealth at the cost of the debtor's well-being was a damnable sin: "Usury is a very great Sin, that is, to lend our Money upon Usury to those who borrow for Necessity and Want, and to exact such Payments with Rigour and Severity, to strip such miserable People of that little that remains, to imprison their Persons, and make them end their Lives in a Goal" (21). Huddleston, even against Jones, would similarly remark that in "extreme Necessity, [there is] no place for *Lending*. The Necessitous having a Natural Right, to take what may relieve their present Want, all things in that occasion becoming Common, and to Refuse a Person, in extreme Necessity, is a sort of Theft . . . and no less Folly, in pretending to Lend, what in extreme Necessity is more another's, then [*sic*] yours" (36). Interest or no, the key issue for Sherlock and Huddleston, as well as for Jones, was whether financial action of any kind—moneylending, foreclosure, and so forth—was helpful or hurtful; if the latter, then it was condemned. It is a simple enough point to make, and one that unsurprisingly finds its way into the mouths and publications of pious Christians, but it is one that gets less attention than it deserves, because it displays a remarkable continuity of opinion across denominational lines: Jones a semi-closeted Dissenter, Huddleston a Jesuit, and Sherlock a nonjuring High Churchman. Jones was one of many contributors to a discussion, thus far uncharted, about the ethics of the changing financial order in which Huddleston and Sherlock also played important if less extreme roles.

What makes Jones's voice unique? There had been far more careful and sustained attacks on usury by theologians in the seventeenth century, and the replies to Jones's sermon provide more sophisticated and subtle arguments regarding usury. Dunton, for example, includes printed Hebrew text evoking the distinction between "*Nesheck* and *Tarbith,* the one signifying *biting Usury,* (or Extortion) the other *multiplying increase*" (*Athenian Mercury* 2). Even so, these replies are not of especial significance; most merely restate or directly cite arguments that had been made by authors in the long tradition of pro- and anti-usury polemic that had been circulating in theological communities for, literally, centuries. Dunton's distinction between "*Nesheck* and *Tarbith,*" for instance, had long been central in defenses of lending, appearing in all of the major usury statements of the sixteenth and seventeenth centuries. There- fore, if Jones is read as a theologian and evaluated according to the strength of his theological case against usury, then he is indeed worth forgetting, for there is virtually nothing of theological interest in it; there is certainly nothing new in it.

What made Jones's sermon unique was that it was seized upon so vigor- ously that "all Tongues are full of it," which could only have happened if the general skepticism it articulated was felt at some level by individuals beyond Jones himself (*Lombard-Street Lecturer's Late Farewell Sermon, Answer'd* A2). Jones has been forgotten because many of his contemporaries, as well as more recent historians, wished to read his sermon as a belated *theological* argument, a late installation in the old dispute regarding the lawfulness of interest and moneylending. It is no such thing; rather, Jones takes it as a given that it is a sin and focuses instead on the emergence of a *culture* of usury that he per- ceives in and around his parish, a culture whose defining trait is not the simple taking of interest but its belief that decisions made about money and wealth can proceed without moral restraint. Jones is concerned with the notions that one can live with the idea of being considered a usurer and that usury can be *thought of* as a legitimate calling. Bishop John Jewel (1522–1571)—whom Jones somewhat surprisingly does not cite despite a shared hostility toward usury actuated by similar Calvinist leanings—had made a similar point in his com- mentary on Paul's first letter to the Thessalonians.[15] But we must appreciate the different contexts in which Jewel and Jones stated their cases. Jewel's com- mentary was published posthumously in 1609, nearly a century before Jones's sermon, when moneylending not only was considered morally reprehensible but was strictly regulated. When Jones, by contrast, attacks the "Trifling and Shuffling Distinctions" erected by dubious moral agents, his aim is directed at an entire system of pro-lending norms and laws that had been adopted

between his and Jewel's own eras as well as the development of new financial
agents, institutions, and instruments whose precise relation to moneylending
per se had not yet been firmly established. Where earlier anti-usury polemics
had provided extensive historical, scriptural, and philosophical evidence and
analysis to demonstrate that usury was an abomination, forbidden by God
in Deuteronomy and elsewhere, and rejected by the wisest of statesmen and
civilizations, Jones is primarily interested in tying his dismissal from St. Mary
Woolnoth to a culture of usury—broadly understood—that cannot tolerate
his censure. Elizabethan and Jacobean opponents of usury had no compara-
ble need to justify their attack on usury; their attacks conformed to accepted
doctrines. Jones, by contrast, was fired for protesting.

Unlike earlier theologians who had focused on usury in soteriological and
hamartiological terms—in terms of salvation and sin—Jones is more immediately interested in the circumstances of his impending dismissal and in shaming his congregation for allowing it to happen. He asks what his parishioners
would say to themselves if, right now, "the Lord Chief Justice of *England*" were
to come to them to tell them that their undertakings are shameful. Elsewhere,
noting that usury has been "Universally *Hated* by all Men of all sorts, and in
all Ages and Countries," Jones quickly particularizes the matter: "Look to it all
ye of this Parish, whose chiefest Employment is Banking and Usury" (David
Jones 32). When Jones, earlier in the sermon, provides a justification for the
length of his sermons—the cause of some complaints against him—he sarcastically asks his parishioners, if his sermons were shorter, would they use the
extra time to go down the street, or indeed across the street, "to the Exchange
or to the Coffee-house to hear News?" (22). It is plain from such efforts that
Jones's concern extends beyond the simple matter of interest on loans to the
kinds of practices—the trading of stocks, for example, or the composition
and sale of insurance contracts—that would take place at coffeehouses, at the
Royal Exchange, and in Exchange Alley (all more or less across the street from
the church). Try as he did, though, to locate his critique of usury in his immediate time and space, Jones's sermon was eventually inserted into a theological
tradition in which Jewel, Sanderson, Shaw, and Jelinger situated their tracts.
Thus his sermon could be (and was in fact) read, not as the expression of a
historical agent witness to a series of current events that troubled him, but
as out of joint with time, as the ravings of a madman committed to the same
superstitious theologies of earlier religious demagogues.

Jones undoubtedly had something of the demagogue about him, but instead of seeing in Jones—and in Jones's respondents—an impassioned reaction to the sudden changes in finance that were happening everywhere, but

most especially in Jones's immediate environs, critics have instead figured him as locked in an increasingly irrelevant past. Most important, Jones displays no interest in discussing usury in the way that his forebears had done, in defining it in one manner or another, in distinguishing it from forms of legitimate commerce; quite the contrary. Usury, for Jones, encompasses a panorama of profiteering behaviors, evident most of all in his utter disregard for the nice philosophical distinctions that had defined the casuistry of the preceding generation and that were increasingly becoming the territory of artful lawyers looking to enable their clients' exploitative commercial practices, which he saw as increasingly definitive of the congregational activity of the parishioners of St. Mary Woolnoth. Put simply, for Jones usury meant nothing more, and nothing less, than financial modernization, understood as the severing of economic life from ethical and spiritual life, the view that economic matters were distinct from spiritual and ethical matters.

When Jones speaks of usury, in other words, he is not solely concerned with the isolated question of the legitimacy of taking interest on loans (usury narrowly defined); rather, he is speaking about a new culture of finance and commerce that would seek to cancel an ethical state of risk and replace it with an all-too-human principle of security: "slipp[ing] the collar" of uncertainty for assured gain (David Jones 31–32). But in employing the term *usury* to designate the great space of the new finance, in which "slipping collars" could be achieved in a wide variety of ways, he would come to be seen by later readers as engaging in an old debate about *usury*'s narrow meanings. Jones can hardly be blamed for this, since the revolution in finance that was under way by the time of his sermon introduced an array of financial practices and technologies that had no history and no coherent vernacular and could therefore only be criticized from an ethical standpoint under the aegis of the umbrella term *usury*.[16] Because of his choice of words—the only words available to him, so not really much of a choice—not only did Jones fail to install a permanent critique of finance when it was most needed but in opening himself up to the charge of being out of joint with time (by preaching where he did when he did) he made *any* argument against usury seem out of joint with time. Jones's remark about "Trifling and Shuffling Distinctions"—attempts to distinguish various forms of commerce from usurious dealing—should be read as an attempt to critique the wider system of finance before there was a sufficiently refined critical vocabulary to do so, an attempt to speak to the problem with new economic practices before names for such practices existed.[17] But his attempt to speak to them was a practical failure. Not only did Jones fail to rectify the inequities and impieties he perceived as inherent to the new financial order but the Jones event in its totality would gradually become the reference point—thanks, no doubt, in large part to Pitt's poem—for a political economy that sought to place the critique of finance in the space of the premodern and the irrational.

Jones clearly anticipated this result. He exhibited neither the intellectual power nor the rhetorical gifts of an Edmund Burke in estimating the nature of the revolution transpiring around him, but in his implacability he attained an equivalent degree of critical distance from the events. For it was this transition, this "belating" or "medievalizing" of usury critique, that Jones attacked. For him, the words of Sanderson were valuable both for their truth and because they came from a time that his banking parishioners would appear to have forgotten. Historical change provides the *occasion* for Jones's sermon, which makes the sermon symptomatic of financial revolution (he was a voice in its midst), but the "revolutionary-ness" of his moment is also the *topic* of his sermon (he was reflecting on the very process of its happening). Jones's sermon, in fact, proceeds from a story of a biblical transition, namely, the moral turning away of the Galatians from the pious but challenging Saint Paul toward the more appealing "Gnosticks," who, in Jones's words, "handled the Word of God deceitfully, and made a Merchandize of the Souls of Men, and thought Gain to be Godliness" (1). Such remarks reveal that Jones was not making universalizing pronouncements about money and usury from the rarefied air of Christian theology but was responding to the unique historical situation and urban space occupied by him and his parishioners. Jones imagines that he might be able to redirect the course of events (to dissuade his parishioners from giving in to finance, from turning "Gnostick"), however difficult such a task might be, and while from a later historical point finance may appear to be destined for ideological and institutional triumph, it did not appear so to him. Nor did it appear so to the many anxious auditors and readers of his sermon who wrote in to Dunton; or to those who sustained the print market for discourses on usury in the ensuing years; or to those who kept the memory of Jones alive, if only in the fleeting capacity of a proverb, byword, or catchphrase. They remembered a time when raving at usurers in Lombard Street had been possible.

Taking as his text Galatians 4:16, "Am I therefore become your Enemy, because I tell you the Truth?," Jones spends well over half his sermon simply preparing his auditors and readers for advice they will not want to hear, insisting that he is merely a messenger. Jones knows, in other words, that he faces long odds in tackling his subject, both because his City parishioners are directly tied into the nascent system of banking and perhaps because the system of banking and finance is already exerting a palpable pressure on cultures beyond the parish boundaries of St. Mary Woolnoth. Jones is aware that the reason for his impending departure is precisely his congregation's unwillingness to face the "Truth" of usury and that his truth cannot be heard by those who have resolved to shut their ears: "Oh what a tuff thing a Usurers Conscience is! Can any thing equal it for Hardness, but his barred, locked Iron chest? Oh how hard is it for such a miserable Wretch to be saved, whom nothing can convince of his sin?" (33). Much of what David Jones has to say—and even more of what his respondents have to say—confirms Norman Jones's view that by 1700 usury had ceased to be a matter of policy concern and instead become a question of conscience. But in choosing to end the history of usury with its moral internalization, Norman Jones overlooks the fact that the transition he accurately describes was itself a matter of considerable worry. David Jones argues precisely that if individuals are allowed to decide whether their profiteering is ethical, they will inevitably follow the "Gnostick" line of reasoning and ratiocinate themselves and their consciences into a state of selfish complacency. In other words, the transition described by Norman Jones is the very target of David Jones's sermon, thus raising the question whether usury had been accepted by the end of the seventeenth century or was thought to have been accepted when in fact it had not been. To put it otherwise: was the acceptance of usury *reflected* in economic writings of the late seventeenth and eighteenth centuries, or was its acceptance *produced* by a secondary literature that cast its critics as medieval, gothic, and out of touch with modern economic realities?

Jones selected a "miraculous" subject for his apocalyptic farewell: usury, a subject of biblical, ancient, medieval, early modern, and immediate historical significance, was on the brink of being routinized, institutionalized, literally steps from where he delivered the sermon. The pressure of history on this moment, and the pressure such a moment places on our sense of history, could not be greater. Preaching on absolute and historical thresholds, Jones requires a scriptural text capacious enough to address both—"Am I therefore become your Enemy, because I tell you the Truth?" What other text suits a moment when what had been expressly forbidden, or hidden, was soon to become the norm?[18] To be fair, the historical importance of Jones's sermon and the outpouring of commentary upon it are virtually negated by virtue of Jones's reliance on scripture that almost willfully announces his own impending irrelevancy. As noted above, it is not surprising that historians of the modern economy have considered the Jones affair inconsequential, for it does not follow the sequence of financial history as that story has been narrated over the centuries. Neither Jones nor his followers could be a part of the "Truth" that historians have described. It is the casting out of figures such as Jones—and the traces he left behind—that enables us to narrate, to comprehend, to think of the transition from a premodern to a modern system of finance as a kind of revolution. David Jones, with and like premodern financial ethics, must first be made to pass away.

In his time, however, Jones and others saw the line between licit and illicit commerce eroding as the sheer number and variety of financial instruments and opportunities rapidly increased. It was not that such instruments were evil in themselves, merely that they created countless new opportunities for innovative forms of abuse. Even in his spirited reply to Jones, Dunton cannot help but admit that a sermon against usury—which Dunton also regards as a "Sin"—makes sense in 1692: "There never was a time wherein 'twas less necessary to teach men *they shou'd love themselves* than now; and perhaps at this time Covetousness is a more Universal Sin than ever, it being observable, that many who pass for good Christians, and abhorr the Excesses of Debauchery, are yet deeply Guilty of this Sin" (97). Notwithstanding Dunton's claim for the unique historical importance of the usury question in 1692, the outcry concerning usury then was an extension of an unbroken line of conversation reaching back to the period covered by Norman Jones. In 1679, to take an earlier example, Christopher Jelinger (fl. 1641–1681) printed his lengthy treatise *Usury Stated Overthrown: or, Usuries Champions with their Auxiliaries, shamefully Disarmed and Beaten.*[19] In 1682 the moderate nonconforming minister Samuel Shaw (1635–1696) had written a treatise highlighting various forms of worldliness. Although he carved some space for moneylending, he held fast to the old line: "To make a Trade of Usury, and to get ones Living out of the Sweat of other Mens Brows, is condemned for an idle wicked Life, even by the favourablest Censors, yea, by the very Patrons of Usury" (354). Connecting this point to the ethical matter of risk, Shaw added that "to bind Men and their Friends, and their Heirs and Executors, to make a certain advantageous Return of an uncertain hazardous Employment of money, is very Cruel, and an Atheistical confronting of Divine Providence" (354).

Even texts in defense of the financial developments of the 1690s labored under anxieties about the lawfulness of usury. For example, an English review of the Dutch jurist Gerhard Noodt's (1647–1725) 1698 defense of usury, *De Fœnere et Usuris,* trots out for yet another ride all of the old arguments made in usury's defense: it is the same as buying and selling; it is the same as renting out property; its prohibition in the Old Testament was limited to usury between Jews specifically and not a universal or timeless prohibition of lending; and so forth. Whatever the arguments, the mere existence of Noodt's book should lead us to ask at least three questions: (1) if the moral issue of usury had ceased to be a matter of concern in Protestant lands by 1698, why was a defense of usury necessary in the first place? (2) what exigencies would have led an Englishman to read, let alone review, such a defense? and (3) to what market would such a defense and such a review have appealed at this time? While these questions cannot be answered with certainty, it seems at least probable that the usury question had not been settled, at least not for the reviewer who enthusiastically recommended Noodt's volume to his readers, who presumably was at some level in need of the justification provided by Noodt.

Just as important as the fact of the review is what the reviewer declines to discuss: the reviewer, who lays out in some detail Noodt's arguments in defense of lending, refrains from a consideration of Noodt's exceptions—moments in which commerce verges on sin and thus requires restraint—on account of, in his words, the "difficult and obscure places of the Law" with which Noodt deals in those sections ("Review" 88). To gloss this point: the reviewer recounts Noodt's explanation of why usury is acceptable but suggests that the reader consult Noodt directly for the reasons why it might not be. This anxious moment of avoidance of the point at which usury becomes wicked should be read in the full context of a culture to which the matter of the new finance was, at a minimum, something that required continuous defense and the strategic use of rhetoric. Was it, as the reviewer explicitly states, Noodt's argumentative complexity that necessitated the reader's direct consultation of the text? Or was it the reviewer's uncertainty about the strength of Noodt's defense of usury in the face of contrary cases that compelled this anxious act of avoidance? Or, to fuse these two possibilities into one, was it the very puzzle itself that bothered the reviewer? That is, why should something (usury) that the reviewer clearly believed to be acceptable, and that he believed others believed to be acceptable, require for its justification vertiginous feats of legal and ethico-logical discrimination—feats so vertiginous, in fact, that they could not be explained or named in the review? Put simply, if it was universally accepted, why was it so difficult to defend? Even if we accept the mundane answer offered by the reviewer—"It's too complicated to explain"—we already catch a glimpse of the possibility that usury meant not one, but two things—interest on loans *and* the criminal attainment of financial certainty—and that these two meanings were often confused by those who wrote about usury. Such confusion bespeaks not a resolution of the question concerning finance but an intensification of anxieties about which forms of financial practice could be considered usurious and which could not. But for all that has been said about the naturalization of usury in the course of the seventeenth century, what stands out upon a cursory survey of the print market for texts concerning usury is that in the 1690s it was still unnatural enough to provoke discussion in the pulpit and debate in print.

The David Jones Affair beyond His Time and Place

In the period just prior to the financial revolution, Jelinger and Shaw had articulated their positions squarely within the framework of Christian theology and debate. The pamphlets surrounding the Jones affair suggest that the debate concerning usury was coming down from that rare air and becoming (or had just become) relevant to a much wider swath of the English populace, which is not to say that it had broken free from its Christian origins. In this section, I attempt to reconstruct that populace, not for evidence of its size or its composition and not to precisely delineate its doctrine, but to point toward an energetic cultural current whose only traces of existing lay at the margins of texts involved in the Jones controversy. It may not even be a populace or demographic that is at stake, but rather a disposition or feeling of ethical panic that could strike anyone at any time and just as quickly disappear again.

To begin, it should be noted that every author involved in that controversy observes in one way or another that the recondite matter of usury—usury as a matter of theological concern—is suddenly the subject of intense popular interest:

> Mr. *Jones's* Farewell Sermon has been the occasion of much Discourse in City and Country, especially that part relating to Usury, a Subject which of late years has not been (as I know) much controverted on one side or another; but now being so zealously opposed by Mr. *Jones* . . . it has occasioned a more than ordinary Concernment of Spirit in many (I hope I may say good Christians, who have a hearty respect for Mr. *Jones*, and have been or are concern'd in the business of Usury) to examine this matter a little more closely than they have hitherto done, and the dealings of Usury are become universal, reaching Nobility and Gentry as well as Merchants and Tradesmen, so that all have need to be satisfied, whether it be lawful or not? (Crouch i)

Scholars wishing to date the end of concerns about usury might draw on just such a passage as this for evidence of the newfound legitimacy of usury. Yet the passage just as strongly suggests the opposite: notwithstanding usury's "universal" employment, a "more than ordinary Concernment of Spirit" predominates in the minds of Christians. The sentiments expressed by Jones had escaped the confines of theological debate and entered into the daily considerations of nobles and merchants, gentry and tradesmen, from both city and country. Similarly announcing the popularity of the sermon, the title page of this same text notes that it was published "at the Request of *several* Judicious and Sober Christians." While that claim may be somewhat self-serving for the author wishing to sell his *Discourse*, the *Vindication against the Athenian Mercury*—a pro-Jones tract that specifically attacks those who believe that lenders to the Crown deserve to be repaid with interest—closes with the author claiming that he too has "*oftentimes* been forced to vindicate Mr. Jones in *several* Companies upon the account of Usury" (7, my emphasis). In collapsing all forms of lending and investment, from the private transactions of merchants to the loans provided to the Crown by goldsmith bankers and wealthy elites,[20] into *usury*, the *Vindication* illustrates that the ethic preached by Jones was not aimed just at the isolated affairs of merchants, bankers, and elites bent on charging high rates of interest, though this group did present special problems. It was aimed at and read as an attack, using the language of usury, on the process of financialization itself,[21] a process that promised (or threatened) to extend into the lives of all members of Jones's parish, as well as into the lives of those who lived elsewhere but regularly made the journey to hear Jones's sermons.

Even texts on the other side of the debate, such as the anti-Jones *Lombard-Street Lecturer's Farewell Sermon, Answer'd*, acknowledged the sermon's extraordinary popularity. Of greater interest, however, is what the author of this tract says of the print *market* for Jones's ideas: it is a text "of no small merit, [since] the Bookseller could afford so many *Guineas* for the Copy, a price rarely given for a Sermon" (1, my emphasis).[22] Returning to Dunton's piece in the *Athenian Mercury*, while he rarely devoted an entire paper to a question from a reader, he devotes all of this particular issue to Jones. It opens:

Quest. 1. *In Mr.* David Jones's *Farewell Sermon p.* 34. *he says, he that taketh any increase, not six in the hundred, but be it never so little, he shall dye for his Usury, and his Blood shall be upon his own hand, and* page 38. *He that gives or takes upon usury may lawfully be cursed: Pray your Thoughts upon this Doctrine?*

> *Answ.* This and several more Questions of the same Nature have
> come to our hands, so that pursuant to our former promises, we have
> oblig'd our selves to answer 'em. . . . (1)

In other words, the question stated here was not the only one about the status of usury that the popular talk of Jones's sermon had raised for the *Athenian Mercury*.[23] Dunton elected to frame the discussion in terms of interest
rates, but did he do so because—and in keeping with the general confusion
about usury that was expressed elsewhere and would be further expressed in
the 1698 review of Noodt's *De Fœnere et Usuris*—those other questions "of
the same Nature" were more complicated or more difficult to address? *The
Lombard-Street Lecturer's Late Farewell Sermon, Answer'd* opens with the following observation: "The Popular Noise of a certain *Farewell Sermon*, Preach'd
amongst you, has Rang so loud in the Town, that all Tongues are full of it"
(A2). What these "Tongues" were saying we do not know, just as Dunton's
unpublished questions "of the same Nature" as the one printed remain obscure. What *is* known, however, is that far from having been turned out for
a lack of parishioners, Jones was dismissed for having attracted too many. In
the *Farewel-Sermon* itself, Jones spent a good bit of time replying to those who
objected to the fact that his church was so "fill'd and throng'd" with strang-
ers from other parishes that his regular parishioners "could scarce get at it
[the church]" (24). Again, while we may never know with certainty what it
was that drew such "throngs" to him, the afterlife of his anti-usury sermon
suggests that for all of his eccentricity, something Jones raved against reso-
nated with the great mass of humanity beyond the confines of his parish. And
given how little was known about him aside from his zealous criticism of
finance—which must have begun prior to his sermon, since he was on his way
out, deemed unsuitable for a City church, when the sermon was delivered—it
seems reasonable to assume that it was at least partly the vigorous stance he
took against usury that encouraged such remarkable attendance at St. Mary's
and also led to his expulsion. While Dunton and others attacked Jones on the
matter of interest, and there is little doubt that many still found even interest on loans problematic, Jones's appeal was also obviously tied to his having
tapped into ethical and spiritual questions relating to the changes occurring
before his eyes that were larger and more complex than questions relating to
interest alone.

Just as Jones's presence extended geographically beyond the confines of St.
Mary Woolnoth, drawing visitors and respondents from other parishes and

faiths, it also extended historically. First, Jones's sermon was printed a second time, in 1703, suggesting that even after the founding of the Bank and the developments in public debt financing that followed, the usury question had not been finally settled, at least in the minds of the masses of individuals who made up the system that was in a state of "revolution." But the second printing of Jones's sermon was by no means the end of the story; Jones and his sermon lived on in the print record of the ensuing century. Cunningham's description of Jones's sermon as having aroused a "passing excitement" turns out to have been quite wrong. Dunton remembered the controversy well enough, and presumed his audience would as well, when he casually referred back to David Jones as having "lash[ed] the Usurers in Lombard-street" in his 1708 *Hazard of a Death-Bed Repentance* (8). The diarist Thomas Hearne (bap. 1678–1735) described the "Farewell Sermon" as "very characteristic" of Jones (409). The sermon would also be alluded to by Thomas Brown (bap. 1663–1704)[24] and Edward "Ned" Ward (1667–1731), who treated it with dignity in a March 1700 issue of *The London-Spy*. More than a decade later, in 1713, Anthony Collins (1676–1729) observed that while usury had been accepted by most priests, it had not been accepted by "the Reverend Mr. David Jones, who takes Usury to be a sin" (60). A decade after Collins, in May 1725, a little over a year after Jones's death, a writer for the *Weekly Journal* compared the futile attempt to defend the virtue of chastity in a culture of lust to Jones's having unsuccessfully "inveigh[ed] against Usury in *L-mb--d street*." Becoming gradually unmoored from the original context of financial revolution, Jones's sermon increasingly became a byword for or idiomatic expression signifying the attempt to resist the ineluctable current of modernity. The idiom may have begun as early as 1699, when Thomas Brown thus described his own futile attempt to persuade some country gentlemen to give up foxhunting: "They mind me no more than the Bankers in *Lumbardstreet* [*sic*] did the zealous *David Jones* declaiming against Usury" (*Collection of Miscellany* 327).

The title of this book, *Raving at Usurers*, derives from a later incarnation of this idiom, which appeared in an oft-printed, semi-satirical Horatian ode penned by Christopher Pitt (1699–1748) entitled "The Art of Preaching. A Fragment" (published posthumously in 1756). "The Art of Preaching" was included in numerous miscellanies, including *The Poetical Calendar* (1763), *The Oxford Sausage* (1766), and Samuel Johnson's *Works of the English Poets* (1779–80). A sort of *ars poetica* for the sermonizing sort, Pitt's text offers preachers advice on what and what not to do to communicate their message. By turns serious and satirical, the poem builds toward its crowning example of who should not be emulated: David Jones, the only preacher Pitt openly names as guilty of bad preaching. Pitt advises preachers to select a topic suitable for an audience:

> Some easy subject chuse, within your power,
> Or you will ne'er hold out for half an hour.
> Still to your hearers all your sermons sort;
> Who'd preach against corruption at a Court?
> Against Church Pow'r at Visitations bawl?
> Or talk about Damnation at *Whitehall?*
> Harangue the Horse-guards on a Cure of Souls?
> Condemn the Quirks of Chancery at the *Rolls?*
> Or rail at Hoods and Organs at *St. Paul's?*
> Or be, like David Jones, so indiscreet,
> To rave at usurers in Lombard-street? (109)[25]

The reference here, written a half century after the sermon's initial delivery, by someone who had not even been born when Jones delivered it, suggests a subterranean cultural life for David Jones. On the one hand, these lines highlight the foolish disregard Jones had for his auditors, and they confirm Brod's assessment of Jones as implacable and singular. But in choosing to align him with preachers who might raise questions about such things as "Church Pow'r" to an archdeacon—the reference to "Visitations"—Pitt paints Jones as somewhat more complex, for churches often do wield power unjustly, politicians do sin, Chancery can be capricious in its procedures and judgments, and the question of ornamentation and music in sacred spaces had in an important sense been the cause of a recent civil war. Pitt later advises "Country Vicars" to shed their "little Band and rusty Wig" when they come to town to preach, and he may have Jones's humble, Welsh origins in mind here. What is not clear is whether Pitt is ironically denigrating homespun, country wisdom to underscore the corruptions of the City or sincerely calling for moderation in rural idealism and pragmatism in modern urban contexts. A similar note of uncertainty had been struck by some of Jones's respondents in the original pamphlet battle, who acknowledged at once Jones's good intentions and bad execution.[26] Pitt's poem, as well as those early respondents, dramatizes the problem this book seeks to address: are eighteenth-century expressions of belief, however mediated, in risk for its own sake, in the ethical necessity of uncertainty, legitimate stances against financial modernity, or are they simply cases of raving lunacy?

That the reference to Jones in Pitt's poem is passing rather than central to the poem as a whole exemplifies the structural tendency of marginalized or radical discourses, figures, and ideas: never fully in or out of consciousness, they are poised exquisitely on the brink, ready to be taken up as a cause or cast into an unforgiving pit of oblivion. The Jones affair reveals a subtle thread of thought, an affect, an evanescent and now-forgotten aspect of eighteenth-century life. David Jones, as a spokesperson against the tide of financial modernization, thus occupies a paradoxical position. Although he cannot be incorporated into anything like an orthodox history, such as those written by Norman Jones and R. H. Tawney, Jones nevertheless continues to survive in history, if only in the capacity of a passing or colloquial allusion.

David Jones and Political Economy

Jones has always been present, but he has also, in a sense, always already been forgotten, branded a zealot, an eccentric, a raving lunatic. How did this happen? Early on, Jones's firebrand tactics made his message distasteful; soon he became a byword for futility. Pitt's poem later represented Jones's foible as an ecclesiastical one; because of the poem's frequent reprinting, later generations would read Jones's words not as a timely critique responding to exigent historical circumstances but as obsolete and impractical spiritual reflections. The pamphlet battle the sermon precipitated and the widespread discussion the sermon provoked attest to the fact that the financial developments of the 1690s raised a series of ethical questions that transcended the religious context in which Jones happened to raise them. But because the sermon came from the pulpit, and because Pitt memorialized the affair as essentially an ecclesiastical blunder, Jones's critique of finance came to seem nothing more than an echo or rehashing of older, obsolete, superstitious attitudes toward money and finance. As much as Pitt's attack on Jones kept his name alive, it also discredited him, and with him, the critique of usury in general.

But here the question again must be asked, whence, in the 1690s, would an ethical critique of finance have come if not from the established tradition of Christian anti-usury polemic? In Jones's time, the language of finance itself had barely begun to enter into ordinary usage; there was even less a robust, non-spiritually-based ethical language to help articulate a posture of resistance. Hawkes claims that the post-Reformation period witnessed the dawn of political economy in the works of William Petty (1623–1687) and John Locke, but stances taken *against* political economy would nevertheless have needed to rely on Christian ethical discourse (192). Further, we must look to

the eighteenth century to see that whatever nascent political economic discourse had been produced in the period between 1660 and 1700, the nature
and even the reality of a discretely financial order remained unclear to even the
most erudite and astute observers of the world (see, e.g., Kramnick 39–40).
Understandably vexed by rapid financial innovation, Defoe could only bluster
in 1701: "These People can ruin Men silently ... and *Fiddle them out of their
Money*, by the strange and unheard of Engines of *Interests, Discounts, Transfers, Tallies, Debentures, Shares, Projects*, and the *Devil and all* of Figures and
hard Names" (*Villainy of Stock-Jobbers Detected* 22).[27] While there is no doubt
that Jones considered his sermon in the context of Christian salvation and sin,
we must not forget that writings against usury provided the only meaningful,
coherent, and authoritative discourse suitable to speak to "the *Devil and all* of
Figures and hard Names." What became of Jones is ultimately less important
than what we are to make of the countless followers, supportive and contrarian authors, essayists, poets, and their readers who in various ways attest to an
ongoing doubt about changing economic beliefs, practices, and relationships
of the last decades of the seventeenth century. Jones's endurance as a figure in
speech and writing over the course of the century suggests that a part of the
modern subject remained in exile from the land of financial progress, from
the land that Macaulay (1800–1859)—who dated the onset of modernity to
the Glorious Revolution and the economic changes that followed it—simply
knew as "England."[28]

As time went on, the normative English subject would trend further and
further away from that occupied and symbolized by Jones and his followers.
In addition to the litany of references to Jones as a sort of madman, by the end
of the eighteenth century objections to finance and usury amounted to nothing more than what Dugald Stewart (1753–1828) called "prejudices." For Stewart, these prejudices had been "completely exploded in every part of Europe,
insomuch that it appears to be almost as absurd to offer a serious argument
against them, as it would be to defend them" (150). Similarly, William Blackstone (1723–1780) had located belief in the sinfulness of usury to the "dark ages
of monkish superstition." But when "men's minds began to be enlarged, when
true religion and real liberty revived, commerce grew again into credit; and
again introduced with itself it's [*sic*] inseparable companion, the doctrine of
loans upon interest" (456, my emphasis). Unlike old false religion—Judaism,
paganism, Catholicism—British Protestantism accepts usury as a matter of
necessity and practical convenience. Happily fled are the "former times" when,
Blackstone sarcastically intones, "many good and learned men ... very much
perplexed themselves and other people, by raising doubts about [usury's]

legality *in foro conscientiae* [in point/forum of conscience]" (455). Later, citing Blackstone's *Commentaries*, Noah Webster wrote from Connecticut in one of his "fugitiv" essays (published in Boston and drafted according to his ideal of a uniquely American orthography) that "in no instance are the laws of England and America more strongly marked with the traces of ancient prejudice and barbarity, than in the prohibition which prevents a man from using hiz *money az he pleezes*, while he may demand any sum whatever for the use of hiz other property" (*Collection* 312–13). "I am so firmly persuaded of [the legitimacy of usury]," Webster remarked,

> that I venture to predict, the opinions of men will be changed in less than half a century, and posterity will wonder that their forefathers could think of maintaining [laws regarding interest on loans]. They will vew laws against usury in the same light that we do the inquisition in Spain, the execution of gypsies and witches in the last century, or thoze laws of England which make 100 l. annual income necessary to qualify a man for killing a partridge, while they allow *forty shillings* only to qualify him for electing a knight of the shire. (*Collection* 315–16)

Hypocritical logic of rank, belief in witches, laws against usury—for the zealously patriotic American Webster, who never missed a chance to indict the failings of British society, the argument against usury was out of joint with time by virtue of being locked into a larger and longer system of feudalism and Roman Catholic superstition, coordinate to Blackstone's "dark ages." (Webster, writing a century after Jones, still perceived lingering doubts about "usury" among his contemporaries: "The opinions of men will be changed in less than half a century.") Given such a powerful narrative of liberation and progress, it is easy to see why Jones, the quintessential anti-usury raver, would eventually be relegated to the realms of barbarity, madness, and irrelevance. The association of condemnations of usury with the belief in witchcraft and the miraculous begins with the pathologizing of David Jones, intensifies and crystallizes in the writings of Blackstone, Stewart, and Webster, and reaches its apogee in the nineteenth century, in William Edward Hartpole Lecky's (1838–1903) narrative of the "rise of rationalism" in the modern world, *The History of the Rise and Influence of the Spirit of Rationalism in Europe* (1866), featuring lengthy discussions of both usury prohibitions and witchcraft.[29]

Such thinking on the usury question was by no means confined to the polite and erudite formulations of Stewart, Blackstone, and Webster. A writer for the *London Chronicle* in 1776 put the matter in remarkable and widely ac-

cessible terms when describing the legitimacy of usury, here couched in terms
of the right to "alienate" property in whatever manner one chooses:

> A free and unrestrained power of alienation of every species of prop-
> erty seems not only to be the characteristic but the parent of free-
> dom; the feudal system that denied it, was a system of slavery, and as
> soon as this basis of its tyranny was shaken, the whole fabric fell to
> pieces; the current of human equality issuing from the exalted source
> of human nature, but choaked up and interrupted in its course by
> the Gothic tenures and manners, after undermining by degrees, and
> finding a silent way through its obstructions for several ages, at last
> broke over its mounds in the beginning of the seventeenth century,
> and seeking its way with fury and impetuosity, overshot the mark with
> its projectile force and overturned the constitution, till after various
> undulations it settled itself at last in that calm and peaceful state in
> which all undisturbed fluids remain when at their level, and at which
> all bodies in creation rest when at their natural stations. (1)

The medieval background to the rise of capitalism that Tawney delineated in
the twentieth century (discussed in greater detail in chapter 2) was already
being scripted in statements such as these, which could be described as an-
thropological corollaries to the biographical degradation of Jones, in the middle decades of the eighteenth century. It is not surprising to find Pitt's poem
anthologized so feverishly in precisely the same decades that witnessed the ef-
florescence of political economy, for it could be argued that the political economists' stadial histories of civilization, in which the usury prohibition serves
to mark premodern irrationality, both influence and are influenced by the
pathologization of Jones's raving in "The Art of Preaching." Over the course of
the eighteenth century, taking a stance against finance was increasingly treated
as an aspect of gothic, medieval, barbaric, superstitious (and often Roman
Catholic) life, but Jones appears to have been the first individual mocked for
clinging to such a stance. In this passage from the *Chronicle*, in which modernity is coded in terms of the essential power of capital bursting its dam with
the unstoppable force of the torrent, Jones would factor as one of the leftover
"obstructions" whose resistance was feudal and futile. The intensely poetical rendition of the rise of finance capitalism here—differing in content but
reminiscent in form of Denham's "gentle, yet not dull" Thames, which earlier
had given form to Augustan ideals of balance and proportion—should alone
open our eyes to the fact that the narrative of the end of usury is as rhetori-

cally constituted as any other such narrative. If the medievalizing of Jones and the critique of usury during and after the financial revolution was the *means* whereby anti-finance was suppressed, it is not difficult to imagine a *motive*. Given the literal importance of capital in colonization and industrialization, it might be said that the actual progress of modernity depends upon the *narrative* of capital's liberation from feudalism, since that narrative is the only guard against the realization that at the core of finance lies something vaguely unmentionable, ethically suspect, and certainly un-Christian.

Given the institutionalization of lending that led up to the 1690s and the "triumph" of modern finance that took place after that decade, Jones's sermon appears in retrospect as the naïve or quaint expression of an Anglican sophister, idealistic fantasy, atavistic lament for a purer Christian world, or simply the lunatic prescription of a disgruntled preacher just fired from his post. However, if Jones's remarks were eventually regarded as obsolete or idealistic, they certainly were neither in 1692. To be sure, they do fit into Norman Jones's narrative of transition, wherein usury gradually vanishes as a matter of public concern because it becomes increasingly a matter of individual intention and conscience. But as Margaret Ellen Newell has put it,

> Classical economic theory has so penetrated our own culture that
> we assume the naturalness of the economic man: rational, active,
> striving, improving, best left to his own devices by a limited state. But
> market-induced "passions" seemed highly unnatural—and sometimes
> threatening—to many seventeenth- and eighteenth-century Euro-
> peans. In the eyes of some contemporaries, the unfettered pursuit of
> wealth threatened to unleash a cornucopia of sins and dangerous social
> crimes throughout the social spectrum. (20)[30]

I would add to this that the Jones affair is important not merely for the critique of finance that it offers but because it was a cultural and discursive location where the naturalness of "economic man" was being established and where the critique of finance became (or was described as being) suddenly inappropriate, irregular, deviant, or, in Stewart's words, "absurd." It is not just that Jones attests to the existence of widespread hostility toward finance in the time of financial revolution (many historians allow this much) but that Jones's and other attacks on usury were read, cited, and repackaged over the course of the century so as to produce the sense that they were merely instances of raving, madness, or backwardness. A growing financial discourse, an *anti*-anti-finance way of seeing—such as we find in Jones's opponents, as well as in Pitt, Stewart, Blackstone, Webster, and other political economists of the late eighteenth century who were intent on occulting views such as Jones's, if not Jones himself, on through to Macaulay and Lecky in the nineteenth century—began to reconfigure the "nature" of commerce. Against the decidedly unnatural world of David Jones/feudalism/medieval thought stood something more real and legitimate: *homo economicus,* or economic man, the object of the analysis of political economy.

CHAPTER 2

Hazarding All for God

The Death of Usury and the Financial Revolution, Reconsidered

[Usury] bringeth the treasure of a realm or state into a few hands.
For the usurer being at certainties, and others at uncertainties,
at the end of the game most of the money will be in the box; and
ever a state flourisheth when wealth is more equally spread.

—*Francis Bacon, "Of Usury"*

JONES WAS doomed by his imprecise deployment of the term *usury* and by the firebrand tactics he employed to attack it. But even Jones recognized that *usury* meant more than simply taking interest on loans. Here it is my intention to discuss what this other meaning was and how significantly it factors into early modern anti-usury discourse and to show that on the basis of this other meaning the financial revolution might be read as having grown out of, rather than in spite of, the ethic put forth in Christian anti-usury literature. In this chapter, divided into three parts, I explore the history of ethical risk-taking up to the point at which moral concerns about usury are said to have been abandoned once and for all (by the end of the seventeenth century, around the time that Jones delivered his futile sermon). In the first part, I aim to sketch the ethic of uncertainty as it unfolds in intellectual history. It is not my purpose, nor is it within my ability, to examine that history in its entirety; for this, readers may turn to Eric Kerridge's economic history of Reformation thought on usury. But because it will prove helpful in demonstrating the continuity this book aims to stress, I briefly relate some of the views of the principal defenders of the risk criterion and, further, describe how those views have been overwritten, pathologized, or erased in orthodox histories of economics. By doing so I reveal how pivotal figures in the story of a *break* in the history of usury, such as John Calvin and Francis Bacon, might be seen as mediating anti-finance rather than rejecting it.

In the second part of this chapter, I address how this ideational continuity can be reconciled with the fact of financial modernization (the appearance of lotteries, banks, a culture of credit, and so forth, in the later decades of the seventeenth century). What sense can be made, I ask, of the development of a series of technologies, practices, and ideas that would appear to conform to the modern economist's idea of a financial system? I argue that at least some of those technologies and ideas might themselves be regarded less as ruptures with a premodern past than as continuations of the ethic advanced in early modern anti-usury discourse. Events such as the founding of the Bank of England can be read from a traditional perspective as confirmation that early modern usury prohibitions had ceased to exercise any influence. But the Bank of England, as well as the Million Lottery, can also be read as an expression of a collective desire to take risks, risks that would likely, if not necessarily, pay off because they would be taken within a just providential order. The events of the financial revolution, I argue, thus cut two ways. On the one hand, they provided enhanced financial security for some (such as the elite financiers who had been burned by Charles II in 1672); on the other, the financial revolution dramatically increased the number of opportunities for individuals to expose themselves to risk. Those who flocked to Jones's sermon may therefore have been opposed to some developments and in favor of others; or they may have supported the new institutions so long as those institutions were constrained by ethical principles or so long as the preeminence of the divine was conceded and it was risk, rather than certainty, that defined one's experiences with those institutions. Jessica Richard has recently rightly highlighted the aesthetic pleasures that risk-taking delivered to seventeenth- and eighteenth-century English subjects and reads the lottery as evidence of "the persistence of gambling within capitalism" (19). I aim to supplement that view and to complicate it somewhat by arguing that such risk-taking could also serve as an expression of faith.

In the final part of this chapter, I attempt to synthesize the first two parts by focusing on how things might have looked to someone who was both deeply devout and commercially active in the latter half of the seventeenth century. Specifically, I look at how one individual, the Puritan merchant Samuel Jeake (1652–1699), expressed his commitment both to the providence that underwrote the early modern critique of usury and to the new instruments of finance that defined the later seventeenth century. Jeake's belief in the providential underpinnings of the commercial order testify to the possibility of reading the financial revolution not as a moment of rapid secularization but as yet one more way in which God's will revealed itself in the world.

To preview the central claim of this chapter, it may be useful to begin with an overview of usury's two meanings and to briefly concretize that differ- ence with a look at the most famous usurer in the English literary tradition: William Shakespeare's Shylock. While usury was often criticized for being at odds with Deuteronomic law—a case of taking interest, or too much in- terest, in return for allowing someone the use of one's money—what made it the worst form of gain in the eyes of countless thinkers in the Protestant tradition was that it implied the making of a claim on the future that could not be reconciled with a providentialist view of personal and human history. An economic practice was considered acceptable if it placed the individual in a sufficiently powerless position relative to the outcome, which, in a world de- fined by Christians, was ultimately a matter of providential grace. Unlike ven- tures involving actual risk of loss, usurious lending was seen as providing the lender with financial security that neither depended upon nor derived from God's protection or authority. Lending and the exacting of interest were in fact subordinated to this more fundamental idea. The loan, textually codified and typically, though not necessarily, interest-bearing, offered the individual lender a degree of security independent of providential decree and influence. Because at some level the risk involved in other sorts of commercial undertak- ings (planting, trading, maritime privateering, venture capitalism, manufac- ture, even the lottery, for some) entailed the willful deliverance of individual futurity into the hands of an interventionist and determining providential authority, simple profiting *could* be folded into the Christian framework inso- far as any profits generated from an exchange or venture that was subject to God's will could be considered a divine gift, a matter of grace rather than will, not unlike salvation itself.[1] According to this view, if one happened to profit, then it was God's will that made it so; by the same token, if a merchant lost his ships at sea, or a farmer his crop to blight, it was the will of God and as such, although unfortunate, entirely just.

Thomas Moisan has shown that the distinction between merchants and usurers was less clear than polemicists of the early modern period made it seem, which I would suggest results from the fact that usury was thought to be taking place not only in the case of the contracted money loan but when- ever this open and uncertain element—providence—was canceled in the transaction. A merchant, for instance, who engrossed a commodity and could thereby firmly control the price of the commodity could fall into the category of the usurer even if he did not take any interest on a loan, even if, in fact, he did not lend anything at all. While the loan contract exemplified this attempt to make the future certain, it was only one of many instantiations of usury.

On the basis of this more flexible meaning of *usury* one can more clearly perceive the difference between the merchant and the usurer in Shakespeare's *Merchant of Venice* (1596). Antonio's decisions to trust his fortunes to wind and wave and then to become "the fool that lent his money gratis" to Bassanio are united in that both moments show him willing to cede his control over the future unfolding of events (48; 3.3.2). Shylock, by contrast, insists upon the execution of a "bond" that he insists cannot be undone and that therefore must be enforced through courts of justice, or with what Portia, in the guise of the lawyer, calls the "sceptre ... of temporal power" (59; 4.1.194). Shylock's real crime is not his desire for Antonio's flesh but his insistence on foreclosing future possibility; or, rather, the reason he desires Antonio's flesh is because for him the future became closed when the contract was issued. While Portia's insistence upon the divine quality of mercy has been aligned with chivalric ideals, it also partakes of the terms of the usury debates of the same decades, wherein the usurer was negatively regarded because of his belief that the economic world of contracts was insulated from the divine.[2]

At issue, ultimately, was whether such a thing as an economy existed apart from the Christian providential realm, and if it did exist, was it not the same as the equally godless—Christian-godless, of course—spaces of pagans, Jews, and Satan? Whereas the restrictive, temporal economy that underwrites Shylock's bond entitles him to execute it, from the higher, general economy of providence mercy "droppeth as the gentle rain from heaven" to show that the one is not, or should not be thought of as, separate from this higher economy (59; 4.1.189). Portia keeps with the reigning theologians' anti-usury logic when she further remarks that "in the course of justice, none of us / Should see salvation," not simply because Christians regard God's mercy as essential to salvation but because neither the soul nor God is a factor in—that is, can be seen in—Shylock's delimited, temporal economy (59; 4.1.1). Risk, or hazard, was the only way of indicating to one's self, to the world, and to God that one's "economic" actions were in the first instance a profession of faith in the workings of providence and a testament to one's willingness to accept whatever fate one was dealt in the course of time.

Usury, Risk, and the Ethic of Uncertainty

In what is arguably the single most important work on religion and economics, R. H. Tawney wrote that the problem with usury was that it implied a future certainty, and he presented this view as characteristic of the medieval mind:

[The lender] may demand compensation—*interesse*—if he is not repaid the principal at the time stipulated. He may ask payment corresponding to any loss he incurs or gain he foregoes. He may purchase an annuity, for the payment is contingent and speculative, not certain. . . . What remained to the end unlawful was that which appears in modern economic text-books as "pure interest"—interest as a fixed payment stipulated in advance for a loan of money or wares without risk to the lender. . . . The essence of usury was that it was certain, and that, whether the borrower gained or lost, the usurer took his pound of flesh. . . . His crime is that he takes a payment for money which is fixed and certain, and such a payment is usury. (42–43)

Tawney's insight into the relation between usury and certainties is important; his relegation of that relation to the "medieval background" of his *Religion and the Rise of Capitalism* equally so. For Reformation and post-Reformation writers just as firmly believed in and continued to promulgate the criminality of financial certainties that Tawney exclusively associates with the medieval criticism of *pactum*. Financial instruments were acceptable so long as they were "contingent and speculative, not certain." Where Tawney goes wrong is in assuming that the only way an individual could attain such "certain" returns was through a contract that stipulated in advance a guaranteed return—interest—on a loan. While Kerridge has already observed Tawney's error in conflating usury with interest exclusively, I would like to draw attention to the fact that Tawney's attempt to locate and thereby confine the argument regarding certainty to a specific, premodern historical moment or epoch suggests that later writers who express similar convictions are out of touch with their present, with their modernity.

The impact of Tawney's characterization of beliefs concerning certainties as characteristic of a premodern moment, echoing Whiggish histories of Western civilization's liberation from the prison of superstition and belief, is difficult to overstate. And the impact is not limited to triumphalist narratives of modernity. To take one example, Maurizio Lazzarato, a thinker who is sympathetically attuned to the problem of risk in contemporary Western financial culture but whose perspective on modernity owes more to Nietzsche, Deleuze, and Guattari than to orthodox economic history, similarly assigns this position to the medieval rather than to the modern era in his 2012 book *The Making of the Indebted Man*. There is a fairy-tale quality to Lazzarato's rendition of the story:

Whereas in the Middle Ages time belonged to God and God alone,
today, as possibility, creation, choice, and decision, it is the primary
object of capitalist expropriation/appropriation. . . . Whereas in industrial societies there still existed an "open" time—in the form of progress
or revolution—today, the future and its possibilities, quashed by the
huge sums of money mobilized by finance and devoted to reproducing
capitalist power relations, seem to be frozen. For debt simply neutral-
izes time, time as the creation of new possibilities, that is to say, the
raw material of all political, social, or esthetic change. (48–49)

It is not that Lazzarato is wrong about finance. He is absolutely right
about how it works vis-à-vis the individual's ownership of and relation to
future time and in much the same way that Tawney is right to see the medieval subject as concerned with the openness of the future. However, there
is no reason to believe that it is only in the context of the current configuration of global capital, or in the medieval context of *pactum*, that a critique
of finance based upon the foreclosure of the future is possible, for the argument that such unlikely bedfellows as Tawney and Lazzarato make about
the need for finance to remain open with respect to time and possibility has
been made throughout the entire history of capital, though it has taken different forms. Allowing for the many differences between the theocentric critique of finance characteristic of the medieval and early modern periods and
the post-Marxian critique offered up by Lazzarato, uncertainty features as
an ethical category in surprisingly similar ways.[3] Moreover, the attempt to
locate belief in the risk criterion—which is another way of describing the
value placed upon an open, non-neutralized time, the condition of "possibility"—in a once-upon-a-time medieval moment of wholeness not only gets
it wrong from a basic factual standpoint but serves to re-create modernity
through an act of historiographic violence. This particular act of belief relegation and historical confinement—the making of the risk criterion into a feature of the premodern or medieval mind—serves as a key technology for the
discursive creation of modernity because it effectually unhinges the progress
of capital from its own, immanent critique. Far from an exclusively medieval belief, the risk criterion was most forcefully articulated by Martin Luther,
and while Luther's position on this matter has been accepted by revisionist
religious historians, their findings have not made their way into the study of
early modern culture more broadly speaking, one result of which has been a
nearly exclusive focus on early modern beliefs about and cultural productions'
engagement with the legal prohibition of interest on loans and the Scholastic

insistence upon the barrenness of money. Both of these anti-usury views, the one grounded in Old Testament law and the other in Aristotle's *Politics*, were important features of early modern thought, of course, but they are by no means the only foundations upon which critiques of the changing economic order were based.

In attempting to formulate a workable distinction between trade and usury, Luther had argued in favor of vulnerability and uncertainty in commerce, because only under those conditions could the agent be said to submit himself or herself to the divine authority over future events in time, as described by Lazzarato. Here, for example, Luther attacks the idea of standing surety for another individual's bond:

> Standing surety is a work that is too lofty for a man; it is unseemly, for it is a presumptuous encroachment upon the work of God. In the first place, Scripture commands us not to put our trust and reliance in any man, but in God alone. . . .
>
> In the second place, the surety is trusting in himself and making himself God (for whatever a man trusts in and relies upon is his god). But his own life and property are never for a single moment any more secure or certain than those of the man for whom he becomes surety. Everything is in the hand of God alone. God will not allow us a hair's breadth of power or right over the future, nor will he let us for a single moment be sure or certain of it. Therefore, he who becomes surety acts in an un-Christian way. (*Trade and Usury* 253–54)

Although this attack appears in Luther's writing on usury, his primary target is not moneylending, which is merely one manifestation of the more fundamental crime of attempting to limit future possibility. Elsewhere in the treatise, Luther complains that by controlling the flow of a given commodity, monopolies are able to raise and depress prices to keep small competitors out of the market. Monopolies, he writes, "do not have to suffer any loss, injury, or risk" (271). This, Luther argues, is "contrary to the nature, not only of merchandise, but of all temporal goods, which God wills should be subject to risk and uncertainty" (271).

Before exploring these views in greater detail, let us first consider how they have been read and how those readings have factored into the "disappearing" of the risk criterion from the historical record. To begin, Luther's position on the subject of risk has been regarded as something of an embarrassment since at least the nineteenth century. For instance, in the January 1897 issue of *Open*

Court, a monthly periodical "devoted to the Science of Religion" and "the Religion of Science," where a lengthy excerpt from Luther's treatise is reprinted, the editor condescendingly remarks of the passage concerning sureties quoted above that Luther's stark distinction between worldly and spiritual matters made it impossible for him to recognize "the spiritual significance of trade as a moral factor in the evolution of civilization" (editor's note on 17). To translate: Luther was a good man, but he did not understand trade. Such a reading of Luther, laden with judgments based on core assumptions about both Luther and the realities of trade, is part of the powerful revisionism exercised by historians who assign civilizational importance to commerce and cannot read the critique of finance, the celebration of uncertainty, as anything other than aberration, error, or delusion. Luther and his followers saw that in usurious dealing the place of God was difficult, if not impossible, to locate, for unlike the adventurous risktaker, the usurer would always be sure of property.

Tawney elaborated, but did not substantially revise, this basic nineteenth-century perspective. Tawney writes that Luther, when "confronted with the complexities of foreign trade and financial organization, or with the subtleties of economic analysis, [is] like a savage introduced to a dynamo or a steam-engine. He is too frightened and angry even to feel curiosity. Attempts to explain the mechanism merely enrage him; and he can only repeat that there is a devil in it, and that good Christians will not meddle with the mystery of iniquity" (89). Such a frenzied incoherency, Tawney claims, results in a text that defies attempts to read it: "It is idle to scan [Luther's utterances] for a coherent and consistent doctrine," for it is the product of an "impetuous but ill-formed genius" who dispenses "with the cumbrous embarrassments of law and logic, to evolve a system of social ethics from the inspired heat of his own unsophisticated consciousness" (88–89). As dazzling as Tawney's insults are, his treatment of Luther fails to grasp one essential point and rides on the back of a profound logical error perpetrated by Tawney himself: Luther's "doctrine"—to the extent that this is even what Luther imagined himself to be writing—is coherently organized under the banner of the risk criterion, and it reverberates throughout *Trade and Usury.* Tawney references risk in Luther's treatise on just two occasions, and only in passing, and thereby fails to grasp the continuity and force of Luther's position. Tawney judges Luther not in terms of the nascent financial system that Luther recoiled at but purely as an ultimate historical failure. Tawney is guilty of a teleological bias that governs and shapes his assessment of Luther's coherency and importance to future opponents of unbridled economic development.

A slightly more complicated but no less important instance of reading

Luther anachronistically is to be found in the introduction to Walther I. Brandt's English edition of *Trade and Usury* in Luther's *Works*. Brandt sets the stage in his introduction to Luther's thought by pointing out that the treatise is important primarily for its "keen observations on the business practices of the early sixteenth century" (233). Brandt adds that when it comes to larger ideas, however, Luther "knew very little about economic laws" (233). As a kind of evidence for this, Brandt asserts that Luther "held to the long scholastic tradition which, following Aristotle, taught that money does not produce money" (233);[4] Luther's "frame of reference was of course the Middle Ages" (233). These remarks, however, appearing on the first page of Brandt's introduction, derive from a Tawney-influenced depiction of Luther's commercial ethics as savage and premodern. To discredit Luther's overarching ethical stance against finance, Brandt invokes the Aristotelian position, as if to highlight the antiquity or obsolescence of Luther's ideas, and he aligns Luther with a Middle Ages that is itself discredited because superseded by a wiser, modern age. In accusing Luther of failing to grasp "economic laws," Brandt, in other words, presupposes the existence of an economic system that admits to laws or codes or that might be discussed in such terms. But the "laws" of economics, as Brandt presumably understands them, were not articulated until some three hundred years after Luther lived, so to accuse Luther of not knowing about them is to say little more than that he was born before Alfred Marshall (1842–1924), who was beginning to publish his field-defining *Principles of Economics* in the 1890s—the same decade in which the *Open Court* editorial was written, by which time Luther's commercial pieties had been rejected and people could congratulate themselves for assuming less naïve, modern attitudes toward economics.

Yet Luther does, Brandt observes, helpfully describe the "business practices of the early sixteenth century." Unable to theorize economic life but long on "practical" knowledge, Brandt fails to appreciate that the two were very much the same for Luther in 1524 and that the emergence of a culture in which "economic laws" could be articulated independent of an ethics is precisely the object of Luther's critique—as it would be for David Jones much later. Luther's theoretical uselessness results, according to Brandt, from an unrealistic approach to commerce: "his concern was religious in the first instance and only secondarily economic" (239); Luther was "the theologian and pastor who laid upon the heart of Christian hearers the uncompromising demands of God" (239); "he was realistic enough" to allow the charging of interest in some cases but was otherwise implacably attached to ideals characteristic of the medieval mind (238). But Brandt is really demanding from

Luther a "realism" that is the product of a much later historical event, to wit, the emergence of economics as a science and method, while the assumption of a fissure in Luther's mind—"religious in the first instance and only secondarily economic"—anticipates the sort of scholarly locution that Pocock would later be guilty of in saying that for Davenant, an "equation" between the commercial and the Christian had to be *made* (see the introduction). More specifically, the idea of economic reality, the idea of economics as a separate reality, as Brandt employs the concepts, emerged only in the discursive, violent, and decidedly unreal world of late-eighteenth- and nineteenth-century political economy, in which such a reality was being forged in the pages of works by Smith, Ricardo, Bentham, Mill, Bagehot, Lecky, and Marshall, to name but a handful of luminaries in the pantheon of political economy. As one recent commentator puts it, this style of political economy is "intended to force social reality into practical purposes: profits, accumulation, power. Economic reality does not exist, it is the result of a process of technical modeling, submission, and exploitation" (Berardi 73). Because liberal political economy had different ideas of what was and was not "realistic" to ask of or expect from commerce, Luther's thought could not be made to square with that reality, rendering him, for Brandt, a bad theorist and an interesting historical curiosity whose greatest achievement was chronicling an age of error. And it was precisely this illegibility of Luther vis-à-vis political economy that made him seem medieval or "savage" for Tawney. More might be said of Brandt's Tawney-inspired negative assessment of Luther's modernity and theoretical relevance to history, but perhaps we should look to Luther himself instead.

Luther had argued that "at no time are we [to be] sure of either life or property, but may await and receive everything from his hands, as a true faith does. And truly we see it every day in many of God's works, that things must work out a certain way whether we like it or not" (255). Building upon this view, Luther lists five types of exchange that could be justifiably labeled Christian: (1) bartering; (2) being robbed and then giving freely; (3) giving freely without expectation of repayment; (4) lending without the imperative to repay but accepting payment if eventually offered; and (5) buying and selling for cash payment. On the other hand, he "who lends expecting to get back something more or something better than he has loaned is nothing but an open and condemned usurer, since even those who in lending demand or expect to get back exactly what they lend, and take no chances on whether they get it back or not, are not acting in a Christian way" (257). What makes the five types of exchange listed above legitimate is that, in Luther's words, they do not involve "presuming upon the future" and instead entail "clinging to God alone" (257). Contracting for, demanding, or even *expecting* remuneration con-stitutes usury for Luther, who was developing Luke 6:34–35: "And if you lend only where you expect to be repaid, what credit is there in that? Even sinners lend to each other to be repaid in full. But you must love your enemies and do good, and lend without expecting any return; and you will have a rich reward" (*Oxford Study Bible*). The central idea—"lend without expecting any return"—grounded the ethical prohibition of lending, but lending was merely an instance or manifestation of a more fundamental crime (hoping for, ex-pecting, or making certain a future return). The contract signified a look to-ward the future, the hope of return, an objectification of future time, but for a writer such as Luther, even *thinking* about the possibility that one might get something later was usurious. Between these two positions—an actual con-tract securing future returns and the bare expectation of receiving returns—theologians staked out their own, but few ventured outside these parameters.

According to the religious historian Joan Lockwood O'Donovan, in writ-ings on usury by medieval theologians in the Thomist/Aristotelian tradition, "retaining of ownership and risk became the decisive criteria for distinguish-ing non-usurious from usurious uses of property" (54), and it was the risk criterion that had been taken up by Luther. According to O'Donovan, Luther "views risk as expressing the divinely ordained structure of humankind's rela-tion to temporal goods, and strategies for the overcoming of risk as endemic to the avaricious corruption of exchange, and so condemns all practices that enable the merchant to 'make safe, certain, and continual profit out of unsafe, uncertain, and perishable goods'" (62). O'Donovan adds that "the argument about risk occupies the pivotal place in Luther's usury theory" (63). Luther was modern, it might be said, not because he embraced the new commer-cial culture of his time but because he *rejected* the Aristotelian bases upon which the medieval and Scholastic anti-usury position had been founded in favor of a more robust ethical system grounded in the experience of risk and premised upon the positive value of uncertainty. If we wish to be anachro-nistic, we might further say that Luther was modern in that he grasped or foresaw the potential *consequences* of separating economic from ethical life: without a coherent and logically prior ethical foundation, economic "laws" as such—the view that there might be "laws" independent of ethical and spiri-tual considerations—would necessarily lead to inequality and exploitation.

Tawney accused Luther of incoherence, and yet it is plain, if one cares to look, that Luther's views are organized around and activated by this central ethical mandate to risk. It appears, as I have noted, in his condemnation of standing surety. It is equally central, as Luther continues to argue later in

Trade and Usury, to his critique of those who engross commodities, those who attempt to secure monopolies, those who sell "on time and credit" rather than cash, those who traffic in what amount to commodity-futures contracts, and those who exploit the absolute needs of the poor and others who find themselves forced to pay whatever merchants demand (*gouging*, in modern parlance). While none of these conform to what is typically described as usury—the taking of excessive interest—for Luther they all partake of the same basic evil, namely, the attempt to make profits certain and shift risk onto others. Each of these individual types of deals, in its own way, effectively removes the chance of loss—as well as what we might today label "market competition"—and in so doing allows for the growth of exploitative systems of wealth and commerce. Luther lists a number of other sinful business practices, all of which reduce, for Luther, to studied and cunning attempts to avoid uncertainties. This is, further, the centerpiece of Luther's lengthy criticism of *Zinskauf*, which he reads as a coded attempt to get around the strictures on loans by merely redescribing what amounts to a loan in terms of a *Kauf*, "purchase." In this light, the biggest impact of Tawney's erroneous claims regarding Luther's commercial ethics consists not only in their having underestimated the internal coherency of Luther's thought and his keen eye for financial chicanery, which Luther saw as a necessary product of economics without ethics, but also in their having occluded continuities between Luther and his successors.

If Luther is classed with Catholic and medieval writers who expressed a similar antipathy toward the criminal certainties of the *pactum*, "we associate the name of John Calvin," writes Michael Wykes, "first and foremost with the liberation of usury from medieval economic thought" (27).[5] This type of reading, which is also evident in Tawney's conception of the changing ethics concerning finance, has by and large situated Calvin in opposition to the old prohibitions. There is good reason for this: in support of lending, Calvin, in his commentary on Psalms 15:5, stated that "the gain which he who lends his money upon interest acquires, without doing injury to any one, is not to be included under the head of unlawful usury" (213–14). Wykes points out that Calvin's broader contribution to the progress of finance was to illustrate the similarity between the Roman *mutuum* (a money loan, long considered usurious) and *locatio* (the renting of a place, house, or field, often considered a legitimate form of profiting), thereby introducing the possibility of money's ability to produce more money.

Wykes crucially observes, however, that the matter is not quite so simple: Calvin allowed for lending but stipulated that the loan must not benefit one party more than the other, that there must be equity in the transaction, and that the loan must not oppress the poor. Hence, the "good" or "evil" of usury becomes a circumstantial and historical affair and does not amount to a theological legitimation of lending, much less the abandonment of ethical guidelines in commerce. Wykes observes this tension in Calvin's general attitude toward usury—he allowed it but did not trust it—and argues that Calvin more or less resolved it with the equity (or fairness) limitation. But by introducing the question of equity, Calvin did no more than place an ethical restriction on a practice regarded as inherently unethical, leaving usury's theologically and ethically repugnant status fundamentally intact. To return to the distinction between writers of anti-usury opinion and writers of anti-finance, Calvin did allow usury in the narrow sense—the taking of interest on loans—but only because he grasped the larger and more fundamental need for risk. It is a "strange and shameful thing," Calvin observed, that

> while all other men obtain the means of their subsistence with much toil, while husbandmen fatigue themselves by their daily occupations, and artisans serve the community by the sweat of their brow, and merchants not only employ themselves in labors, but also *expose themselves to many inconveniences and dangers,*—that money-mongers should *sit at their ease* without doing any thing, and receive tribute from the labor of all other people. (213, my emphasis)

As Roger Fenton (1565–1616), a translator for the King James Bible and a prominent early modern opponent of usury, put it, Calvin exploded his apology for usury by placing countless restrictions upon it: "even where he is most favourable" regarding lending, Calvin did nothing to "relieve" the conscience of the usurer (63).

Complicating matters further is a noticeable but frequently overlooked tension between the form and the content of Calvin's various comments on usury. Generally speaking, his prose style is as suggestive of opposition to usury as his argument for equitable lending is of belief in its acceptability. That is to say, his tentative, equity-constrained, occasional allowance of lending contrasts sharply with the rhetorical energy displayed in moments of hostility toward usury and usurers: "all bargains in which the one party unrighteously strives to make gain by the loss of the other party . . . are here condemned" (223); "let [my readers] not imagine that any thing can be lawful to them which is grievous and hurtful to others" (223); "it is scarcely possible to find in the world a usurer who is not at the same time an extortioner, and addicted to unlawful and dishonorable gain" (223); "Cato of old justly placed the practice of usury and the killing of men in the same rank of criminality, for the object of this class of people is to suck the blood of other men" (223); it "is not . . . without cause that God has, in Leviticus 25:35, 36, forbidden usury" (224). Depending upon a rhetoric of absolutes and universals that constantly threaten to envelop all particular deals—"all bargains," "any thing . . . which is grievous and hurtful"—Calvin pairs such abstractions with the grossly material image of the blood-sucking demon, a trope that was ubiquitous in anti-usury literature. So while his text offers a counterweight to the biblical condemnation of usury in the form of the argument that lending is bad only when it is unequal, there remains a decided imbalance between, on the one hand, Calvin's rhetorically excessive, enthusiastic condemnation of it and, on the other, the philosophical argument that is quietly and almost imperceptibly inserted within that broader condemnation.

This is as much as to say that if Calvin was able to rationalize usury to himself, there is ample reason to believe that it would *not* be rationalized by his readers. Calvin's rhetorical exuberance may have been designed to discourage would-be usurers, who might seek justification in the commentary's distinctions, but the result would have been the same: the text functions primarily as an attack on usury. In any case, it seems likely that zealots could locate in Calvin's tone ample reason to distrust the distinction, while later readers who wish to locate Calvin in the positive history of capitalism's progress have to draw upon subtle and undeveloped remarks scattered throughout Calvin's writings (such as the equity provision in the commentary on Psalms 15:5). Whatever we ultimately make of Calvin's position, against Nelson's claim that by "the middle of the seventeenth century the traditionalist forces [against usury] had been thoroughly routed in Protestant lands" (95), Calvin*ists*, particularly those in seventeenth-century England, "thundered from the pulpits and presses of England the most powerful and consistent *anti-usury* doctrine ever known to that Christian commonwealth" (George 462). Reading through the Puritan Robert Bolton's (1572–1631) writings against usury, for instance, one is immediately struck by the number of times Calvin is invoked for support. Whatever later historians may have made of Calvin's "pro-usury" posture, it is undeniable that his English successors read him as arguing precisely the opposite.

If Calvin managed to erect a clear and legible distinction between usurious and non-usurious lending—which I am suggesting his rhetoric, if not always his logic, resists—it was the result not of logical progression but of displacement. Calvin merely shifts the emphasis toward an equally vexing arrangement of new terms. What, now, one might ask of Calvin, constitutes an *equitable* loan, and what an *inequitable* loan? What is the difference between simply gaining from poor people and devouring them? How does one define injury to others? All such "economic" questions could only be answered by contemplating one's ethics first. Calvin closes the comment on usury specifically with a specific reference to the Golden Rule, arguing that were the rule universally followed, a defense of usury would not be necessary, which is as much as saying that lending for profit proceeds ethically only from the standpoint of a corrupted and sinful world.

So if Calvin did allow usury, because he did not precisely define who was included under the term *poor*, because he did not specify the nature of an equitable loan, because he still clung to the risk criterion, because his abstract terms made nearly every deal or bargain or exchange somewhat suspect, and because he only allowed lending in light of the fallen-ness of the world, readers might fairly interpret Calvin as prohibiting usury in virtually every conceivable circumstance. Far from a tension, however, what Calvin's argument shows is how impossible it was for him to regard "economic law" as separate from spiritual or moral law, since all economic decisions had to be made with spiritual ends in mind. Regarding Max Weber's once-popular view that Calvinism was determinant of capitalism's progress, Joyce Appleby points out that Calvinism's heyday was well past by the time of accelerated economic modernization[6] and that Calvin therefore could not have had a positive impact on such progress, but this should not lead us to forget that Calvinism may have continued to provide a basis for arguments *against* new capital formations. Via their sixteenth- and seventeenth-century successors, Luther's and Calvin's views remained the active ingredients of an anti-finance discourse that went underground, bubbling up whenever the villainies of financiers became most apparent.[7]

Like Calvin, Bacon makes allowances for lending, and so he too has been classed with those who brought about key transformations in ethical thought respecting usury. But also like Calvin, Bacon reveals how it was possible for someone to support the charging of interest on loans and still embrace a medieval, Lutheran, and Calvinist ethic of uncertainty. I should stress that I am not calling into question Bacon's modernity in general (which is, in any event, largely a semantic dispute about the meaning of modernity); what I am questioning is the idea that Bacon's attitude toward usury was the articulation of a thoroughly rational, innovatory, secular spirit. The triumph of capitalism greatly enjoys being a part of that story of the triumph of rationality, innovation, and so forth, which is why Bacon's words on usury loom large in

Whiggish narratives that assert Western civilization's transcendence of older anti-usury ideas. There are good reasons for Bacon's place in such narratives, but his view concerning usury should not be one of them. To show this, however, it is necessary here to dispense with the two dominant ways in which Bacon's modernity with respect to finance has been understood, vis-à-vis the Aristotelian sterility hypothesis and vis-à-vis the idea that usury was rejected for its displacement of real work.

I will return to Bacon in a moment, but with regard to Bacon's time more generally, scholars of recent date have increasingly interested themselves in the notion that usury was once viewed as a case of wealth generating more of itself through a kind of unnatural monetary onanism or sodomy.[8] Crucial to such reflections is a comment made by Aristotle in the *Politics*: "For money was intended to be used in exchange, but not to increase at interest. And this term interest, which means the birth of money from money, is applied to the breeding of money because the offspring resembles the parent. That is why of all modes of getting wealth this is the most unnatural" (1997). As important as claims about interest and reproduction would turn out to be in validating norms regarding commerce and sexuality, however, anxieties about usury's unnatural tendency to breed were not "the major ideological obstacle to the accumulation of capital"; at least they did not feature as centrally in early modern anti-usury tracts as recent scholarship might lead one to believe (Hawkes 97). In its full context, Aristotle's remark relates rather to his larger concerns about the procuration of money and the function of money in binding society together and keeping it harmonious, which is a point that Wennerlind reminds his readers of in his recent work on seventeenth-century neo-Aristotelian political economy (33–37). Aristotle's views on money were important in early modern attacks on the unequal and improper distribution of wealth in society, but writers involved in the usury controversy in England rarely relied on the sterility claim—that money could not produce or should not produce more of itself—in their formulations of ethical and religious guidelines for commerce. And so to put it bluntly: scholarly emphasis on early modern preoccupations with the sterility of money, while revealing much about the early modern attitudes toward the body and sexuality, not only tells us very little about early modern commercial ethics but actively mystifies and obscures other legitimate foundations upon which Reformation and post-Reformation anti-usury opinion had long been based.

Unlike the risk criterion, which touched on virtually every form of "economic" activity, the sterility hypothesis not only was limited in being exclusively applicable to money loans but, as a logical nonstarter, *appealed* to pro-

ponents of lending since it could be so easily mocked. In "Of Usury" (*Essays*)
Bacon mentions Aristotle's remark, only to summarily ignore it and thereby
show how toothless the dictum really was. Had it been worth refuting, Bacon
would have done so. He was not the only one to ignore it, and if we look to the
major anti-usury polemics of Bacon's time—nearly all of which were written
by devout churchmen of one stamp or another—it becomes apparent just
how small a place the Aristotelian "argument" occupies in those texts. In its
proverbial form, it increasingly became a joke, albeit one with serious, if distant, consequences. For the claim that anti-usury opinion of the "premodern"
era relied upon nothing more than Aristotle's decontextualized proclamation
about money's sterility enabled later writers to articulate the distinctive modernity of finance and to thereby tacitly proclaim their own intellectual superiority over such outmoded and dogmatic ways of thinking.

Whatever the impact of the Aristotelian view on the history of usury may
have been, clearly there were tactical reasons for casting it as central to the
views of anyone opposed to finance. As the author of an otherwise serious
early-eighteenth-century apology for usury put it, "As for the saying . . . that
it is Monstrous for Money to beget Money, it's a trifling Reason . . . I know of
nothing else that begets Money more than Money, and he that will fish for
Money, must bate with a Silver Hook, or else he may bob long enough till he
is ready to Starve" (*Common Law Treatise* x). The author refutes the maxim
concerning the monstrosity of monetary autoproduction by employing an
equally valid metaphorical construction of money as a sort of fish; neither line
of reasoning holds up, though they are equally good as metaphors. The sterility hypothesis, in short, *became* an antiquated position by being abstracted
from its complete context, in which the question was not the ontology of
money or the sexuality of metals but the social function of money. By the end
of the seventeenth century, Aristotle's argument was not even an argument;
it was a metaphor that when unhinged from a more comprehensive framework could be undone and reworked without any ethical, political, or spiritual
cost.[9] The most that can be said, at least with respect to Christian anti-usury
of the seventeenth century, is that while anti-usury polemicists frequently *referenced* the sterility hypothesis, few did more with it than cite it to provide one
more authoritative, classical attack on usury. On the other side of the debate,
defenders of the new financial order enthusiastically portrayed Aristotle's
claim as *central* to critics of finance, for doing so would discredit those critics'
opinions wholesale, even when those other opinions did not logically depend
upon the validity of the sterility hypothesis. That Bacon ignored the sterility
argument shows that he was not in league with Aristotelians, but that is no

reason to conclude that he rejected the risk criterion, which was the more fundamental issue relating to finance. The sterility argument is, to risk a pun, a red herring. The real roots of the usury problem were grounded elsewhere, in the problem of risk, which ramified deeply into the soil of Christianity and foliated into a far more diffusive and sheltering ethic of uncertainty.

Anti-usury polemicists more commonly drew upon exegetical commentary on biblical commands and directives, particularly those found in Luke 6:34–35, "Lend, hoping for nothing again"; and Genesis 3:18–19, "You will get food from [earth] only by labor all the days of your life; it will yield thorns and thistles for you. You will eat of the produce of the field, and only by the sweat of your brow will you win your bread" (*Oxford Study Bible*). In the latter, the operative word in the context of the usury debates was *sweat*: the lender circumvented the sweats of labor as well as, by extension, the anxious sweats associated with the contemplation of loss.[10] By using banks, contracts, and courts to secure profits, the usurer effectually stole the bread that had been naturally produced by the "thou" of Genesis 3:19, the interpellated Christian laboring subject.[11] To extrapolate Genesis's link to Luke 6:34–35, it was thought that expectations concerning future remuneration for present action implied that one was attempting to circumvent the determinations of God and seeking to avoid the harsh, hazardous, and uncertain progression of the self through the world. Although there are superficial similarities between Genesis's focus on work and Aristotle's line concerning money's sterility, the metaphysics of money—whether it can produce more of itself or no—was not essential to the line of reasoning that developed out of Genesis 3:19 or Luke 6:34–35. If the sterility hypothesis did carry some weight in the early modern period, it did so only insofar as it referenced and activated a more fundamental belief that one's profits should not be determined in advance. A system of pure finance—money generating money, if one wishes—was problematic because it was predicated on a system of external supports that effectively and determinately foreclosed the chance of loss and suffering, not because of a belief in some strange, metaphysical attribute of coin. Lands are subject to loss, houses to decay, laborers to illness or injury, and ships to wind, wave, and piracy; a financial scheme, by contrast, in which the courts or the state might intervene to secure a stream of revenue into the future, is not subject to loss, at least not in the same ways.

Returning to Bacon, although such scriptural sources would not have provided him with a sufficient reason to reject usury, he was keenly aware of them. In "Of Riches" he writes that "usury is the certainest means of gain, though one of the worst, as that whereby a man doth eat his bread *in sudore*

Bacon

vultus alien [in the sweat of another's face/brow], and besides, doth plough upon Sundays" (*Essays* 166–67).[12] For Bacon, what made usury the "worst" means of gain was that its certainty was predicated upon the sacrificial gestures, adventurous journeys, and/or grueling labors performed by others who signed away the benefit of those gestures, journeys, and labors to lenders who refused to assume the risks themselves. Even though Bacon presents it as a "besides," his reference to "plough[ing]" on Sundays is a crucial index of this larger meaning. For Bacon, when the laborer would rest (Sunday), the usurer would continue to reap his benefits, because the loan term (and interest generated over that term) factored in the Sabbath whether the laborer worked or not. The money, that is, would continue to "work," in the sense that it would continue to yield revenue for the lender, while the laborer himself was paying heed to mandatory times of rest and repose.[13] The laborer, who refuses to "plough upon Sundays," admits to and allows for pauses in work. The laborer does so not simply because of the need for rest or because it exhibits a formulaic piety but because in devoting portions of the week to God, he or she symbolically gifts a portion of the possible future (revenue, harvest, etc.) to God. What might have been earned on the Sabbath would have more tightly secured the laborer, but the laborer virtuously elects instead to give the gift of this time to God. So the sacrifice of the future in the form of rest on the Sabbath is, in effect, a de-securitizing of the laborer's future. This de-securitization is what Bacon tacitly praises by promoting rest on Sundays.

But there is more. As easy as it is to assume that what Bacon is here praising by way of contrast is labor, trade, or manufacture—productive work instead of unproductive finance—the distinction between legitimate and illegitimate commercial behavior in the early modern period is equivalent to our modern distinction between "real work" and "unreal finance" only insofar as it is the *security* that the financier gains through the work of others that marks the illegitimacy of the transaction.[14] It is the *security* provided by finance that is ethically tainted, not its "unreality" or its "unproductivity." Had productivity been paramount for Bacon, it would have made little sense for him to remind his readers that there were more important things than work, that they ought not work on the Sabbath. Central to anti-finance, in other words, was a conception of work that was not reducible to productivity. In chapter 3, I will discuss how this conception figures in *Robinson Crusoe*. But even in Bacon, an element of sacrifice, or what the political economist might call "wasted time," has its place.

In other words, if the sterility hypothesis was not the primary basis for the early modern critique of usury, neither was the claim that usurers simply avoided labor. The distinction between work and usury invoked by early modern English writers should not, therefore, be simply mapped onto a modern productivity/nonproductivity binary, as this binary's hierarchically privileged term depends on whether one is discussing, say, the efficiencies of a factory or the ethical experience of Christian subjects. More important was an antecedent distinction between, on the one hand, economic activity that entailed risk and placed the self in a condition of vulnerability vis-à-vis the future (the laborer or merchant who exposed himself or herself to loss) and, on the other, economic activity that sought to eliminate contingency from fallen, human existence (the usurer).

It was neither money's inherently nonproductive nature nor finance's displacement of real work that constituted problems for Bacon; rather, it was that usury "bringeth the treasure of a realm or state into a few hands. For the usurer being at certainties, and others at uncertainties, at the end of the game most of the money will be in the box; and ever a state flourisheth when wealth is more equally spread" ("Of Usury" 75). Bacon argues that moneylending should be allowed, but this is because it *prevents* usury, which for him was the illicit attainment of certainty. Moneylending, therefore, should be allowed because it prevents the hoarding of wealth, which is bad for the commonwealth and disastrous for real commerce. He allows, in sum, for usury in its narrow sense (the charging of interest) in order to prevent usury in its broader sense from becoming the norm. While scholars have, with a few notable exceptions, overlooked the importance of this distinction, the problem with certainty that Bacon's essay takes as a given—it need not even be argued or independently articulated—is widely available in the archive of early modernity, and writers of the seventeenth century emphasized that in addition to subverting the postlapsarian mandate to work, the usurer also circumvented the risks inherent to a fallen world. As Kerridge puts it, "The essence of usury was that it was not merely gain, but certain and assured gain. The borrower bore all the risk and uncertainty, the usurer none" (58). This is what properly defines the ethics of commerce and finance, from Luther all the way to Bacon.

In reading Francis Bacon anti-financially, I hope to have shown that the term *anti-finance* is not intended to apply solely to writers who were opposed to commerce or wealth. In his praise and admiration for wealthy individuals, the wildly popular evangelical preacher Anthony Horneck (1641–1697) also fits within the tradition I am charting. For Horneck, profiting was by no means an evil, and commerce could be sacrosanct under certain conditions: "that . . . many of those who truly fear God, have a very large share in temporal Plenty and Prosperity; and that many times Men thrive the better for a serious Life, and a secret Blessing attends them, Plenty steals upon them beyond expectation; and as if some good Angel were at work for them, Riches flow insensible upon them, and every thing they undertake doth prosper, insomuch that themselves cannot but wonder at their increase" (153). What Horneck registers in his remark is not a doctrinal, illegible, premodern religiosity but a traditional need to feel as though one's profits are not guaranteed from the outset, that things might have turned out otherwise, that wealth flows from complex and oftentimes inscrutable sources, and that it does so to the extent that one has behaved in an ethical manner. His remark that "plenty steals upon them beyond expectation" is not simply a different way of saying that they get more than they could expect in their wildest dreams; rather, it means that plenty comes as a result of its not being expected.

The calculated expectation of returns—the mental or intellectual modality of the contract—was considered by many to be just as problematic as written contracts, since even bare expectation was an attempt to decipher (and possibly master) what was to remain inscrutable and uncertain. Miles Mosse makes this point particularly clear in his *Arraignment and Conviction of Usurie* (1595).[15] While his tract aims to refute virtually every extant defense of usury, Mosse writes at length on the problem of the calculated anticipation of future return (a view echoed in eighteenth-century attacks on prudence):

> Not only hee who in lending convenanteth for gaine, or whose usurious practices may be discovered of men, is such an usurer as is condemned by the word of God: but even hee which lendeth without any convenant at all, and doth onely *expect* an increase, or *hope* for gaine at the hand of the borrower, he is judged of men and condemned of God as a committer of usurie. And therefore, if I lend without convenanting for gaine, but yet *hoping* that he to whom I lend wil in regard therof speake a good work for me, helpe me to a good marriage, procure me a gainfull office, or such like: this *expectation* and *amendment* maketh me to become an usurer. (385)

Heightened attention to and the rational calculation of future contingencies was for Mosse a modality of the contract; although immaterial, calculation was no less criminal than contract. In the case of the contract, the future was made certain; in the case of the expectation of return, the individual attempted to manage and direct the future in a manner that, for Mosse, attempted to cut providence out of the equation just as obviously as did a contracted money loan.[16] Also damning both, John Blaxton (fl. 1634) distinguished hoping for return from contractual lending, calling the former "Usury of the heart," as opposed to "formall Usury" (5–6). Interestingly, a potentially pro-usury argument—that the anticipatory calculus employed by the money-lender could be put toward wholesome rather than sinister ends—rarely entered the debate at all, and when it did, counterarguments were made.[17] The ethical taint of usury arises from the *form* of the act, not from its content or goal. Even ostensibly wholesome uses of usurious profits were therefore condemned. Pointing to Roger Fenton's 1611 *Treatise of Usurie*, Natasha Korda has observed that "far from being a manifestation of God's charity," the widow's attempt to support herself by lending money for interest "precludes charity and expresses a lack of faith in providence" (135). Although providential grace launders profits for the merchant adventurer who sends his ships to sea, or for the farmer who reaps a bountiful harvest, or for the *uncalculating* lender who ends up with more than he expected, providence is incapable of laundering paybacks for the *calculating* lender, no matter whether those paybacks are intended for self-aggrandizement, simple subsistence, or even charity.

The anti-usury polemicists of the early modern period held the view that anticipation of future returns entailed a usurpation or circumvention of divine, determining authority. This view culminated in laws that regulated lending, laws that increased the risk taken by lenders, which at least mitigated that usurpation to an extent by pushing usury closer to more readily identifiable commercial risks such as farming, maritime exploration and venturing, and trade.[18] The fundamental belief in the value and importance of risk in theological terms was confirmed by the 1624 Usury Act, which limited interest to a maximum of 10 percent per annum and is regarded as a paramount formalization of lending in England. As much as this would appear to have transcended the medieval criticism of *pactum*, however, the formalization of lending did no such thing, since the act's passage could just as easily be attributed to the fact that it forced many lenders into a position of having to take *greater* risk. Mandating lower rates of interest—and 10 percent per annum was lower than what was sometimes charged—forced lenders to assume a larger risk when putting forward the principal loan amount and to profit less from that risk over time (increasing the impact of the risk on the lender by reducing the amount the lender would be paid to assume it). The act's full text, along with similar acts passed under Henry VIII and Elizabeth I, stressed that they were all passed *against* usury. That language was not merely a moralistic veil intended to conceal an ulterior pro-finance imperative or a rhetorical patina inserted to appease the churchmen. By limiting interest rates, these laws put usury, in its broad sense, under attack. If one were to contemplate the passage of statutory restrictions on credit-card interest rates today—nearly impossible given the financial sector's commitment to charging as much as possible—the significance of such a restrictive regulatory effort may be apparent.

So, as much as they contributed to the naturalization of lending practices in the seventeenth century, the laws passed in the early seventeenth century did not materially alter the conversation about sharing risk, the importance of moderating finance with ethical constraints, and the desire to keep the future open. In his 1682 discussion of usury, the moderate Nonconformist minister and teacher Samuel Shaw could still confidently proclaim: "To bind Men and their Friends, and their Heirs and Executors, to make a certain advantageous Return of an uncertain hazardous Employment of money, is very Cruel, and an Atheistical confronting of Divine Providence" (354). What Shaw was arguing decades after the legalization of lending was, in essence, a continuation of arguments made during the theological disputes about usury that had characterized the first half of the century. It was the same remark that Bolton had made in the wake of the Usury Act: "For in the contract of actuall Usury there is an absolute covenant for certaine gaine, which the Borrower, whether He shall gaine or loose is absolutely bound to pay together with the Principall" (18).

John Blaxton made the most complete case for the importance of risk in commercial dealings. In the opening of his 1634 compilation of anti-usury views he defines usury as follows: "outward and actuall Usury is, when the creditour doth not onely intend certaine gaine by lending, but also covenanteth for a certaine summe to be allowed him at a certaine time or times" (5). The repetition of *certaine* in Blaxton's definition means both a precisely predetermined amount (a "specific" sum) and an assured amount (a "guaranteed" or "secure" sum). These are two sides of the same coin: the definition of a specific amount to be returned is a codification and thus restriction of future possibility, just as the legal requirement to repay at a specific time requires the specification of the amount to be paid at that time. Underlying this view, as always, was the claim that usury required the borrower to assume all risk. What specifically defines usury, Blaxton writes, is that in a usurious contract

the property is translated to the borrower, [and] so with the property also *the hazard wholy appertayneth to the borrower*: for the very contract of mutuation includeth in it an obligation, binding the borrower, that whatsoever becommeth of this particular which he borroweth, he shall restore the full valew thereof at the day appointed, in the same kind. And to this promise, either by word or writing, entreth into bonds, and statutes, laying his goods to pawne, or his lands to mortgage, giveth sureties, to assure and secure the creditor for the principall. (8, my emphasis)[19]

By contrast, when one loans to a borrower an object that is liable to break-age, damage, spoilage, or decay, both the lender and the borrower share in the loss potential. Money, however, is not subject to breakage, spoilage, and so on; if the money is lost, the borrower is still obliged to pay, for bonds do not discriminate between one parcel of money and another (what will later be described as money's *fungibility*). Even in cases other than lending, as in the insuring of money being transported, Blaxton allows that such a contract "is not unlawfull, provided, always, that there be an adventure or hazard in truth, and not in pretence only; and also that the gaine be proportionable to the hazard" (9). Bolton was likewise concerned with the "pretences" that were employed to make a certain gain deceitfully *appear* to be hazardous (64). And, a "Mr. Wheatly"—included among Blaxton's list of witnesses against usury—stipulates that the "Law of Charity" dictates that "he which will have part in wealth, must also have part in woes; and he that will divide the sweet, must also divide the sower; he that will take of the good successe, must also take of the bad" (39). The usurer, defying this law, "makes sure for himself to have a part onely and infalliably in the profit, and therefore serves himself alone, and not also his brother" (39). The fair distribution of risk is recognized as not simply a matter of living in accordance with biblical *law* but a matter of living in accordance with an *ethic* of Christian charity. The cruelty of usury did not consist merely in profiting; that much could be accomplished in ethically cir-cumscribed ways. Rather, a relatively separate series of theological and ethical precepts, having to do with the need to experience the future as uncertain, led to the determination that its cruelty consisted in the unwillingness to share in the risk of loss.[20]

For seventeenth-century writers on the subject, usury was not simply con-demned by God (i.e., it was not merely dogmatic allegiance to the Aristotelian sterility hypothesis or to the Deuteronomic prohibition that actuated resis-tance to usury). More fundamentally, the very worlds, values, and practices entailed by usury had no need for a god. In this respect, *usury's* meaning was closer to "secularity" or "worldliness" than to "interest on loans." As late as 1679, Jelinger would add that "the Usurer is for Earth, and leaveth the Church be-cause he cannot abide the hearing of the Word" (*Usury Stated Overthrown* 126).[21] Three years later Shaw wrote that the "world in general is, whatsoever is not God," and that to value "riches more than God . . . makes an idolatrous lover of the World. To seek these more then [*sic*] the Kingdom of God, to hunger after them more than after righteousness, to confide in them *more than in the Promise and Providence of God*, doth denominate the accursed person here spoken of" (48–49, my emphasis). Because the usurer secures his money without a felt need for providential assistance, Shaw goes on to argue in a series of chapters, the usurer exemplifies this spirit of worldliness. For Luther, Calvin, Mosse, Blaxton, Fenton, Bolton, Jelinger, Shaw, and countless others—writers who came from virtually every quarter of the Christian tradition—profits were legitimate so long as they were not expected at the outset. In fact, an argument could be made that the worse the loan or investment looked from the standpoint of its return potential, the more likely it was that the return would be granted, since in making the deliberate choice to trust in God and the goodness of others—neither of which was an especially quantifiable or calculable variable—one was performing the role of a dutiful, Christian, ethical subject, who, in some cases, as Horneck put it, might therefore be rewarded with wealth "beyond expectation."[22] As Jeremy Bentham (1748–1832) put it derisively, but not inaccurately, in his 1787 portrayal of the Christian subject of the premodern era, "The better the terms [of the deal], the worse it was to lend upon them" (letter X, x.2).

An Anti-Financial Revolution?

In an underappreciated essay published in 1957, the Puritan and Protestant Reformation historian Charles H. George sought to reconcile the widespread anti-usury posture of many of the writers I have discussed with the economic modernization that took place in the later seventeenth and eighteenth centuries, observing that far from promoting financial capitalism, as Weberians might argue, "Calvinist social theory, as it appears in England, is no more, and possibly less, permissive of usury than is Roman Catholic social theory" (474).[23] Although George did not focus on the risk criterion as I have done in the preceding sections, he rightly sensed that even as modernization occurred something continued to sustain the Protestant, especially Calvinist, practical theology that had long prohibited usury. Overlooking the dynamic that I have been calling "anti-finance," the fact that writers against usury were aiming at something other and more fundamental than interest on loans, George argued that a modern financial regime had eventually won out by quarantining the ethical debate, by simply stating that usury's ethical legitimacy was a recondite matter best left to theologians. This leave-it-to-the-divines mentality enabled modernization, according to George, by compart-mentalizing the ethical question altogether. George may have been right: this tactic may have worked for a time or for some people. But compartmental-ization could only delay the resurfacing of the ethical question and could not itself be a solution to that question. In again falling into the trap of believing that what Protestant theologians objected to was strictly interest on loans—usury in the narrow sense, which, admittedly, the theologians themselves often conflated with the broader ethic—George missed the more important fact that his research seems to inevitably suggest: that the legalization of lend-ing was a confirmation of anti-usury polemic, a confirmation, in other words, of the desire for risk and for resources to be more fairly distributed than they had been under an elite, quasi-oligarchic, goldsmith-backed financial system. Again, to state an obvious but often disregarded reality, this was Francis Ba-con's argument. Thus George came to overlook the important continuities between anti-finance and, as paradoxical as it may sound, the financial revo-lution. In other words, George—one of the few historians to recognize and take seriously the puzzling fact of a pervasive *seventeenth*-century anti-usury discourse—presupposed that anti-usury polemic and financial revolution could only exist in an antithetical relation to one another, and therefore he did not consider that the financial revolution may have represented, at least for some, an extension, rather than a denial, of early modern commercial ethics.

Being "at certainties" was construed as usurious; usury meant being "at certainties." If either party to a transaction stood to lose in ways that the other party did not, the exchange or arrangement was rejected, for writers leading up to and including Bacon, Bolton, Jelinger, and Shaw. Bearing this in mind, I suggest that what the seventeenth century witnessed in terms of usury law was, first, merely a codification of extant values rather than a change in the temper of the times. Second, sixteenth- and seventeenth-century Par-liaments legalized moneylending, but the new laws did not challenge, or seek to challenge, the widely held view that usury was ethically abhorrent. The very texts of these laws often said as much, which would only have been possible if the laws themselves were seen as consistent with an underlying ethical im-perative. The perceived mutual exclusivity of the legalization of "usury" and an anti-usury ethical culture is also a function of historical revision: later writ-ers, reflecting on seventeenth-century attitudes toward usury, assumed that it was moneylending, interest, or the barrenness of money that constituted the usury problem and that once moneylending was legalized, and money's ability to produce more of itself acknowledged, the critique of usury was rendered obsolete. But as I have noted, we are dealing with two different problems: usury qua interest and usury qua certainty.

Here, I wish to attempt to account for a series of events that are often read as confirmations of the erosion of old beliefs concerning usury: the fallout from the 1672 Stop of the Exchequer; the ensuing transferal of fiscal authority to the Parliament; the Glorious Revolution; the establishment of the national debt; and the consequent institutionalization of borrowing and lending in the forms of the first national lottery and the Bank of England. Although in her work on the Enlightenment Lorraine Daston has shown that risk as a moral factor in commerce would continue into the eighteenth century in the form of developments in probabilistic sciences, and although Daston connects those developments to usury law and courts of equity, there has been no attempt to understand how the events of the financial revolution could have taken place in and among a devout English people, a people for whom the cutting-edge speculations of Continental mathematicians would have been quite alien if not altogether unintelligible and a people who would have regarded the attempt (through probability or otherwise) to manage or control risk as unsavory, if not itself a form of usury. I would like to suggest that the events of the financial revolution not only are consistent with the view that risking defeat and loss was the most ethical approach to commerce but logically proceed from that view insofar as many innovations either aimed at or could be justified by (a) those innovations' correction of systemic risk imbalances (as attempts to undercut or minimize illicitly attained financial security) and (b) their delivery of new risk opportunities to an ever greater portion of the English populace (attempts to give more people an opportunity to take risks). I will briefly summarize these events and explain how they figure into the narrative of financial progress.

I do not aim to provide a new history of these events, but merely to explain how they can be made to square with a culture in which risk and uncertainty were deemed ethically necessary, or at least preferable to the calculative, rational, selfish economism that is often uncritically applied to the subjects of the financial revolution. As such, this might be considered groundwork for an alternative financial history, one that reads the development of the modern economy in terms of the continuity between the premodern or early modern ethical privileging of risk and the financial revolution. One caveat: It is undeniably the case that many understood the development of finance as part of secularization; and it is probable that many believed that the purpose of finance was to generate as much wealth as possible for one's self and one's family, regardless of the ethical or spiritual consequences of doing so. I aim to do nothing more than explain how events that seem from one perspective to anticipate the ascendancy of *homo economicus* may also be read as anathema to the emergence of that very figure.

Prior to the Bank of England's establishment in 1694 the Crown had been able to borrow from a variety of sources, but without clear protocols for doing so. In the fourteenth century Edward III had borrowed from Italian bankers such as the Bardi family; more than a century later Henry VIII had gone to Antwerp to borrow money to support his war against the French; and seventeenth-century lending institutions were composed largely of local, private, domestic sources, particularly the goldsmith bankers of Lombard Street, who were the recipients of deposits for many citizens of London and its surrounding communities. When money was short, the Crown would occasionally simply refuse to repay loans, thus damaging the credit of the sitting monarch as well as his or her immediate successors (Roseveare 8). If the king was the law, and the law declared that the king would not pay, there was little anyone could do aside from refusing to lend additional money (which, for those who were financially ruined in such processes of "legalized default," would have been impossible anyway). In the seventeenth century, the state of Crown finance was so deplorable that when the Civil War erupted, Charles I seized the entire sum of money contained in the Royal Mint, located in the Tower of London at the time. The outcry was substantial, and the king, in a portentous moment of capitulation, returned the treasure on the condition that he could keep forty thousand pounds as a loan (Giuseppi 7).

This asset seizure was succeeded some thirty years later when the restored king, Charles II, issued a similar order, this time to the Exchequer to cease payments on all outstanding loans that had been made to the Crown. The motivations for doing so were quite different from those of his father, as Charles II had ample funds to continue repaying his debts (Roseveare 21). But Charles II was planning war against the Dutch, and he anticipated the need for greater future revenues to outfit his military. The order to "stop" the Exchequer from issuing payments to creditors—which would consequently increase the amount of wealth available to the Crown—was issued on 18 December 1671,[24] and although it certainly ruined some of the major creditors involved, historians have found its ultimate consequences rather difficult to assess.[25] The individuals to whom the Crown owed money were a small, close-knit group of London financiers, but as Scott observed a century ago, "It is to be remembered that most of the funds, lent by them to the Crown, had been borrowed from their depositors," so that when these primary lenders failed, "the area of ruin extended to the merchants, until it reached many widows and orphans, whose income was derived from the interest on their capital" (287).[26] As Scott's rhetoric suggests, the Crown's credit with lenders had as much to do with the public spin put on the Stop—the much-discussed "widows and orphans"—as it did with the actual number of individuals affected, for as P. G. M. Dickson put it, after the Stop "there was always a question-mark against Charles' financial reputation" (250).[27] If Charles II's credit was not damaged generally, his credit with two parishioners of St. Mary Woolnoth must have been. Of the approximately £1.3 million frozen by royal decree, approximately 80 percent was owed to four individuals, a full 32 percent to the benefactor of St. Mary Woolnoth—Sir Robert Viner, now a baronet—alone. Edward Backwell (1618–1683), another goldsmith banker from St. Mary Woolnoth, was owed nearly £300,000, not including interest.[28] The latter's career as a banker was through.

The eventual settlement reached by the king and his lenders was sufficient to ensure that the king remained solvent, although thanks to the complicated repayment strategy designed to allay this lack of confidence, he had unwittingly created a permanent national debt.[29] Charles II agreed to borrow a large sum of money from the treasury with the proviso that the state would repay the sum, plus a specified rate of interest, over an extended period. By shifting toward long-term, low-interest loans, the state could use the funds allocated to it by private creditors to immediately improve the state of the nation (militarily, socially, commercially, or otherwise) without imposing dramatic increases in taxes or duties on the citizenry to begin repaying the principal. Instead, the Crown could simply maintain its current level of taxation and pay down the debt as circumstances allowed. In reality, as interested parties had suspected and feared, the likelihood of the principal ever being repaid was rather small. This perpetual debt altered the perceived relation between the king and the state, for the king's debts could no longer be conceived of as localized acts of trust involving those on the inside, but were seen as an indefinite bond with the people, dependent upon the future strength of England as a nation (which would prevent the bonds from being canceled or nullified), and hinging upon the view that the financiers to the Crown were, in at least one sense, more integral to the maintenance of the state than was any particular monarch (Pocock, *MM* 425–26; Wennerlind 169). Under these conditions, a marginal amount of interest was not seen as detrimental to the functioning of the state, nor was it thought to present a long-term burden on national finances, since the interest payments were to be strategically calculated to accord with the probable future income of the state.

Thanks to several years of prosperity in England subsequent to the Stop, which resulted in a net increase in the revenues of the Crown, as well as vigorous attempts by the goldsmith bankers to reclaim what was owed to them, in 1677 the king was able to regain some credit by funding an annuity of £140,000 for the creditors he had swindled in 1672, Viner and Backwell among them (even so, Backwell was bankrupt by 1682). Each of the bankers was allowed to allocate 6 percent annuities—in the form of transferable documents composed and witnessed by the Exchequer—to depositors whose claims for withdrawal of funds the bankers had been forced to deny as a result of the Stop. These documents, referred to as bankers assignments, were stamped with the Great Seal and were authorized to be paid out to those creditors with the monies collected from the hereditary excise tax, which was "the securest portion of the royal revenues" (Carruthers 64; Roseveare 22).[30] Charles II was basically mortgaging his own personal future income to repay the money he owed to the bankers in 1672. This unusually high degree of security was intended to produce in both the bankers and the depositors a faith in the Crown's promises to repay. As one contemporary encomiast to the arrangement put it, "*The Sacred Honour and Declarations of the King, the Common Faith, and the Laws of the Nation . . . will be hereby preserv'd Chaste and Inviolate. . . .* This Royal Balsome, Sir, hath now perfectly heal'd up the Wound, and a new and more vigorous *Phoenix* of Credit and Reputation will arise again, as it were, out of its own Ashes" (Turner 9). For every statement to this effect, however, there was a contrary assertion. By the second decade of the eighteenth century, it could be said without hesitation that the shutting up of the Exchequer caused Charles II to "lose all his Credit for ever of borrowing Mony again, otherwise than on the branches of his Revenue, or Acts of Parliament; and would deter the Parliament from venturing to be so profuse and liberal as they had formerly been to him, any more for the time to come, upon ever so pressing occasions: at least without binding his Hands, and reserving to themselves the care of laying out as well as raising any Monies to be given to him" (D. Jones 75).

The Stop, we are frequently reminded, was the product of a culture wherein the lives and fortunes of the people could be interrupted by the arbitrary decisions of a monarch. It is a version of events, in fact, that conforms in many respects to the depiction of arbitrary power that unfolds in the second of John Locke's *Two Treatises of Government* (1690). It is even possible that Locke was thinking of the Stop when he wrote that when a subject's "Property is invaded by the Will and Order of his Monarch, he has not only no Appeal, as those in Society ought to have, but [it is] as if he were degraded from the common state of Rational Creatures [and] denied a liberty to judge of, or to defend his Right, and so is exposed to all the Misery and Inconveniences that a Man can fear from one, who being in the unrestrained state of Nature, is yet corrupted with Flattery and armed with Power" (327). The story goes that as long as kings retained exclusive control of the nation's financial condition, individual investors had to hope that the future would bring them returns on loans granted to the state.[31] In turn, the larger group of less wealthy individuals who placed their savings into the hands of the king's creditors— individuals who were depositors to the goldsmith banks—had equal reason to hope for, but no reason to expect, the king's fidelity to his promises. The Stop revealed that the king was simply a man whose position of authority enabled him to, in effect, lawfully erase debts whenever he wished to do so.

Thanks to the efforts of writers in the ensuing decades, the story of the Stop of the Exchequer and arbitrary power gained further energy, but it developed from a critique of monarchy into a commentary on insider dealing more generally. Although rumors of the Chancellor of the Exchequer's complicity in the Stop arose immediately, by 1712 the Whig historian John Oldmixon (1673–1742) and others could openly complain that the Stop was not so much Charles II as a cabal of ministers who surrounded and influenced him. Oldmixon blamed Lord Ashley (1621–1683) for the idea, Thomas Clifford (1630–1673) for communicating the idea to the king, and Charles II for executing it (7–11). Charles Hornby (d. 1739) said much the same in 1711 (26). Another Whig historian, Bishop Gilbert Burnet (1643–1715), reported that Ashley, anticipating the Stop, had withdrawn his money from the goldsmith bankers before they were stunned by Charles II's proclamation; two centuries before laws explicitly prohibiting insider trading were passed, Burnet was claiming that Ashley was doing precisely that to secure his own financial position (171). When Charles II damaged the credit of the monarchy, he surely contributed to a heightened awareness of the need for a more representative means of deposit and credit, but the entire incident revealed how those in positions of power—king or ministry—could circumvent laws to guarantee profits by removing themselves from the risk cycle altogether. What Whig historians of the post-Stop era registered in their complaints respecting Charles II's decision to cease payments was a natural outgrowth of a widely held view that financial arrangements were valid only to the extent that all parties shared equally in the risk of gain and loss. Of course, the fact that this particular arrangement to cease payments to the king's lenders negatively impacted some of the most wealthy men in England encouraged Oldmixon and others to publish their views. But these Whigs were also drawing upon an older tradition to articulate their sense of economic justice, to the anti-financial ethical expectation that certainties in matters concerning money, such as those attained in 1672 by the king and his ministers, especially Ashley, were an abomination.

Owing to a subsequent surge in trade and increases in tax revenues, the Crown's financial position gradually improved.[32] Under William III (1650–1702) and Mary II (1662–1694) the state was to reap even greater monetary rewards from a type of revenue-generation device referred to as "aids." The aids established in 1689 were essentially land taxes levied according to both the resources and the physical land possessed by the property owner or renter, as well as according to the improvements the tenant made upon the land (Roy 16–18).[33] I say that these rewards were reaped by the state rather than the Crown because when William and Mary took the throne, Parliament saw to it that they would not establish financial independence on the basis of their considerable royal revenues.[34] The aids gradually became known in the 1690s as the land tax, which, combined with revenues brought in by the excise and customs taxes, amounted to roughly 90 percent of the state's income in the hundred years following the ascension of William and Mary (Brewer 95).[35] The massive increases in revenue under James II (1633–1701) and then William and Mary after the aids of 1689 were sufficient to guarantee that the Crown would not return to the fiscal chaos of the 1640s, but they were by no means sufficient to fund England's full-scale engagement in the Nine Years War, which began almost immediately after the Glorious Revolution.[36] While the tax and tax-collection procedures of the 1690s ensured that the Crown would have a large and steady source of income, those funds were simply inadequate to meet the demands of war; more was needed.

Short-term loans from goldsmith bankers and private financiers meant high rates of interest for the Crown, so alternative solutions to the financing problem were sought. The first part of the solution was to implement a massive national lottery, the Million Lottery, which allowed anyone with £10 to purchase a ticket that was guaranteed to procure the owner something, if not the full amount of the original stake or one of the prizes. Those who could not afford the price of a whole ticket, however, could purchase shares or percentages of individual tickets, a practice referred to as "riding horses," which expanded the number of people to whom the lottery and its prizes might apply. Appalled by the avarice it suggested, Edward Ward was nevertheless fascinated by the lottery's attractions:

> People were running up and down the streets in crowds and numbers, as if one end of the town was on fire, and the other were running to

help 'em off with their goods. One stream of coachmen, footmen, apprentice boys and servant wenches flowing one way, with wonderful hopes of getting an estate for threepence; knights, esquires, gentlemen and traders, married ladies, virgin madams, jilts, concubines and strumpets, moving on foot, in sedans, chariots and coaches, another way, with a pleasing expectance of getting six hundred a year for a crown. ("Lotteries" 252)

We must remember that these were not Viners and Backwells, wealthy and connected elite financiers, but the masses, come to partake of newly available risk opportunities. Ward decries the change because he sees this rush as symptomatic of the greed and foolish hopes of his age; but he also tacitly identifies a new configuration of risk vis-à-vis the English economy. As the economic historian Anne Murphy puts it, "Players [in the Million Lottery] came from all walks of life and all social backgrounds," and they took part because they had previously been unable to partake of such large-scale risk opportunities ("Lotteries" 238).[37] These opportunities, as well as the opportunity to invest in the Bank and the stock of chartered companies, extended to include as well a great number of women, who had previously been unable to invest with such freedom, a fact that has been documented and explored by Nicola Jane Phillips, E. J. Clery, Anne Laurence, Josephine Maltby, and Janette Rutterford.[38] Given this influx of new money, the subscription to the Bank, which was formed shortly after the lottery, was completely filled within two weeks. Shortly after being chartered, the Bank became the place where winning tickets for the Million Lottery were processed.

As a function of parliamentary activity, the Bank was a reflex of the public, not the whimsical scheme of a ministry or monarch, which economic historians therefore often consider to be the vital difference between old and new financial regimes. The Bank's security relied on the credit of the nation, not on William or Mary. Making the most forceful and convincing case for this is Craig Muldrew, whose words I quote again here: "The Bank of England . . . created a new type of security which was based on the politics of taxation, and not the credit of individual bankers. The stop of the Exchequer in 1672 had caused many of the goldsmith bankers to fail, and the creation of public funds and the expansion of opportunities to invest in joint stock companies provided a more secure form of investment" (116). It seems absolutely right to describe changes in public and private finance as an "expansion of opportunities," but in what sense did these changes introduce a "more secure form of investment"?

For that small handful of individuals including financiers such as Viner and Backwell, banks and public funds were certainly subject to greater scrutiny and less disruption than scattershot loans made to Charles II, whom one eighteenth-century historian described as "the deepest dissembler that ever sat on the English throne" (Dalrymple 38n). There is certainly nothing incorrect, that is, about Muldrew's assessment of the financial revolution as improving investment "security," which, of course, more or less repeats what has been said of the post-Stop changes in investment opportunities since the first decades of the eighteenth century, when Whig pundits like Burnet and Oldmixon congratulated themselves for liberating the purse from the tyrannical hands of the Stuarts. But if we are to speak of the "expansion of opportunities" to invest, we must also consider this an expansion of opportunities to take risks in the world of investment and thus also as an expansion of opportunities to sustain losses. Given their experiences with Charles II, Viner and Backwell surely would have welcomed the Bank from the security standpoint Muldrew focuses upon, but in the eyes of the masses, who had no history or point of comparison for their investment, the Bank, the lottery, and the joint stock companies mentioned by Muldrew would have appeared, at some level, as nothing more than a new risk to take (particularly for those individuals who had to rely upon the purchasing of shares of tickets, who constituted an entirely new pool of financial resources for the state). Confronted with an excess of wealth born of developments in trade, those in possession of mobile property were faced with the question, not how to get and keep money, but how to get rid of it. The lottery and the Bank provided the perfect conduits for channeling their wealth into spaces of uncertainty. Individual investors in these various schemes no doubt *desired* to win or profit, but when they are considered as a collective, to describe Ward's lottery-playing throngs as seeking out "secure" investment opportunities seems problematic, and not simply because these throngs had never been able to invest in anything whatsoever before.

From a distant, cultural standpoint, the financial revolution is important not simply because it securitized assets and asset streams for elite financiers—whether it in fact did so or not—but because it converted assets, wealth, or specie into risk opportunities for English men and women. Assets that had formerly been secure—if dormant, locked away in chests, for example—would now be vulnerable, subject to the will of God, new elements in an open system of circulation that might, given the justness of the providentially ordered universe, bring one the return he or she perhaps thought was deserved. Again, this is not by any means to say that individuals entered into the Bank—or the lottery, or any commercial venture, for that matter—with the intention of los-ing but rather to observe that the Bank and the lottery served as opportunities to repurpose monies that had been tied up elsewhere, to turn money into a sign whose value exceeded its pure material utility. While the rise of banks and modern finance are typically read as signs of the emergence of the mod-ern, selfish, acquisitive individual, this extra-material signification means that acts of investments are also critically, perhaps fundamentally, self-abnegating gestures. And, of course, self-abnegation is not just a feature of investment; it is the very essence of Calvinism.

Samuel Jeake's Commercial Providentialism

Narratives of the rise of rational capitalism account for religious belief and self-abnegating behavior in a variety of ways, but virtually all hold that such beliefs and behaviors needed to subside or transform themselves before cap-italism could truly flourish. As the foregoing discussion suggests, however, it may have been possible for someone to relate to financial experience as provi-dential, or, rather, to read the uncertainties of finance as fundamentally reduc-ible to the same uncertainties that structured the totality of life and thus not, strictly speaking, an autonomous space of uncertainty. There is no reason, in other words, to regard capitalism—if that is the right word—as exclusive of so-called irrational forms of thought, belief, and practice. It is the extraction of economic life from its rootedness in a broader spiritual and ethical frame-work that creates the appearance of its comparative rationality. Theoretically speaking, this abstracted "economy" is defined not by a profit motive or any particular commercial practice but by the fact that its autonomy from the providential order means that it is made up of—or *is*—a field of objects that are seen as outside of God and thus to some extent both manageable and predictable. Only when an individual disregards the constraints of ethical un-certainty does it become possible for him or her to imagine, if not necessarily realize, a perfect management and prediction of the objects that compose this determinable field. This individual will eventually be called "economic man." Economic man aims to eliminate all uncertainty and minimize risk, which is the name for the thing that eludes control or mastery (there is no "economic man" without this goal). In contrast, anyone who embraces the uncertainty that is operative at the higher, providential order can only be perceived as mad. Here I would like to consider one such individual—Samuel Jeake, a Nonconformist astrologer, merchant, and sometime moneylender—as a way of illustrating how the ideational claims of anti-finance and the institutional developments of the later seventeenth century might have worked themselves out in the life a single individual.

Samuel Jeake was born in the ancient coastal town of Rye, customarily associated with the Cinque Ports of Sussex (Hastings, New Romney, Hythe, Dover, and Sandwich), and spent his entire life there. Because of its association with the Cinque Ports, Rye had historically been granted particular privileges, not least of which were rights of self-governance and exemptions from certain taxes to the Crown. By the early eighteenth century, however, when Defoe arrived in Rye for the tour described in his *Tour Thro' the Whole Island of Great Britain*, it was plain that the town had lost its former glory.[39] Owing to silt accumulation in the harbor, Rye's ever-changing shoreline, and the need for larger and more stable port accommodations for the increasingly larger ships employed in foreign trade, Rye and the other Cinque Ports suffered economically and politically. Anticipating the decay that Defoe would later record, in 1678 Jeake's father (also Samuel [1623–90]) had written that the term "Ports . . . implies them all Sea Towns, in whose Havens and Harbors Ships may safely arrive and unlade. And no doubt but at first thus they were, though now the restless Sea hath shut it self off from some of them, to the spoiling their ancient Harbors, as in *Romney* and *Hithe*" (6, note q). Although happy to report that Rye still enjoyed its original situation (not having had to actually relocate its town center), surveying the changing topography of his world, with his eye constantly upon the "restless Sea," the elder Jeake could not have raised his son without communicating to him some anxiety about Rye's future.[40] Further, having witnessed in his life the execution of a king, a civil war (in which he was actively engaged on the Puritan side), and the restoration of the Stuarts, he must have perceived the changing landscape as a sort of ecological object lesson for his son, communicating the fragility and uncertainty of the world.

It was in this unstable town of Rye—a town almost entirely surrounded by water, but that so saline as to render it undrinkable—that the younger Jeake established himself as a merchant and composed his diary (Holloway 333–34): "The theme that occupies more space than any other in Jeake's diary is his activity as merchant, money-lender, and investor" (Hunter and Gregory 58). If we approach Jeake from the standpoint of *homo economicus*, the rational, self-interested, calculative individual who views risk as something that must be avoided and the future as needing to be controlled through prudent economy and who experiences the unfolding of events in time as so many confirmations of one's ability to plan for the future, Jeake's diary might be read as a seminal document in the history of financial revolution. But his diary is not a book of accounts; recording swings in the fortune of his health and wealth, the diary parallels at a personal level the larger-scale upheavals of his geographical and political worlds. Given his upbringing in an evangelical, Dissenting household, his abiding interest in horoscopy, his daily prayers and frequent invocation of providence in his entries, it is possible to instead place emphasis on Jeake's positive appreciation of what John Bunyan in *The Pilgrim's Progress* (1678) called "hazard." Toward the end of that eponymous pilgrim's travails, Christian informs Good Will that he finally gets to "reap the benefits of my hazzards" (159); elsewhere, Bunyan praises those who "are for hazarding all for God, at a clap" (221). Comparably, Bunyan offers us loathsome characters like Pliable and By-Ends—echoes of Ben Jonson's usurious character Security—who impiously prefer security and comfort to the hazards of a world suffused with spiritual significance and teeming with opportunities for divine validation or disappointment. For it was precisely the possibility of disappointment, suffering, and loss that made occasional validations meaningful. As David Hawkes argues, Bunyan's allegorical abstractions illustrate that Christian's world is suffused with divine meaning. Mr. Badman's "reprobation," by contrast, "is conveyed through his delusion that he is no abstraction but an independent, autonomous agent" (Hawkes 219). Risk, or hazard, I would suggest, is the means whereby the individual Jeake—who always threatens to become "an independent, autonomous agent"—can commit himself to higher meaning and avoid the "reprobation" associated with the assertion of self.

Readers familiar with Jeake's extraordinarily valuable documentary account of a seventeenth-century commercial life will know that his testimonies to a higher power are manifested most plainly in his casting of horoscopes and in his professions of faith in astrological determinants and significations.[41] Such moments stand out as recognizably irrational or premodern, and when placed alongside his blunt reportage of loans, lawsuits, shipments of wool, and other commercial matters, they produce a bifurcated experience for readers or a sense that Jeake was somehow divided against himself. But the praises Jeake showers upon providence throughout the text, in both horoscope readings and commercial reflections, bind together these dimensions of Jeake's diary and suggest the presence of a spiritual and ethical substrate more meaningful than horoscopes or money. To close this short history of anti-finance, I would like to restore the presence of this unifying substrate in Jeake's diary, not simply to resolve a textual tension but to indicate the dangers of abstracting what might be called the "economic moment" from his more totalizing vision and the errors that might arise as a result.

Early in the diary, Jeake's invocations of providence and God's mercy feature in the context of his recording of illness and accidents resulting in bodily
harm. He introduces providence in relation to agues, cloudy vision, a ringing in his ears, headaches, violent diarrhea, as well as a fall into a cellar, two
unfortunate nighttime encounters with a woodpile in the road, a fall into a
beer barrel, and a stumbling "out of [a] neighbour's Garret" (135). It was a
"great mercy," he writes, that he "did not break [his] Leg" (135). As Jeake at-
tains maturity and enters into the commercial world, providence increasingly
serves to explain and justify his successes and losses. Shortly after the incident
in the garret, Jeake reports the following: "[Feb.] 20 News of a Ship worth
£30000 sterling coming from Morlaix for London, cast away neer to Calais,
all the men, & most part of the goods lost. Supposed to be one of the Ships
that Procter & Sedgwick, advised T[homas] M[iller] & me to have goods
by; in December last, before the war. But we being apprehensive of no war,
gave no order: & so providentially escaped the Losse" (137). To explain, Jeake,
along with his friend Thomas Miller, was being advised to invest in a ship to
transport goods, which, for reasons left unexplained, would have been a wise
investment in the event of war. Because Miller and Jeake did not believe war
would erupt, they declined to invest and so "providentially escaped the Losse"
(the ship was sunk). The word *providentially* refers to both Jeake's foresight
(his own prudence) and his belief that the foresight he employed was itself
sacred: God had given him the wisdom to know and to see, and thus to escape
financial ruin. Or, rather, God had given him the wisdom *not to see* that war
would break out. Jeake's failure to predict the future thus becomes a cause for
celebration.

It is tempting to dismiss such passing references to providence as casual
piety, but Jeake's invocation of providence is frequent and always heavily
weighted (we ought not blame him too of simple raving).[42] Jeake reports that
walking home one night, just as he was about to fall "over a Load of Wood . . .
it pleased God to send a Flash of that Lightening . . . to shew me my danger
& prevent it. Which wonderfull Providence I shall never decline to acknowledge" (224). Jeake goes on to speculate that the way in which he would have
fallen would have resulted in the loss of his eyes owing to the specific positioning of the logs and sticks. Having suffered from poor vision throughout
his life, Jeake reports falling over this same pile of wood later that same night,
but when he did, it was in a different spot, resulting therefore in only minor
injuries to his legs. Jeake then returns to the woodpile the next morning "to
contemplate the mercy of that Providence that delivered me" (224). In visiting
the site a second time to meditate and in memorializing the event in his diary

Jeake follows through on his promise to "never decline to acknowledge" the workings of "wonderfull Providence." It is worth appreciating this moment, to consider the frame of mind in which one would need to be in order to make a deliberate effort to revisit a place of deliverance, to kneel beside it and issue forth a prayer, to quietly contemplate the mysteries of life and deliverance, and then to record that act of contemplation (providing a meta-contemplation of his act of contemplation), and then, more importantly, to consider the possibility that the motivations for Jeake's actions were not always, and quite possibly only rarely, reducible to economic needs or desires.

If we allow that Jeake is serious when offering such praises, then we ought to ascribe an equal degree of seriousness to such praises when they are raised in the context of commerce. Happening to be in London, he learns from his friend Miller of "the Act for the Million Adventure" (the newly contrived state lottery of 1694). He decides to invest: "Looking upon it Providential that I should come at this time: for had I staid at Rye I believe I should have put none in [i.e., would not have invested]; for want of being animated by the Example of the Londoners" (232). Jeake goes on to state that notwithstanding his reservations about the legitimacy of lots and lotteries, he is reconciled to this sort of investment given that the Million Lottery is "not a Lusory but a Civil Lot: & the putting the Act in Execution (when once made) being now become necessary for the support of the Government in the War against France, I was the better satisfied to be concerned in it; & after many deliberate Reflections with my self at Leisure times after my return to Rye, I concluded this might be lawfull" (232). He writes that to determine whether his investment was justified, he had consulted the writings of Thomas Gataker (1574–1654) (*Of the Nature and Uses of Lots* [1619]) and William Ames (1576–1633) (*The Marrow of Sacred Divinity* [1642]). Jeake states that he prefers the latter, and though he does not say precisely why, it is almost certainly because Ames argued that lots were subject to "the singular, and extraordinary providence of God in directing of an event meerly contingent" (W. Ames 298).[43] "After many deliberate Reflections with my self at Leisure times after my return to Rye," Jeake writes, he elected to invest in the lottery. What might the substance of these reflections have been? It is not possible, even with the benefit of the diary, to say with any degree of certainty, but it is no good pretending that these "Reflections" were less important to Jeake than his economic motivations or desires.

Very shortly after this, Jeake learns of the establishment of the Bank of England, but in the same letter he is also told that the subscription is filling rapidly. Apparently low on funds and having to execute some errands, he set out and "providentially met Robt. Brown by the Fishmarket" (241). Brown was willing and able to immediately lend Jeake a hundred pounds at 6 percent interest, which Jeake promptly carried with him to Grocers' Hall in London (he had been in Rye) to buy bank stock. Given how rapidly the subscription was filled, Jeake was right to consider his chance opportunity to invest as providential. On another occasion, a series of individuals "providentially" delivered some funds to Jeake, all of which went toward East India Company stock that was trading at a favorable price. He repeats shortly thereafter: "Providence sent me [these] bills very opportunely" (246). Jeake also, it is important to add, invokes providence in the event of his losses. Having embarked on a trading venture with France after Parliament's 1678 embargo against that country, he points out that he was forced to sell the goods he received at "some Loss," but he is thankful for the loss nevertheless. Describing the illicit trade with France in which he was engaged as being full of "Snares and Temptations" to profit, he writes: "I esteem my self happy, that the Providence of God always prevented me from being imployed & engaged in the smugling Factoryes" (147). Jeake's sense of personal worth—how he "esteem[s]" himself—is a function not of any material index, but of his belief that his economic opportunities are productively thwarted by ethical, legal, and spiritual constraints.

For a moneylending merchant such as Jeake it was necessary to construe success in terms of an uncertain and more open system of causality than is allowed within the paradigm of the contracted money loan. Jeake was a merchant, and he seems to have dealt with contracts on a near-daily basis; but he had also read Robert Sanderson (David Jones's reference point) and Robert Bolton, both prominent early opponents of usury in the broad sense that I have been defining it here (229, 160).[44] Jeake, therefore, could not but have recognized the dangers of seeking certain gain and expecting returns, and so his professions of faith in providence may be read as so many anxious apologies for doing precisely that. But they can also be read as evidence of the belief that it was not the contract that mattered so much as one's orientation toward commercial activity. Such professions, in other words, should not be ignored or swept under the rug as a mere figure of speech or Puritanical tic; they are vital to how Jeake frames and interprets his commercial life. It is more than probable, in fact, that Jeake would have been able to reconcile his identity as a merchant, investor, and moneylender with his identity as an ethical Christian by regarding his acts of finance as non-usurious because those acts exposed him to potential loss. To reiterate the larger point about the two meanings of *usury*: usury was always regarded as a sin, but lending money for interest could be justified so long as the individual was not guilty of having been usurious in the broad sense of seeking illicit certainties.

As Michael Hunter and Annabel Gregory, the editors of Jeake's diary, wisely caution us in their introduction, "The way in which Jeake's account of his life juxtaposes astrology with the new aspirations of late Stuart England should illustrate the dangers of uncritically presuming that all the progressive forces of his day were equally antithetic to astrology" (76). In light of the emphasis that sixteenth- and seventeenth-century writers on the ethics of finance placed upon the need to remain in a state of passive vulnerability with respect to the outcomes of commercial transactions, I believe that an even stronger case can be made for the harmony of these two modes—which even the editors describe as being bound only through the awkward figure of "juxtapos[ition]." References to providence in accounts of commerce and astrological interpretations of rising and falling profits serve to show that "forces of progress" are only legible from the standpoint of a later historiographic disembedding of those forces from the more complex and robust reality of which they were at first merely parts. That Jeake could cast one horoscope regarding the financial settlement of his father's estate and his resultant "increase of Figure" (i.e., Jeake's newly gotten wealth from the estate) on 11 August 1693, another horoscope regarding a "little fit of a Quartan Ague" eleven days later, a third regarding the woodpile incident, and a fourth a few weeks later regarding a near fall from his horse into a river testifies to his sense of a unifying force underlying all the evanescent and uncertain experiences of the living (222–28). This is not merely to say that Jeake believed in God; it is to observe the dangers of abstracting economic moments from the larger pattern of devotion that defined his relation to the "economic" part of life.[45] His editors are right to say that astrology and commerce were not "antithetic" in Jeake's time, but it cannot be denied that they were increasingly *seen as* antithetical, the discourse of astrology suffering from "a failure to retain credit as a belief-system among the leaders of opinion of the day" (Hunter and Gregory 75). This is absolutely true; and so much might be said as well of belief in the sinfulness of usury. If we broaden our understanding of what usury meant, however, we will find that while Jeake's providentialism may appear antithetical to his commercial practice, he felt absolutely no need to apologize to himself.[46]

CHAPTER 3

Risk and Adventure in the Age of Projects

Noah, Defoe, Crusoe

I N T H E previous chapter, I remarked that the ethical value of uncertainty has been available and operative throughout the entire history of capital, notwithstanding Tawney's relegation of that value to the Middle Ages and Lazzarato's claim that it is only because of the current configuration of global capital that such a value has any meaning. Between these two economic moments, the one "premodern" and the other in some sense "post-modern," we presumably find ourselves in the territory of economic "modernity." In this modernity that bridges pre- and post-modern economic orders, belief in the ethic of uncertainty (the medieval frame of mind) gives way to a form of rationality in which risk is perceived as that which must be eliminated (the supersession of the medieval frame of mind) until such time as the social and economic consequences of that elimination become so painful or so painfully obvious as to awaken in us a renewed desire for open and uncertain futures (the post-modern frame of mind). In this and the ensuing chapter I will argue against such a depiction of modernity by demonstrating that in the eighteenth century, when secular economic modernity is so often said to have taken shape, uncertainty continued to inform ethical ideas and ideals.

It did, of course, take on new forms, so that we must look for it in texts that do not immediately announce themselves as economic in character or content. Had the ethic of uncertainty been expressed in such texts, it would have been disqualified from the outset as a Jones-esque case of raving at usurers in an era of finance (in the epilogue, I will look at one example of a nineteenth-century raver). This is because the discourse of usury—the only robust ethical discourse with which one might have confronted the emergence of a financial culture—suffered the same fate as Jones, which Jones suffered in part because of his own conflation of usury and interest in his sermon at St. Mary Woolnoth. The shaming of Jones and the delegitimation of usury critique meant that the ethic of uncertainty needed to find a new way to express itself. In the next chapter, I will show how debates about prudence picked up much of the slack and provided an opportunity to debate the ethics of calculative rationality and to again call into question the autonomy of the economic field. Here, however, I will focus on the rhetoric of projects, focusing on Daniel Defoe, the writer most associated with that rhetoric.

More specifically, this chapter explores how risk and providence work themselves out in two vital texts in the Defoe canon: *An Essay upon Projects* (1697) and *Robinson Crusoe* (1719). Defoe's *Essay* was a pivotal statement regarding the human ability to manage the future and, though they are often underemphasized, the ethical implications of attempting to do so. The opprobrium heaped upon projectors in Defoe's time owed much to traditional understandings of the usurer's unsavory regard for future reward and their sinful attempt at eliminating uncertainty. Thus, Defoe's attempt to rescue the projector from criticism serves as his attempt to mediate between ethical strictures relating to finance and the new commercial opportunities of the later seventeenth century. I argue that the figure of Noah—described by Defoe in both *An Essay upon Projects* and his *General History of Discoveries and Improvements* (1725–26) as the first projector—plays a vital role in this mediation owing to the biblical patriarch's unique relation to God.

I then turn my attention to *Robinson Crusoe* (1719), which many scholars regard as having laid the grounds for later formulations of *homo economicus*, bearing in mind that the risk taken by Noah is not unlike that taken by Crusoe, and argue that Crusoe's decision to leave England, far from being an evil violation of the law of his father, constitutes the essential spiritual moment for Crusoe and sets Defoe up for what might be called the text's *ethical challenge*, when Defoe himself must assume a risk of being misunderstood. Neither novel of individualism nor spiritual autobiography of conversion, *Robinson Crusoe* is a novel of ethical becoming. Whereas the individualist reading foregrounds the becoming at the expense of the ethical (or regards the two as hopelessly divided or only tactically conjoined), the conversion reading implies a spiritual finality or perfection (that he *is converted*) that overlooks how important it is for Crusoe to continually unsettle and disrupt his own sense of security and feeling of certainty. To show that it is this process of unsettlement, rather than merely worldly accumulation, that is Defoe's focus when he writes of Crusoe's initial decision to leave England as well as his later decision to procure slaves to further secure himself, I look at certain passages from the Puritan writer Richard Baxter (1615–1691), some of the same passages that Max Weber used to delineate the Protestant ethic that eventually led to capitalism. By reading Baxter anti-financially, by recognizing the ethic of uncertainty that underwrites his theology, it is possible to see a Defoe who is different not only from the one imagined by Ian Watt, who was explicitly indebted to Weber, but also from the one projected in the "spiritual autobiography" tradition of reading *Crusoe*. At stake in this reading is a reconsideration of Defoe's role in the history of financial modernity, as well as a demonstration of one of the ways that the ethic of uncertainty was mediated—and thus propagated—in the decades of financial revolution.

Providence in the Age of Projects

Defoe is often enlisted in the service of delineating the character of a modernity in which avoiding risk is taken to be rational, but he himself, as Paula Backscheider describes him in her deeply insightful biography, appears to have actively sought risks out. Faced with the decision to either follow in his father's footsteps and become a merchant or enter into the ministry, for which his previous several years of education had prepared him, in 1681 he selected the former option, entering into the burgeoning trade in hosiery (30).[1] Perhaps discontented with the hosier's life, a few years later he took up arms in defense of his faith and the Duke of Monmouth (1649–1685), risking nothing less than his own life and freedom (38–40). As time went on, he "bought and sold goods from Spain, Portugal, and the New World," all in the face of continual "dangers to shipping because of the Nine Years War with France" (52).[2] "Deep, even emotional convictions" drove him into the dangerous debates over occasional conformity at the close of the 1690s (86). He frequently confronted established authorities in print, and suffered memorably for his pamphlet *The Shortest Way with the Dissenters* (1702) by being placed in the pillory; undaunted, he continued his assault on the injustice of his time with his satire *A Hymn to the Pillory* (1703). His various investments, too numerous to list in toto, included everything from civet cats to protosubmarines, investments more often risky than prudent or profitable. To push the cause for union in 1706, he went to the "frightening city" of Edinburgh, rife with "Jacobites, Highlanders, seamen," and others fiercely invested in the sovereignty of Scotland (211). "As an Englishman and one whose presence was a matter of speculation, Defoe himself ran a fair amount of risk" in undertaking this journey (217). It is unsurprising that after the Treaty of Union, in his letters to Robert Harley he displayed "a desire for challenge and variety" (227). To accept a dull administrative position "when he could have done something more valuable to his religion or country would have been, in his opinion, irresponsible and perhaps even sinful" (230). Deeply invested in his country and his religion, Defoe simply could not rest content.

Defoe's risks signified primarily within the terms of a universe he understood to be providential. Just as the critique of usury was predicated, in Luther's words, on the importance of "clinging to God alone," so does Backscheider observe that throughout his life Defoe too depended on and had perfect faith in the existence of an intervening and organizing providence and consciously avoided states of rest or ease for this very reason. Defoe wanted to serve God, believing that whatever success or failure he experienced in the process was part of a divine plan (321–22). Defoe went on to make his most famous character, Robinson Crusoe, perfectly "trust [God's] purposes and benevolence" (420). Defoe's "part was played on the stage of Great Britain and in a providential world that he knew he could never fully understand or predict. Over and over he refers to 'changes and disasters,' to 'new scenes of life,' to 'unseen Mines' blowing up tranquil lives, and to 'mysteries of Providence.' As the future and his part are unpredictable, so are the roles that Defoe will be called on to play" (534). More than simply attempts to account for particular changes in fortune, Defoe's words reflect his sense of the world as infinitely variegated and the future as constitutively beyond the eye of human reason.

A risktaker who understood his actions in relation to God, Defoe was thus well positioned to mediate between the old and the new. Not only was he a devout man trucking wares in an age of commerce but his teacher, the Reverend Charles Morton (bap. 1627, d. 1698), likely exposed Defoe to the difficulty of reconciling Christianity with the financial order.[3] Morton attempted to do just that in a brief treatise on usury written shortly after his young student's departure from Newington Green:

> As *Moses* thus taught his Disciples, so does our Saviour teach his,
> Luke 6.35, 36. *Sinners lend to sinners to receive as much again; but love
> ye your enemies; do good and lend, hoping for nothing again.* . . . Make
> it not your only motive to lend (as sinners do) hoping to receive as
> much again: That is, the like kindness upon occasion at another time,

when they are able to lend and you need to borrow; but in a Christian Benignity, and in obedience to the command, with expectation only of Gods future reward, and *your reward shall be great.* . . . (13)

Morton does seek to establish the legitimacy of expecting a return of the loan principle, but he admits that the only unequivocally acceptable expectations are those that are oriented toward God.[4] As in Jones's sermon, there is nothing remarkable from a theological standpoint in Morton's tract, but insofar as it again represents that distinctively Protestant unwillingness to allow the economic to split apart from spirit, it shows how the ethic preached by anti-usury writers might have made its way to Defoe and shaped how he understood such problems.

 While Morton's focus is on usury, the context for the development of anti-finance in the later seventeenth century was more often that of the "project." Many of the objections leveled against projects and projectors in the years leading up to Defoe's age-defining *Essay upon Projects* derive from the view that projection, like usury, falls outside the scope of natural and Christian ethical behavior. Consequently, projectors frequently are to be found in company with other figures of dubious moral integrity, limited social worth, and questionable sense. In a 1694 English translation of Rabelais we find "Projectors" on a ship loaded with "Astrologers, Fortunetellers, Alchymists, Rhimers, Poets, Painters . . . Mathematicians, Watchmakers, Sing-Songs, *Musitioners*, and the Devil and all others that are Subject to Queen Whims" (83). In another text, projectors are with, simply, "Prodigals . . . and Poets" (Motteux 53). Elsewhere they are linked to "Intreaguers," being "the very *Machiavels* of their Age" (Norris 201). And around King's Bench Walk we find

> Poor *Pettifogging Pimps* o'th' Law,
> *Trav'lers* who ne'er Salt-water saw,
> *Alsatian Biters* and their *Cullies,*
> Pretended Wits and Sharping Bullies,
> *Projectors* and their *Undertakers,*
> *News Writing 'Squires* and *Ballad Makers.* . . .
> (R. Ames 18)

The King's Bench Walk, located in the Inner Temple, is here a figure for the common ideological space occupied by both projectors and "Biters." More than just a generic term for "cheat" or "thief," *biter* was interchangeable with *usurer* for Elizabethan and Jacobean theologians, because the Hebrew word for usury was *neshek*, meaning "biter." "*Alsatian Biters*" may therefore refer generally to the growing number of Yiddish-speaking Jews in the Alsace region, whom anti-Semites regarded as singularly fixated on wealth, or more particularly to the Alsatian-born Protestant reformer Martin Bucer (1491–1551), who had invoked the distinction between *neshek* and *tarbith*, illegitimate and legitimate forms of taking profit from a loan, to permit certain forms of money-lending for Jews in his territory (N. Jones, *God and the Moneylenders* 20–23). Either way, usury was routinely figured as a biting or consuming of the other (while satirical references to Alsace almost always serve as code for dubious forms of finance).

To distinguish the usurer from other economic agents, Blaxton, for example, offered a litany of figures allied to the usurer, many of which explicitly or implicitly evoked this "biting": "the usurers money is like the biting of an Aspe," or like "the poison of an Aspe"; "the usurer is like a Pigge," or like "the worme *Teredo*, soft to touch but consumeth hard timber," "as a Worme in an Apple or Nut," "a blood-sucker of the people"; as well as "like a bever" and "a moath"; and the usurer "pricks with sharp thorns till the blood followes" (Blaxton 47–51). The recurrent image of the usurer as a biter depended in part upon the perception that usurers stole the land out from under impecunious overmortgaged landed aristocrats whose titles reached back immemorially and in part upon the way that the usurer's profiting robbed the individual bodies of debtors and collectives (such as cities or governments) of their "substance."[5] Defoe drew on such imagery when he described stockjobbers as "biters." Underscoring the similarity of the immoral world of speculative finance to the godless world of usury, Defoe juxtaposed the Latinisms of scholastic theology to the decidedly vulgar world of exchange: "Thus the Jobbers bite their Friends, and these Men bite the Jobbers, *qui Sharpat Sharpabitur, Exchange-Alley Latin*" (*Anatomy* 40). Such figurative potential meant that usurers could be likened, and were, to a wide assortment of individuals operating in the space of finance (returning us once again to Mosse's dictum that the usurer appears sometimes in one form and sometimes in another). The language of "biting" thus served to bridge the early modern critique of usurers with a modern critique of projectors.

Usury was employed indiscriminately and loosely; *biting* encompassed a panoply of financial crimes (including cheating, as at cards, for example); *projectors* were defined by their association with other, equally plastic types, such as poets and jobbers. It is clear that critics of finance—though they would not have been able to comprehend themselves as such—were seeking the right way to describe the target of their resentment and resistance. The pliancy of *projectors*, for instance, allowed this inchoate figure to assume multiple roles simultaneously, to be projector, astrologer, rhimer, and so forth, all at once. The founder of a failed land bank, Hugh Chamberlen (1630–after 1720), is a combination of such dis-figures:

> To give you his Character truly Compleat,
> He's Doctor, Projector, Man-Midwife and C[heat]
> Who has Cunningly manag'd a subtle Device,
> Beyond the poor Parson, or *Auberry Price*.
> And all that I farther can say of the matter,
> He's gone to the *Dutch*, and the Devil go a'ter.
>
> (Aveling 171)

The author, possibly Ned Ward, earlier in the poem wonders how, "Considering how often the Nation is bit / by Projects," projectors like Chamberlen manage to attain any credit at all (Aveling 170). Through a strange alchemy of financial projects—involving lies, paper currency, and a series of bait-and-switch tactics—Chamberlen does the work of the devil. This basic point, which the poem repeatedly and unimaginatively rehearses every few lines, was something of a cultural cliché.

The specific version of the devil that this cliché evoked was the scheming one who took the form of the serpent. And the door swung both ways. Not only would the devil be enlisted to describe projectors but projectors were equally serviceable in rendering the satanic. Richard Allestree (1619–1681) described the enemies of the soul, including the devil, as this sort of scheming, polymorphic projector: "What are Hell Gates, but the deep Plots of those Infernal Powers? The *Serpent* is the *Emblem* of *Subtilty*: The *Serpents* of the *Egyptian* Sorcerers, were devoured by *Moses* his Serpent [*sic*]. Wherefore, but to shew that all crafty Counsels and Machinations of hellish Projectors, are easily destroyed by the Power and Wisdom of the Almighty: It was the Rod of God that swallow'd 'em all. . . . And when Satan thought to have won most honor to himself, attended him with shame and loss" (155). Allestree does not say that all "Projectors" are "hellish," but the fact that the term is used in reference to dark magic—"*Egyptian* Sorcerers"—suggests that they are intertwined concepts for him. The satanic quality of the projectors is marked by the fact that God, as providence working through Moses, enters into the world to interrupt or disrupt their "crafty Counsels and Machinations," the word *machinations* emphasizing their belief in and devotion to the idea that the world is an autonomous material or mechanical space. The devil is a pro-

jector not simply because he is "crafty" but because his craftiness blasphe-
mously presupposes a controllable space that is apart from God.

The satanic associations of the projector dovetail with another common
figure for the projector, Icarus. In 1698 Sir John Vanbrugh (1664–1726) associated clergy in search of financial wealth with projectors who "owe their Fall
to their Ambition; [for] their soaring so high has melted their Wings" (42).
Sir William Killigrew (1605–1695) spun out the connection in his poem "On
Vain Projectors" (1694):

> No mortal man can limit or restrain,
> The boundless fansies of another's brain;
> But may such Fetters on his own Thoughts lay,
> As will keep them from wandring much astray;
> But naturally, Men add wings to try,
> How high their vain ambitious Hearts can fly,
> Until like Icarus, their waxen Wings
> Do melt, and their hopes to ruin brings.
>
> (*Mid-Night and Daily Thoughts* 98)

Keeping with the tendency to oppose projectors with submissive Christian
subjects, Killigrew's collection places "On Vain Projectors" immediately prior
to the poem "On God's Wondrous Works," which emphasizes the human inability to understand or control God's creation—not an uncommon juxtapo-
sition.[6] "On God's Wondrous Works"—one of two different poems bearing
this title in Killigrew's collection—indicts the projecting spirit by praising the
value of passivity and submission to providence. Icarus thus has both the-
matic and formal implications in projector discourse. Thematically, Icarus
signals the delusional aspirations of projectors; formally, drawn from pagan
tradition, the mythical Icarus also suggests that projects are associated with
pagan desires attempting to darkly outmaneuver the Christian, providential
order of the natural world. In project literature, Icarus becomes an emblem of
the act of separation from a world of contingency under God's sway.

Part of Defoe's task in the *Essay upon Projects* was to illustrate that not
all projects proceed from the perspective of the infinitely aspiring and that
projectors could be "fettered" by reasonable epistemological and atmospheric
constraints. Defoe was arguing not simply for certain particular projects or
plans for future improvement but for projects generally in a climate in which
anticipatory planning or scheming was relentlessly associated with ethical,
epistemological, and spiritual deviance. While there had been attacks on pro-

jectors for as long as there had been projects, in the 1690s the term *projector* was deployed in the context of a range of financial and commercial undertakings that were often left unspecified and thus might well be anything from founding a bank to crafting wings to fly. The projector was thus intelligible as a form of subjectivity rather than as a professional type. What unifies this subjectivity—in this, bad sense—is the range of associations that connect him to the older figure of the usurer as I have outlined it in previous chapters: one who attempts to circumvent or avoid divine or natural laws; to secure some kind of profit by displacing or unequally distributing the risks the project must face onto an unknowing, ignorant, or helpless individual or population; and to gain without respecting proper ethical boundaries.

It is in this context that Defoe's *Essay upon Projects* should be understood. Defoe needed to meet the ethical demands of his readers and to show that the projector was not necessarily a swindling sort of Josiah Child (bap. 1631, d. 1699), or member of a cabal ministry (such as the one that was said to have perniciously influenced Charles II), but a true risk-taking and therefore deeply *believing* sort of commercial being. Backscheider writes that some of the projects he discusses give us "insight into Defoe's conception of a divine plan built into the details of creation," and it might be added that the entire *Essay* depends upon the existence of such a plan, for only within such a context could projects be considered as being in any way legitimate (70). The solution to the problem, therefore, was to successfully incorporate the idea of the project within a more expansive, even infinite framework of causality, justice, and morality. The problem, at theological, philosophical, and, indeed, rhetorical levels, was that the idea (and language) of projects supposed a manageable terrain of causality, whereas the idea (and language) of providence insisted upon the impossibility of such a terrain. The frequent charge that projects were doomed to failure was not, in other words, separate from claims that projectors were dishonest; these two claims were causally connected. The dishonesty of projectors consisted in their unwillingness to avow the more complex system of invisible causes that were the true reasons behind a project's success or failure. And the success or failure of a given project depended on whether the project's undertakers paid due respect to the contingencies of a providential order. To avoid the charge of abstract, fanciful boundlessness, upon which the poetry of Killigrew and others insists, Defoe understands that the projects he presents must be limited in scope (i.e., realistic), but they also needed to recognize the existence of an "invisible world," a "supernatural world existing at the same time and in the same place," to use words Robert

Folkenflik employs to describe a quite similar problem posed by the real in *Robinson Crusoe* (117).

One sign of Defoe's desire to accommodate the impious manageability of the project to the infinite causality of providence is his attempt to capture and represent reverberations of projects beyond their original purpose or goal. Defoe rarely limits the basis for his advocacy of a given project, in other words, to a single advantage or to a single social benefit. In fact, it is possible to read Defoe's shift toward the sociality of the project—as opposed to the private, isolated, closed, "for profit" project—as a preliminary indication of his desire for the project to in some way reverberate or echo; like a rock thrown into a pond, the project's meaning ought to radiate outward. For instance, by establishing a pension fund for the benefit of wives of seamen who die in battles with pirates, Defoe hopes to benefit not simply those wives or those seamen but also *other*, unrelated seamen by inspiring them with added courage so that should the need for battle arise at sea, they will be more likely to courageously defend their vessels (not having to worry themselves with thoughts of leaving their wives and families destitute). It does not stop there, however. That courage, in turn, benefits merchants, whose goods would be liable to seizure by pirates and who can now trade with greater confidence in the security of their goods.

In another of Defoe's proposals, undertaking highway improvements will benefit travelers, but highway improvements, perhaps surprisingly, will also benefit the poor people whose common land would need to be appropriated in order to make way for these new, wider, improved roadways. Each poor common-dweller, Defoe proposes, would be given a "Cottage" on "an Allotment of Land, always sufficient to invite the Poor Inhabitant, in which the Poor shou'd be Tenant for Life *Gratis*, doing Duty upon the High-Way." These "Poor Inhabitant[s]" will, Defoe continues, go on to further benefit the traveler by making it so that he "might Travel over all *England* as though a Street, where he cou'd never want, either Rescue from Thieves, or Directions for his way." These merchants, in turn, will contribute their part to the economic good of the nation, whose horizon presumably entails the happiness as well of the poor common-dweller whose common land had to be appropriated (*Projects* 35). Both of these projects are designed to first benefit a primary group that then, because of this benefit, transfers more value to another group, which often repays the first group for its efforts, taxes, sacrifices, or time. As Defoe describes this ever-expanding system of effects, he vainly tries to represent the theoretically endless chain of events that a single project sets in motion.

"Widening roads reduces theft" is a way of encapsulating Defoe's consideration of what economists today refer to as "externalities," a concept that continues to pose challenges to economic analysis, as externalities are, theoretically speaking, impossible to fully incorporate into the model: since externalities themselves have effects, and those effects have effects, and so forth, the model would only be sufficient were it infinite and thus no longer a model but the thing itself (the problem of the set that contains all sets). From one perspective, Defoe's projects appear to account for externalities. Or one might say that his projects are designed for their externalities, since not only are the external economic side effects of Defoe's projects frequently folded back into the original plan to appear rather as advantages to or justifications for the original project but they call into question the intellectual point of origin for the project. Whether, for example, Defoe designed his pension fund to help widows or to help sustain trade routes remains ultimately unclear. Placing in the reader's mind the contingent unfolding of distant and uncertain future events, each project comes to be justified on the basis not of what the project claims to do (widen roads or assist impoverished wives) but of what each project might eventually become.

That this was not itself a solution to the problem posed by the tension between projects and providence is evidenced by the fact that Defoe goes to lengths in parts of the text to create a morally legitimate status for projectors, but he never offers a project that is motivated by profit. He writes that "'tis necessary to distinguish among the Projects of the present times, between the Honest and the Dishonest" (9). Dishonest projectors include (1) the progenitors of joint stock companies whose projects miserably fail but who manage to profit from the trade in stock; (2) stockjobbers; (3) brokers guilty of defalcation [fraud or misuse of investor funds]; (4) certain unscrupulous engineers and patentees; and (5) inventors whose projects are "fram'd by subtle Heads, with a sort of a *Deceptio Visus*, and *Legerdemain*" (*Projects* 11).[7] Other than stockjobbers and brokers, who *perhaps* can be identified and avoided, Defoe defines dishonest projectors as those who attempt to secure profits through dark, mysterious, even magical channels, echoing in certain ways Allestree's "*Egyptian* Sorcerers." Part of the problem for Defoe is that while the projects covered in the *Essay* are clearly distinct from for-profit enterprises such as treasure hunting, he does not wish to make it seem as though the *only* honest projectors are those who exclusively seek the public good. These sorts of projects, by virtue of their social value and charitable aspect, did not need to be defended. It was the for-profit, private venture—definitive of his commercial practice—that required defense.[8]

Whether he was successful in doing so depends on whether we believe that Defoe considered the culture of projects to be unfolding in a secular or spiritual world. Steven Pincus has rightly noted Defoe's more historically minded claim that the modern "Original" of the "Projecting Humour" dates back only as far as 1680 ("Revolution in Political Economy?" 118). But it is nevertheless important in ethical terms for Defoe to reach back in the *Essay* to the Bible, to Noah and Nimrod, however strange a historical argument that might be.[9] There are two reasons for this. First, Noah and Nimrod speak in fundamental ways to the view that projects were the outgrowth of an ostentatious humanity, one inclined to plan and direct futurity without the assistance or guiding principles of God. As Backscheider notes in her reading of *Crusoe*, there is a sense that God's providence makes it "futile for human beings to plan" (428). While it is tempting to read Noah and Nimrod as supplemental to Defoe's more practical efforts in the *Essay*, they are crucial in light of the satanic and Icarian associations of the project that pervaded the commercial and the cultural imagination of the later seventeenth century, which themselves were extensions of the accusation that usurers too were in league with the dragon or devil or serpent. At the simplest level, then, Defoe allows his reader to read projects back into the Bible and to situate them in a space other than one that had come to define the modern project (Icarus, the serpent, Satan, tricks, magic, the polymorphic projector/astrologer/cozener/poet/ etc.). Defoe's biblical references enter the projector into a longer civilizational and spiritual history, freeing that figure from the taint of recent anti-projector discourses and entering it into a framework expressly understood as providential. Defoe does date the beginning of the modern project to around 1680. But in having emerged under the watch of, and guided by, the inspiration of Charles II, who Defoe loathed, the modern project was precisely the problem. Pincus's claim that Defoe located the modern project in recent history is, in other words, absolutely correct, but the modern project is precisely why Defoe looks to Noah: to write an alternative history of the project, one more in line with the ethic of uncertainty than those of the modern era.

In lieu of openly resolving the projects/providence dilemma, Defoe offers the example of Noah, that eminently submissive biblical figure, whom he narrates, however briefly, as the original projector. In a preliminary section of the *Essay* entitled "The History of Projects," Defoe playfully discusses the problem with the Ark's antithesis, the Tower of Babel:

> The Building of *Babel* was a Right Project; for indeed the true definition of a Project, according to Modern Acceptation, is, as is said before,

a vast Undertaking, too big to be manag'd, and therefore likely enough
to come to nothing; . . . if the People of the Old World cou'd have Built
a House up to Heaven, they shou'd never be Drown'd again on Earth,
and they only had forgot to Measure the Height, *that is,* as in other
Projects, it only Miscarri'd, or else 'twould have Succeeded. (13)

What are we to make of the fact that Defoe positions the Ark and the Tower of
Babel as the two possible forms that a project might assume? And if these are
the two archetypal project formations, why does Defoe not clarify the reasons
behind their respective success and failure? Finally, inasmuch as the Tower of
Babel was built specifically to consolidate and strengthen the descendants of
Noah, and notwithstanding its ultimate failure, would the Tower not serve as
a better analogy for the social and collective projects Defoe endorses in the
Essay? Or to put this in different terms, given the social and collective aspects
of the projects he describes in the remainder of the *Essay*, why would Defoe
choose the one obviously constructive collective act of building to represent
the "bad project"—the Tower—and the one "individual" effort of Noah as the
"good" version of the project?

Defoe has two things in mind when he selects the Tower as the perfect
example of the modern project. First, the Tower of Babel was a very big and
therefore very unviable project, one doomed to fail simply by virtue of the
practical impediments to its accomplishment. Second, though, Defoe bears
witness to a tendency in projecting culture of his time—along the lines of
the Icarian and satanic/serpentine project—to challenge the preeminence of
the divine in this world. God destroys the Tower because he fears humanity's
growing strength, its ostentation, its belief in its ability to complete tasks without his approval and guidance. Rather than offering reasons for the failure of
the Tower project, Defoe presents the Tower as a definition of the *modern*
project, a "Right Project . . . according to Modern Acceptation." Against Nimrod's modern Tower, Defoe positions Noah's Ark, a project, he writes, that
"seem'd so ridiculous to the Graver Heads of that Wise, tho' Wicked Age, that
poor *Noah* was sufficiently banter'd for it; and had he not been set on work
by a very peculiar Direction from Heaven, the Good old Man would certainly
have been laugh'd out of it, as a most ridiculous Project" (13). To make sense
of these ironies: Defoe understands modern projects as failures because they
are undertaken against all that is good and holy. In contrast, projects that are
oriented toward the greater good, though they may appear to be laughable,
are preferable because they are underwritten by providence.

Turning to the Old Testament enables Defoe to envision and narrate a sequence in which the connection between the project and the divine is made explicit, thus countering the view that projects are a case of simple irreligion. But doing so also enables Defoe to describe a population that is out of touch with God (the "Graver Heads" who dismissed Noah). In this way, Defoe locates a form of commercial agency that falls somewhere between the godless freedom of the Icarians and a state of being fully controlled by God. As important as the fact that God and Noah are in league with each other, in other words, is the fact that Noah's building of the Ark is figured as an act of will, one in defiance of the "Graver Heads" of that "Wise, tho' Wicked Age." Coyly alluding to divine guidance rather than asserting it—"a very peculiar Direction"—and casting the patriarch as a "Good old Man," Defoe navigates between outright determinism and atheistic freedom, placing Noah's project in the space of what might be called the ethical. As any reader of the *Essay* would know, of course, the reasons for the Ark's success and the Tower's failure consist solely in the extent to which their principal architects submit to the "very peculiar Direction" of God. This omission on Defoe's part only makes sense if we see it as part of a broader strategy to defend projects *against* the providentialist strand of argument seen in the anti-projection literature of the period, which stressed the way projectors attempted to circumvent a natural Christian order. Projects unhinged from an authentic and proper original purpose—to serve God—and oriented toward the triumph of man's ingenuity and power are to be resisted as a basis for the new commercial order.

Defoe would go on to make extensive use of Noah in later writings as well, often juxtaposing him to Nimrod, as he had done in the *Essay*, and always committed to the relevance of biblical to modern history. Noah, he reminds us in a prelude to a discussion of shipping and oceanic travel, was also the first shipwright.[10] Defoe begins his *General History of Discoveries and Improvements*, a kind of guidebook to the history of projects, with "*Noah* and his sons coming out of the Ark upon the Mountains of *Armenia*," the lone survivors of a providentially ordained project that had entailed ridicule and risk (9). In 1706 he praised Noah's "Courage" in taking such a risk—otherwise "he had certainly been drown'd"—but lest such courage be read in terms of romance heroism rather than in a spiritual context, Defoe quickly adds that it was really "his Faith" that saved him from destruction (*Caledonia* 12).[11] In 1704 Defoe juxtaposed Noah and Nimrod in an attempt to challenge the Jacobite Charles Leslie's (1650–1722) political absolutism.[12] Arguing against the divine right of kings, Defoe points to the fact that both Noah and his sons were "commanded by *God*," whereas *Nimrod* "inveigled the *People* into Subjection" (*Caledonia* 12). Nimrod's sin was blasphemy: "And the *Power* he promis'd to protect them against was, he told them, the *Power* of *God;* who by dividing them into *Colonies* only design'd to destroy them" (12). Nimrod is "a prudent and ambitious Man," but for all of that, God blasts his scheme (11).

Looking forward to *Robinson Crusoe,* Defoe's use of biblical narrative and ironic understatement in his rendition of Nimrod/Noah allow him to endorse projects without having to positively affirm this endorsement. He allows his reader to complete the process of thinking or reasoning about projects and, in turn, to determine what sorts of projects would be acceptable in the eyes of religious and ethical authorities. Had Defoe made his advocacy of projects explicit, he would be rhetorically manifesting that deviant, all-too-human quality of projects that had created public-image problems for the culture of projects in the first place. By refusing to say outright whether projects were good or bad, human or divine in origin, Defoe manages to locate them in providential history, on the one hand, and in the projecting culture of his time, on the other. To openly speak of the Ark as a divinely ordained project would be to require divine ordination for all projects, while to explicitly speak of Babel as a challenge to God would damn projects altogether. Satire and parable—evasive forms of expression, ways of saying without saying—come to the rescue where an axiomatic logic or principle could have only further delegitimized the Age of Projects. Defoe was not generally antipathetic toward the making of money, but he did have specific ethical concerns about commerce at a turning point. Would it end up godless, ministerial, and would it entail the consolidation of wealth in the hands of sharpers and biters, as had happened, with great public outcry, no fewer than twice in the previous thirty years? Or would friendly societies and bankruptcy reform, to name two projects Defoe proposes, create the basis for a new kind of providential economy, of the sort that Jeake could comfortably align with his extremely mystical religiosity? Noah allows Defoe to recover the project from imputations of gross presumption and cozenage, its modern form, and to depict it as a risk taken with an eye toward the larger providential economy, in which such risks might meet with reward.

As any reader of Lemuel Gulliver's visit to the Academy of Projectors knows, attacks on projects continued well into the eighteenth century, becoming a subject of renewed importance during the South Sea Bubble, when one writer, humorously invoking Seneca's "Man is a reasoning animal," defined an "English-Man" as "A Projecting *Animal.*"[13] What has not been fully appreciated is the extent to which the seafaring Noah, the risk-taking man of God, would also continue to serve as a counterbalance to the impieties of the modern projector. Defoe's novelistic practice, as recent scholarship has demonstrated, did not crystallize in the decade following the South Sea Bubble by accident.[14] But whereas some scholarship has emphasized the way in which his fiction helped readers to deal with the epistemological crisis generated by the uncertainties of a credit economy, I would suggest that his fiction, *Robinson Crusoe* in particular, was an attempt to reestablish the importance of risk to ethics. The South Sea crisis did not expose the problem of risk; it showed, yet again, that the *absence* of risk in commercial affairs could horribly mangle the nation. It was not just that the experience of Noah provided a template for Defoe's narrative plots. Defoe's resolution of the providence/projects division in narrative—a formal resolution that neither required nor allowed for a full determination of what makes projects good rather than "modern"—could serve as the basis for more sustained narrative efforts. Backscheider writes that Defoe "habitually, even characteristically, thinks about God in the world and, therefore, thinks typologically" (530). By juxtaposing Noah's dangerous and, in the eyes of others, ridiculous project to the ostentation of Nimrod and Babel, we can see just how deeply that typological reading influenced his sense of the past and his vision for the project of the future.

Robinson Crusoe: Noah contra Weber; or, Calvinist Desire

While Crusoe's resemblance to the biblical figure of Jonah has been detailed by G. A. Starr, there has not been, to my knowledge, any sustained scholarly consideration of Defoe's use of the Noah figure. This is somewhat surprising given Defoe's interest in apocalypse, extreme weather, oceanic travel, and the theme of providence, as well as the advertisement at the end of several of William Taylor's early editions of *Robinson Crusoe* for a series of maps of "Sacred Geography," showing, among other things, "The peopling of the World by the Sons of *Noah*" (2nd ed., after 364).[15] *Crusoe* has been described as a fantasy of apocalypse, and its hero as a forerunner of the "last man" motif.[16] If this is so, Crusoe's island, then, replete with animals, cut off from all other human life—as if there almost were no other human life—in this way also comes to seem a figure for the Ark, carrying him until 1687, on the eve of the Glorious Revolution, when (Eng)land is finally cleansed of (Stuart) wickedness.[17] What all this might suggest is that Defoe liked to think with Noah. In 1697 it helped him to resolve certain tensions in the culture of projects. It may have been a previous commitment to Noah that inspired such thinking about projects, or perhaps Defoe's understanding of projects led him to Noah, but either way the story of Noah intersects with the culture of projects at the point of risk-taking and providentialism. Situating *Robin-*

son Crusoe in this history—of risk and the ethics of uncertainty—makes two things clear. First, Crusoe's spiritual conversion, if that is the right word, does not happen on the island; it happens when he decides to leave England. Second, the story Crusoe tells his readers about his religious development—its progress on the island—is both disingenuous (a lie) and also ethical for this very disingenuousness. This will become clear, but it all depends on how we read Crusoe's father's words prior to Crusoe's venturing out onto the wide and uncertain sea and how we account for Crusoe's rendering of his decision to leave as his "Original Sin."

I position my reading of Defoe against two general ways of reading *Robinson Crusoe*. On the one hand, there is the claim that Crusoe has something to do with selfish individualism.[18] While Ian Watt's narrative of the rise of the novel has been largely superseded as a way of understanding the history of the novel as a genre, his analysis of Crusoe as modeling economic man continues to exert a profound influence on the novel's readers. On this reading, Crusoe bodies forth as an exemplary protocapitalist, marshaling both human and nonhuman resources for profit and improvement: "Robinson Crusoe has been very appropriately used by many economic theorists as their illustration of *homo economicus*" (Watt 63). He leaves England to seek wealth and rejects the dull life promised to him by his conservative father, of which decision Watt writes: "Crusoe's 'original sin' is really the dynamic tendency of capitalism itself" (65). His isolated status on the island mirrors the condition of the individual in the modern world; his work ethic raises him above others; his skills in accounting manifest the calculative rationality and information technologies of the new financial order; and his preoccupation with accumulation testifies to a prudential, thrifty, industrious, and ascetic character. Writing against Watt, John Richetti rightfully restored the significance of the spiritual aspects of Defoe's text, arguing that Crusoe's piety must emerge in tandem with his selfish economism in order to offset the piratical/criminal potential of the modern individual: "Crusoe may be said to have purified the secular values which are implied by the spirit of the book through the religious values which are its letter" (*Popular Fiction* 96). Both Richetti and Watt, however, see Defoe as essentially advocating an economic spirit, though in Richetti it requires spiritualism to offset and limit that secularity's dangerous potential.

Reading Crusoe as an economic subject extends even to Marxist and postcolonial readings of the novel, which stress that the novel critiques the selfish individualism manifested in the figure of Crusoe or that the novel is complicit in empire via the economically selfish figure of Crusoe.[19] Weaving together the traditional reading of Crusoe as economic man and newer readings of the colonial context for Defoe's fiction, Aino Mäkikalli, for instance, writes that "depictions of slavery and colonialist action [in Defoe's fiction] can be interpreted as part of the *homo economicus*–ideology, that is, the principles of the human being who acts by economic terms" (261). Good, good but needing limitation, or capitalist/imperialist—Crusoe is in these and many other cases viewed as somehow representative of a modern form of economic life, for better or for worse.[20]

On the other hand, many have read *Robinson Crusoe* in religious and spiritual terms. On this reading, Crusoe's narrative conforms to the pattern of the spiritual autobiography. His bibliomancy, his prayers, and his journey of spiritual discovery and self-understanding are read as primary, while his experiences as a trader, a plantation owner, a farmer, and a hunter are secondary (as either allegorical vehicles for a higher realm of spiritual significance or worldly challenges to salvation). Most of all, Crusoe's recognition of his disobedience toward his father is read as Crusoe himself reads it: as his "Original Sin." Crusoe is the prodigal son, a rebel, a transgressor: "By a single act, Crusoe thus defies the joint authority of family, society, and Providence" (Starr 79). But underlying even these spirit-centric readings is the belief that Crusoe's decision to leave is in some ways an economic one: he prefers to seek wealth, to pursue worldly goals, rather than obey the Law of the Father. In this respect, those who have read *Crusoe* as exposing the criminality at the heart of international trade and slavery have a great deal in common with those who brand his choice to leave England as his "Original Sin." For the former, the decision to leave results in pain, exploitation, and suffering for Crusoe, Friday, and/or the many nonhuman victims of Crusoe's selfish, slavish, or imperial impulses. For the latter, the decision to leave results in possible damnation; this is ultimately avoided, they argue, by Crusoe's spiritual conversion, which takes place on the island.

Michael McKeon's adroit management of the tensions of the novel, its staging of the conflict between spiritual and secular concerns, has the virtue of treating both in tandem, of recognizing the impossibility of an exclusive focus on either. McKeon does not, however, see them as reducible to the same underlying set of assumptions, because he regards their copresence in Defoe's fiction as ultimately a case of contradiction that requires negotiation. For McKeon, desire must be "limited and therefore detoxified" by a spirituality that places desire in a new light (*Origins* 324), and the secular desire that initially leads Crusoe to travel must be "transvalued" by "spiritualization" (318). This reading, the most sophisticated of its kind, is nevertheless predicated upon the political economic notion of the autonomy of spiritual and economic life, and more specifically upon the Weberian notion that "spiritual and secular motives" are "inseparable, if ultimately contradictory, parts of a complex intellectual and behavioral system" (*Protestant Ethic* 319).

In order to understand, however, why Crusoe's desire does not require any naturalization and why Crusoe's "wand'ring inclination" at the novel's outset is not in need of transvaluation, much less motivated by a selfish economism, it is necessary to return to the Weberian establishment of Calvinism's supposed internal contradictoriness (*Protestant Ethic* 319). By focusing on and reactivating the importance of taking risks in Protestant English culture— rather than on the importance of securing wealth, for better or worse, as a sign of greed or as evidence of election—we can see how what McKeon presents as a tension is not, in fact, a real tension. First we must remember that readings of Crusoe as *homo economicus* are the product of nineteenth-century political economic applications of Defoe's novel rather than an emanation of eighteenth-century commercial ideology; this is a point that most Defoe scholars would accept as true, but it is one whose implications have not been sufficiently addressed in readings of the novel.[21] Defoe was fully steeped in older traditions, as the spiritualists rightly observe. On the other hand, Defoe had to interrogate how spirit functioned and what it meant in new commercial contexts. Novak, unique in having foregrounded early on questions of money, commerce, and trade in the analysis of Defoe's works, could not have put it better when he wrote in his biography that "the notion of a God who was incapable of intervening in the affairs of human kind was something Defoe could never accept. However much his God may have remained hidden behind the physical nature through which He worked, Defoe never appears to have doubted His continued presence" (*Daniel Defoe: Master of Fictions* 660). Similarly emphatic about the fact that Defoe believed in God, as it were, *all of the time*, not simply when it was convenient or when he forgot to be a man of commerce, Backscheider remarks that Defoe "may not have been a regular part of any congregation . . . but he was never out of communion with God" (530). If these biographical accounts of Defoe are true, how is it possible to think of Defoe's "economics" apart from such a "continued presence" and such a communion? By placing the ethics of uncertainty at the core of an analysis of Defoe's novel it is possible to see what the novel looks like before it is divided into its respective "spiritual" and "secular" parts. Risk, I will argue, enables us to comprehend the relation between the purportedly antithetical worlds of ethics and spirit and the tangible worlds of commerce and trade, between which Defoe's fiction is said to reside. Risk is vital insofar as it serves as a bridge between the world of matter and the unseen world of secret causes and unknowable tomorrows; in giving oneself over to risk, one comes into contact with and validates his or her commitment to things unseen and undetermined. And it is only in and within that worldly order that such an act of commitment can take place.

Before turning to the novel itself, it is worth exploring how these two positions—the economic and spiritual readings of *Robinson Crusoe*—emerged as antithetical, how reading *Crusoe* became an either/or practice. The nineteenth-century appropriation of Crusoe by political economy, with its own implicit and explicit attempts to represent economics as external to matters of spirit, superstition, and the divine, surely paved the way. In other words, the very opposition between the realms of spirit and money is itself the product of a later historiographic construct—encouraged by economistic thought and writing—that conforms to neither Defoe's novel nor his historical time period. Watt's characterization of Crusoe, which was grounded in this antithetical understanding of the relation between matters of spirit and the economic, is therefore central here and requires fuller treatment in view of its influence on twentieth-century interpretations of Defoe's fiction.

Watt's Crusoe, a laboring individual attempting to master the natural world and generally incarnate the spirit of bourgeois capitalism, depends in large measure upon his application of Max Weber's theory of the Protestant, specifically Calvinist, ethic of work to the novel. On this reading, Crusoe begins the novel an impetuous rascal intent on defying the wise advice of his father and gradually becomes a sober and pious laboring man of God. God blesses this newly accounting and accountable exemplar of the Protestant capitalist by rewarding him at the novel's end with a considerable fortune. This portrait of Crusoe is the one that continues to shape many basic understandings of the novel and therefore of Defoe's commercial ideology, extending, as I have noted, even to readings that are critical of Crusoe's colonialist mentality and appropriative spirit. Even those readings critical of Crusoe, that is, read his adventures and experiences in Watt's terms—or, rather, Weber's terms, and therefore the terms of a nineteenth-century economistic division of spirit and money—never questioning the Weberian substrate upon which Watt's reading is based. So let us briefly consider Weber's approach to Calvinism's ethic of work, bearing in mind what has been argued in earlier chapters about the hostility that English Calvinists often and openly expressed toward usury understood as the avoidance of risk.

For Weber, capitalism is a mode of rational organization of society that is premised, ultimately, on an *irrational* mandate to work. "One may," Weber writes, "rationalize life from fundamentally different basic points of view and in very different directions" (38). The particular form of rationalization that occurs under capital is, however, "positively irrational" if we believe that what people generally want is happiness, since capitalism and its mandate to work for work's sake is in fact anathema to happiness (eudaemonia) (38). So Weber goes about reading Calvin and his followers in terms of this central command to work, which, in light of Defoe's Calvinist or quasi-Calvinist upbringing, eventually leads Watt to conclude that what Defoe inherits from the tradition of Calvinism is the work ethic as described by Weber. On this reading, Crusoe bodies forth as an exemplary Calvinist whose unceasing labors serve as an ongoing consecration of time to God but also look forward to the coming age of capital.

Consulting Weber's sources, we can see that Watt's reading of *Crusoe* is, ultimately, an expression or specification of Weber's reading of the English Calvinist Richard Baxter's *Saints Everlasting Rest* (1650), with which Defoe was almost certainly acquainted. Weber (and Tawney, as it happens) read Baxter as champion of an ethic of work, and since, it is argued, Defoe coincided theologically with Baxter, it is clear that Defoe must have embraced the idea of the calling; and so, it is further argued, Crusoe's "work" is what saves him (or might save him). We will explore these various logical steps, but first it is important to note that Novak wisely advises caution when applying the Weber-Tawney thesis to Defoe given that Defoe at one point—in writing his life of Daniel Williams, to be exact—came out against Baxter and Williams on the matter of justification by works (Novak, *Daniel Defoe: Master of Fictions* 125–26). This is a rather thorny matter, but Novak's sense that Defoe does not seem to fit within the Weber-Tawney thesis is as good a place as one will find to begin sorting things out.

The problem, however, goes even deeper than the somewhat contained dispute over justification by works, for it is possible to see that however much he may have objected to Baxter's opinion on this matter, Defoe might have embraced *another* aspect of Baxter's thought, a part that was in fact *at odds* with the mandate to work that Weber claims is central to Baxter's and, by extension, Calvinist theology. To state this more clearly: Defoe did reject the idea of justification by works, as Novak has pointed out, but he may have embraced a different aspect of Baxter's thought, namely, Baxter's attack on *living a restful life*, with which the so-called Calvinist doctrine of work might easily be confused. It is certainly possible that Baxter confused them himself—I will clarify this distinction in a moment—but there is enough in Baxter's writing to say that he advances at least *two* lines of argument concerning the purpose and meaning of work in a Christian life. (At the risk of further muddying things, I must note that these two lines of argument concerning work, or labor, are unrelated to the entirely separate issue of justification *by* works, which might be more properly styled "justification by good deeds.")[22] In any case, to avoid confusion, when speaking of these two lines of argument in Baxter with which I am concerned, we should be speaking not about the problem of work but about the problem of *rest*. At times, it seems that Baxter is arguing that one should work, labor, produce, and so forth, and not rest (this is what Weber gets out of Baxter). At other times, however, what Baxter is arguing is that one should avoid the feeling of content, ease, or restfulness, *whether one is working—that is, productively laboring—or not*. Although these might appear to amount to the same thing, they are in complete opposition to each other: in the former, work is oriented toward producing or a building up of the self; in the latter, work might lead us into a state of restful complacency every bit as spiritually toxic as idleness. So we are dealing with not one binary, but two: production/idleness and restlessness/restfulness. And for Baxter, production was opposed to restlessness, since one could produce and be restful (in the sense of being at ease) at the same time. In any case, Baxter would appear to have been more interested in the latter of these two binaries since for him it went without saying that producing for its own sake was nothing more than sinful worldliness.

Another way of describing this opposition would be to say that on the one hand there is a work that is oriented toward production, accumulation, and security and on the other hand there is a work that aims to unsettle the self precisely when production, accumulation, and security begin. In making his case for the connection between Protestantism and the work ethic, Weber clearly has the former of these two theories of work in mind. It is *not* clear, however, that the passages from Baxter that Weber uses for support defend that interpretation of work. To be exact, Weber draws upon the tenth chapter of Baxter's *Saints Everlasting Rest*, in which Baxter enjoins his reader to resist the temptation to rest. At first glance, it looks to be a classical statement of the Calvinist mandate to work, in the sense of produce, evidence in support of Weber's reading, but that is only if we assume that the alternative to rest is work in the sense of production. Here is an excerpt from Baxter, one to which Weber draws his reader's attention. I present it to illustrate that Weber's is only one reading of Baxter's thought, though I see it as the wrong one. This excerpt also anticipates in important ways a significant passage in *Robinson Crusoe*, to which I will shortly turn. To preview: what appealed to Defoe the novelist was not so much Baxter's ethic of work, but Baxter's belief in the spiritual value of keeping oneself in a state of uncertainty:

What wonder then, if God cut me off, when I am just sitting down in
this supposed Rest?[23] and hath not the like been your condition? . . .
Many a servant of God hath been destroyed from the Earth, by being
overvalued and overloved. I pray God you may take warning for the
time to come, that you rob not your selves of all your mercies. I am
perswaded, our discontents, and murmurings with an unpleasing
condition, and our covetous desires after more, are not so provoking to
God, nor so destructive to the sinner, as our too sweet enjoying, and
Rest of Spirit in a pleasing State. If God have crossed any of you, in
Wife, Children, Goods, Friends, &c. either by taking them from you,
or the comfort of them, or the benefit and blessing, Try whether this
above all other, be not the cause: for wheresoever your desires stop, and
you say, Now I am well; that condition you make your god, and engage
the jealousie of God against it. Whether you be friends to God, or
enemies, you can never expect that God should wink at such Idolatrie,
or suffer you quietlie to enjoy your Idols. (*Saints* 563–64)

When this passage is viewed from a Weberian standpoint, it is almost impossible to see how it could be read as anything other than a call to produce
and a chastisement of idleness. Yet, the passage makes no such claim. In fact,
it refuses to make such a claim, because the "settled" state that allows one to
say "Now I am well" might be marked by productive work.[24] Watt wrote that
"Calvinism in particular tended to make its adherents forget the idea that
labour was God's punishment for Adam's disobedience," but in overlooking
such moments as this one in Baxter, Watt himself forgets that the punishment for Adam's disobedience was not a steady job as a middle manager in
midcentury America but unending self-denial, physical struggle, and existential discombobulation (73). Watt conflates these two meanings of *work*—the
work of production and the work of unsettling the self—and therefore reads
Crusoe's many labors in terms of self-affirming and self-maximizing productive activity. For Baxter, but perhaps even more for Defoe, true Christian subjectivity was marked by a constant anxiety or uncertainty about one's true
state, while labor was intended to express one's commitment to uncertainty,
not to ameliorate, palliate, or forget about it. Many a man or woman, Baxter
might say in response to Weber (or Watt), has said "Now I am well" precisely
because he or she had some kind of gainful employment, some easy and settled state in which to "rest" comfortably in this world.

    The work Baxter endorsed was that of undoing wellness: "Consider, if
God should suffer thee thus to take up thy Rest here, it were one of the sorest

plagues, and greatest curses that could possibly befall thee: It were better for thee, if thou never hadst a day of ease, or content in the world. . . . To have their portion in this life, and their good things on the Earth, is the lot of the most miserable perishing sinners" (564). Introducing this nuance into a consideration of Calvinism also helps to surmount the puzzling conundrum introduced by Weber concerning the relation between work and election. Weber argues that the existential and spiritual anxieties produced by Calvinist uncertainty about election are the reason for work and economic activity. Behaving in what amounts to an "economic" fashion, according to Weber, serves as a kind of coping mechanism for the unique psychic stress engendered by the Calvinist twin doctrines of absolute depravity and predestination. Weber takes the passage quoted above to mean that Baxter advised his readers to undertake some kind of economic behavior or other, which forces him to detect an anxiety at the heart of Calvinism concerning the seemingly paradoxical fixation on worldly matters (economic life) and the recognition of one's inability to control one's life and salvation. This puts Weber in the difficult position of having to assume that Calvinists simply could not admit this contradiction to themselves (lest they articulate and thereby expose the contradiction of spiritual life and economic work that constituted their fatally flawed worldview, leading to the collapse of their unstable theological structure). The question—the *key* question—is, why did they not articulate it? If Calvinists saw that their constant labors generated varying degrees of material wealth, why would they have refused to acknowledge as much? Weber's answer—and his argument fully demands that he make this apology—is that the last thing Calvinists would *say* was that they worked in order to be productive. In other words, Calvinists were lying to themselves: they refused to admit that underneath their appearance of piety was a deep fascination with the wealth that their labors generated. Perhaps this was the case for some. But another way of looking at it, a way that does not require so much insinuation, is that Calvinists would never have worked in order to be productive because they simply did not believe that productivity was the end of work.

A brilliant reader and thinker, but one deeply influenced by a century of political economic reason that had proclaimed a division between spirit and world so loudly and so frequently that it could not be unheard or unseen, Weber likely would have found such a hypothesis untenable. Weber concedes that labor as productive resource emerged only at a later date, when the origins of the mandate to work for work's sake—to work for God—had been suppressed and all that was left was the habit of work itself (the irrational core underlying the process of rationalization). But this process of suppres-

sion and forgetting could only have been possible if in the original theology
work meant a building up of self, which, at least in Baxter, appears not to have
been the case: "As we [Christians] have not yet obtained our end, so are we in
the midst of labors and dangers; and is there any resting here? What painful
work doth lie upon our hands?" (565). And so it is clear that Weber has been
reading Baxter anachronistically, in terms of this postsuppressive condition of
modern capital, not in the terms that Baxter himself used, which were more
closely bound up with the ethic of uncertainty and the idea of a determining
providence than they were implicated in industry/idleness or productivity/
nonproductivity binaries. Anachronistically supposing the centrality of these
binaries in Calvinism, Weber reads the Calvinist criticism of rest as the same
thing as the mandate to (productively) work. But Baxter encourages nothing
more than remaining unsure as to the morrow and being therefore dependent
upon the workings of an open system that for him was thoroughly suffused
with providential justice and grace. Far from anticipating later attempts to
organize and exploit human labor, Baxter is legible in anti-financial terms insofar as the only sure recommendation he offers his reader is to allow oneself
to relate to the future as utterly unknown, undetermined, and unfixed. Just
as Luther had argued that standing surety for another man raised the surety
to the status of a kind of idol, compelling the second man to, in a sense, worship the first, here Baxter positions the self who has found no more need to
change against a self whose settled state eliminates desire. "That *condition* you
make your god," writes Baxter. On this reading of Baxter's words, Weber gets
it wrong, reading Calvinist anxiety as a by-product of uncertainty respecting
election. But for Baxter, and I think for Defoe as well, anxiety was the entire
point. Anything that placated anxiety, including productive labor, was to be
regarded as highly dangerous. Security must be sought, but when attained, it
must be discarded, and then sought again.[25]

    There may well be better support for Weber's hypothesis than these par-
ticular passages; I introduce them only because Weber himself calls our attention to Baxter and because they promote the ethic of uncertainty in ways that
are strikingly similar to the ways in which that ethic is employed in anti-usury
literature. The themes of faith in adversity and the necessity of unsettlement
run throughout *Saints Everlasting Rest*, and they are pronounced in the ded-
icatory statement, where Baxter lays out his principal purpose in writing his
treatise. He charges his parishioners, when he is gone, to find a minister who
will not appease them or make them rest easy. And when he asks them to be-
ware of "loitering" and "Laziness," he is referring not to the work of the body,
or not just to the work of the body, but to the work of the mind. "Spare not

any pains," he remarks, "in *working* out your salvation." Failing to break the self down continuously results in pride:

> If once you grow wise in your own eyes, and love to be valued and preserved, and love those best that think highliest of you, and have secret heart risings against any that disregard you, or have a low esteem of you, and cannot endure to be slighted, or spoke evil of; never take yourselves for Christians, if this be your case. To be a true Christian without Humilitie, is as hard as to be a man without a Soul. (*Saints* a3)

This is a fairly ordinary statement about the sin of pride, of course; what makes it important here is Baxter's explicit criticism of those who seek to be "valued and preserved," because it gives us reasons to doubt the Weberian understanding of Calvinist work as oriented toward a building up. I would suggest that it was this erroneous interpretation of Baxter that influenced Weber's understanding of Calvinism, which then influenced Watt's reading of *Crusoe*, which has led us to make certain assumptions about the nature of Crusoe's journey and the work he performs on his island, where attempts to ground the text in seventeenth-century spiritual traditions have relied upon Weber's anachronistic, economistic readings of Calvinist thoughts on work.

One final, important word on Baxter will return us to McKeon's influential post-Wattian reading of *Crusoe*. Specifically, what are we to make of Baxter's clear approbation of "desire" toward the end of the passage quoted above? He writes that "for wheresoever your desires stop, and you say, Now I am well; that condition you make your god." Of course *desire* is a vague and imprecise term that encompasses a wide range of phenomena related to the will, but where in Weber's understanding of the seventeenth-century Calvinist is there room for desire of any kind? How would the Weber-Tawney thesis accommodate Baxter's clear acknowledgment of the positive ethical value that Baxter confers on desire without reducing it to something antithetical to Calvinism as they describe it? Weber's Calvinist is ideally ascetic and only accidentally and problematically productive, inclined toward eradicating desire rather than responding to it, and desire for material goods is a later corruption of this ideal. But Baxter's encouragement of some forms of desire was in fact easily reconciled to providentialism insofar as the desire of which he writes could be taken to mean the desire to unsettle oneself, or the putting of oneself into positions in which one needs to keep desiring (and simply making more money to shore up the self is obviously *not* conducive to such forms of unsettlement). For McKeon, Crusoe's "desire" requires "naturalization" through the discourse

of spirit; but for Defoe, as for Baxter, desire was an entirely natural thing to
begin with, a salutary thing, and a moral state of being, not to mention an
excellent jumping-off point for novels and a very good reason for novelistic
sequels or continuations. Defoe's Crusoe provides us with a good sense, that
is, of Calvinist desire as articulated by Baxter. It is entirely unrelated to the
idea of productivity, desire for worldly goods, or work as productive activity
and has a great deal more to do with making it impossible for him to say to
himself, "Now I am well." Wellness is the end of desire.

Bearing this reevaluation of Baxter in mind, I will argue that *Robinson
Crusoe*'s spiritual moment, the vital point at which the latent spirituality of
Crusoe is revealed to the reader, takes place not in one of his moments of
pious reflection that characterize his later reformed states but much earlier, in
his reaction to his father's speech:

> My father, a wise and grave man, gave me serious and excellent counsel
> against what he foresaw was my design. He called me one morning
> into his chamber, where he was confined by the gout, and expostulated
> very warmly with me upon this subject: He ask'd me what reasons
> more than a meer wandring inclination I had for leaving my father's
> house and my native country, where I might be well introduced, and
> had a prospect of raising my fortunes by application and industry,
> with a life of ease and pleasure. He told me it was for men of desper-
> ate fortunes on the one hand, or of aspiring, superior fortunes on the
> other, who went abroad upon adventures, to rise by enterprize, and
> make themselves famous in undertakings of a nature out of the com-
> mon road; that these things were all either too far above me, or too far
> below me; that mine was the middle state, or what might be called
> the upper station of *low life*, which he had found by long experience
> was the best state in the world, the most suited to human happiness,
> not exposed to miseries and hardships, the labour and sufferings of
> the mechanick part of mankind, and not embarrass'd with the pride,
> luxury, ambition and envy of the upper part of mankind. He told me,
> I might judge of the happiness of this state, by this one thing, *viz.*
> That this was the state of life which all other people envied, that kings
> have frequently lamented the miserable consequences of being born to
> great things, and wish'd they had been placed in the middle of the two
> extremes, between the mean and the great; that the wise man gave his
> testimony to this as the just standard of true felicity, when he prayed to
> have neither poverty or riches.

He bid me observe it, and I should always find, that the calamities of life were shared among the upper and lower part of mankind; but that the middle station had the fewest disasters, and was not expos'd to so many vicissitudes as the higher or lower part of mankind; nay, they were not subjected to so many distempers and uneasiness either of body or mind, as those who, by vicious living, luxury and extravagancies on one hand, or by hard labour, want of necessaries, and mean or insufficient diet on the other hand, bring distempers upon themselves by the natural consequences of their way of living; *that* the middle station of life was calculated for all kind of vertues and all kind of enjoyments; that peace and plenty were the hand-maids of a middle fortune; that temperance, moderation, quietness, health, society, all agreeable diversions, and all desirable pleasures, were the blessings attending the middle station of life; that this way men went silently and smoothly through the world, and comfortably out of it, not embarrass'd with the labours of the hands or of the head, not sold to the life of slavery for daily bread, or harrast with perplex'd circumstances, which rob the soul of peace, and the body of rest; not enrag'd with the passion of envy, or secret burning lust of ambition for great things; but in easy circumstances sliding gently through the world, and sensibly tasting the sweets of living, without the bitter feeling that they are happy, and learning by every day's experience to know it more sensibly.

After this, he press'd me earnestly, and in the most affectionate manner, not to play the young man, not to precipitate my self into miseries which Nature and the station of life I was born in, seem'd to have provided against; that I was under no necessity of seeking my bread; that he would do well for me, and endeavour to enter me fairly into the station of life which he had been just recommending to me; and that [if] I was not very easy and happy in the world, it must be my meer fate or fault that must hinder it, and that he should have nothing to answer for, having thus discharg'd his duty in warning me against measures which he knew would be to my hurt: In a word, that as he would do very kind things for me if I would stay and settle home as he directed, so he would not have so much hand in my misfortunes, as to give me any encouragement to go away: And to close all, he told me I had my elder brother for an example, to whom he had used the same earnest perswasions to keep him from going into the Low Country wars, but could not prevail, his young desires prompting him to run into the army where he was kill'd; and tho' he said he would not cease to pray for me, yet he would venture to say to me, that if I did take this foolish step, God would not bless me, and I would have leisure here-after to reflect upon having neglected his counsel when there might be none to assist in my recovery. (5–7)

We might begin a reading of the father's lecture to Crusoe—which serves as the basis for many readings of the novel as a tale of a prodigal son or an as-piring man of commerce intent on a vast fortune that the middle state would deny him—by asking what it means for a man who is, we are initially told, "confined by the gout" to, at the close of his speech, warn his son against tak-ing a "foolish step." Why does the speech, in other words, open and close with phrases that significantly contrast with the substance of the speech? Defoe's decision to confine the father to a sitting position is interesting enough, his choice to assign responsibility to gout all the more so. A disease born of leisure and sedentary existence, consumption of too much rich food, lack of exercise, perhaps too much wine, for its sufferers gout is an affliction of no laughing matter, but literary conventions dictate that it can only ever be a hallmark of a life badly lived, or barely lived, precisely because it has been lived with ease. Defoe's decision to bracket the father's counsel—beginning with a reference to his gout and closing with an admonition against foolish steps—ironically frames the totality of his advice and thereby encourages attention to the more subtle ways that Defoe undercuts nearly every word issuing from his mouth. And if, as I believe, Defoe meant to criticize the father, and not Crusoe, what is to be made of the latter's decision to leave his father? And finally, how are we to account for the fact that Crusoe accounts for it as his original sin?

The self-satisfied oration is delivered by a father who, returning to Baxter, can truly say "Now I am well." This is the mark of that dangerous complacency that Baxter precisely cautions against in *Saints Everlasting Rest*. In fact, the father's speech is an encomium to wellness, as he specifically repudiates the feelings of both "misery" and what he describes as the "bitter" state of being "happy." Everything in his "middle state" conduces toward a life of settlement and comfort, but never the extremes of success or failure, poverty or wealth; nothing is entirely "good," but everything is more or less well. To take a hand-ful of phrases from his address, he encourages a life of "ease and pleasure," a life of being "very easy," a life of "peace and plenty." The father would have his son live in "easy circumstances" and wants him to "slid[e] gently through the world." It is a point that he repeats: he would have Robinson go "silently and smoothly thro' the world," untouched by "vicissitudes" that have an impact on the "higher or lower part of mankind." Such vicissitudes, the father avers, will "rob the soul of peace, and the body of rest." As Baxter cautions his reader, "If the Lord see you begin to settle in the world, and say, 'Here I will rest,' no wonder if he soon, in his jealousy, unsettle you." Hence his title, *Saints Everlasting Rest*: there is to be no such resting as that promoted—commanded!—by Crusoe's father. That phantasm rest is the thing that leads men to damnation; rest is to come later and for saints, not now and not for the embodied being. The father confuses rest in this world with the sort of everlasting rest toward which all, in Baxter's view, should aspire. Unfortunately, aiming toward the former interferes with the latter of these two aspirations. The father's mistake, in other words, is the mistake that Weber makes when reading Baxter. He believes that if one works, then one is not resting, and yet as his speech plainly illustrates, and his sitting posture while delivering it emphasizes, his life is nothing but a state of rest. And just as Baxter prognosticates, just when someone believes that he or she has attained a state of rest, something happens to unsettle everything. Robinson, shortly after the speech, runs away from home, leaving his erstwhile comfortable mother and father to ruminate upon the loss of their last surviving son: "If God have crossed any of you, in Wife, *Children*, Goods, Friends, &c. either by taking them from you, or the comfort of them, or the benefit and blessing, *Try whether this above all other, be not the cause*: [because] you say, *Now I am well*" (my emphasis).

Typically sensitive to the ambiguities of Defoe's language, Novak remarks of the speech that "the father might be seen as little more than a representative of dull, conservative ideas of the past which the enterprising son must sweep aside to achieve his success" (*Daniel Defoe: Master of Fictions* 543). But when read in the context of a tradition that privileges not work but risk, the father's speech comes to seem a great deal worse than what Novak asserts. The father's words are those of the tempter, more closely akin to Satan's subtle address in the Garden, where an original rest was forfeited and human existence was therefore to be defined by the experience of "vicissitudes" and "perplex'd circumstances," from which Crusoe's father impiously promises his son deliverance. It is for this reason that the assessment of Crusoe as undergoing a fortunate fall is somewhat problematic, since that reading, like the prodigal-son reading, depends upon the notion that Crusoe's decision to leave is, in the final analysis, a fall or sin of some kind.[26] I suggest that in electing to resist the sinful recommendation of the father, Crusoe does not give in to temptation, as Adam and Eve do. Rather, Crusoe chooses to live a life against the sinful condition promised and promoted by his father. In the Calvinist tradition to which Baxter and Defoe belonged, the pious life was achieved not through work, much less through work that aggrandized the worker, financially or otherwise, but by struggling to avoid settling into circumstances that led one into a state of rest, ease, or comfort.

This is not the limit of Crusoe's father's impieties so far as Baxter's warnings against rest and settlement are concerned, for the promises he makes to his son respecting his ability to support him in his endeavors are the real reasons why his words are to be read with caution. He tells Robinson that he will "do well for [him]" and "endeavor to enter [him] fairly into the station of life" into which he was born and that by virtue of that station, want of necessities will be "provided against." McKeon observes that for Crusoe it is "not strictly required ... that one remain in the station of one's birth," while it might be said that within a Calvinist vision of personal, individual spiritual responsibility, it would have been strictly required to *not remain* in the station of one's birth if doing so meant the eradication of desire (*Origins* 322). And a life without desire is what the father is secretly promising to his son. In these suggestions, the father in some respects ends up revealing the sometimes violent and often fraudulent bases of the middle state: nepotism, patronage, and a social infrastructure that precedes its individual members, leading to an ossification of that infrastructure, while all the while making it seem as though one has achieved middle-class status on one's own.

Although the father is good and upstanding, we are led to believe, he more closely resembles the bad master in the second of Defoe's dialogues in *The Family Instructor*, a text to which Novak points as an indication of Defoe's development of fictional form ("Defoe as an Innovator" 43–46).[27] Whereas Robinson endeavors to enter into a system of rewards entirely unsecured (going to sea), his father, who like the bad master is proficient in business but entirely lacking in religion, wishes to confer upon him ease using the resources and power he has gleaned in his own trade (setting him up). Considering how confident he is of his ability to make life easy for his son, the father's speech also unveils the inequities of a commercial system that refuses to allow for the possibility and the necessity of loss, discomfort, stress, and anxiety. Crusoe's decision to reject his father's advice is not the *fulfillment* of the ideology of individualism but an ethical critique of that ideology and the faux meritocracy it promises. There would be nothing meritocratic about Crusoe's life of comfort were he to remain in England; insofar as it would be predicated upon the support structure provided by his father, his success would be guaranteed from the outset. *Robinson Crusoe* is not an advertisement for the middle state, as it is so often claimed to be, but a punishing critique of the middle state and the selfish complacency it engenders.

For Defoe, if work does have any positive value, it must be the kind of work that is undertaken from the standpoint of what the father calls "desperate fortunes" and Baxter describes simply as "desire," not from the standpoint of ease and comfort. Crusoe's father's work is not of this kind of anxiety-laden working to avoid rest; rather, it is that selfish and economistic work whose only ends are personal satisfaction and the avoidance of suffering. Those seeking to find in Defoe's novel something like the political economists' merchant would find it here, in the figure of the father, not in Robinson. Far from being a rearguard holdover from an aristocratic age of social stability, the father represents still more dangerous forms of stability: the concentration of wealth and the perpetuation of power through the institution of the family and mechanisms of commerce and finance. This is not to say, of course, that the father is *typed* as villainous, for Defoe goes to lengths to stress that all of this was delivered and warmly pressed in a most "affectionate manner." Vis-à-vis Robinson, however, he is sinful. As Baxter suggests, such filial devotion, perhaps most of all when it discourages the taking of risks on one's own, can lead to damnation: "Many a servant of God has been destroyed from the earth by being overvalued and overloved" (*Saints* 563). If we read the father's speech as a dangerous temptation toward the middle state rather than as the commercial ideal to which Crusoe can aspire but never truly realize given that he rejected it initially, then Crusoe's decision to leave is the sign that he has the spiritual purity to know, even against his own well-being, that staying will put him on the path toward damnation. Instead of settling for contentment (whose evil is symbolized by the father's gout), he chooses vicissitudes that may well lead to death (whose virtue is symbolized by the death of his brother in the wars against the Dutch). Against those readings that focus on Crusoe's "conversion" later in the narrative, I would submit that it is here, in his initial choice to refuse settlement, rest, ease, and pleasure, that his conversion begins.

That decision—to potentially die or to potentially realize wealth beyond dreams—is then strategically brought into alignment with his father's final reflection upon the death of Crusoe's brother in the "Low Country wars." Crusoe's elder brother, we might surmise, also ignored the admonitions of the father. Critics have been less inclined to describe this dead son as in any way prodigal; in fact, they have been disinclined to describe him at all. If that son does receive mention, he is a footnote, a detail. And yet the two brothers, importantly, share a predilection for occupations in which sacrifice is meaningful and valuable. Both refuse the father's advice in precisely the same way, and they therefore serve as mirror images of each other.

Their very resemblance anticipates quite strikingly a series of remarks made a century or so later by John Ruskin, who was as much an *opponent* of any economics that was conceived of as being separate from religion as Defoe was *unable to consider* them as distinct from one another. Rather than anticipating, though, we might surmise that Ruskin, who fondly reflected on *Robinson Crusoe* in his autobiography, had this very moment in Defoe's text in mind (*Præterita* 13). In "The Roots of Honour," the first of the four essays that make up his withering 1862 critique of political economy, *Unto This Last*, Ruskin observes that the true vocation of the soldier is not to slay but to be slain, meaning that the significance of an occupation consists not in what is gained (heads of the enemy, glory, money, etc.) but in what is risked in the act of performing that occupation. Being slain is the "due occasion" of death for the soldier (175). On this logic, Robinson's brother's vocation, his calling, was to *be slain* in war. What of Robinson himself? His father promises a life of ease, rest, settlement, comfort, pleasure, and contentment; instead, he chooses to face death, providing the answer to Ruskin's question: "The Merchant— what is *his* 'due occasion' of death?" The answer, against all odds, is the same as Robinson Crusoe's: he would rather die at sea than remain at home to work at ease. Crusoe nearly dies at least four times, ends up fabulously wealthy, works along the way, gains an island kingdom and expansive plantations, gets married, and so forth. His brother, by contrast, dies in the war. Defoe seems to be saying that their fortunes might have been reversed; such is the uncertainty of the world. Or Crusoe might have ended up like the middle brother: "What became of my second brother I never knew any more than my father or mother did know what became of me" (5). We will return to him in a moment, but for now, we have the two "heroic" brothers who choose risk and a middle brother who is an absence, a nonentity. But his nothingness as an entity is nevertheless a substantial nothingness. Why would Defoe tell us of a character only to tell us that nothing about him can be told? Who is this textual exile?

Reading Crusoe as selfishly motivated—oriented solely towards gain, for better or worse—fails because Crusoe's decision to leave is made on the basis of his *doubts* as to whether he would gain or not. For if Crusoe had been animated by mere desire for lucre, he would have remained at home, where a cozy network of merchants and financiers might have supported and sustained his commercial interests; at a minimum, he would never have had to work, as his father insists, for his "daily bread" (6). Instead, Crusoe opts to take the radical risk on no other basis than that of a "secret over-ruling decree" (13) that compels him. Crusoe figures himself as ultimately passive with respect to this decree: "Not bred to any trade, my head *began to be fill'd very early with rambling thoughts*" (5, my emphasis). What moves Crusoe is a "propension of Nature"

(5), a "wandring inclination" (5), a "current" of desire (10), an "irresistible re-luctance" to going home (15). While the "calm reasonings and perswasions of my most retired thoughts" (14) direct Crusoe back into the fold of his doting parents, something propels him outward and away. Its object remains elu-sive, if only because it is only on the back end of his success that he is able to characterize his "inclination" as oriented toward "raising his fortune," when, in other words, his communion with God is confirmed for him in the form of a "fortune." Observing the obscure way in which Defoe characterizes Crusoe's motivations, Jay Fliegelman has argued that Crusoe's decision to disobey his father is the right thing to do because behind this obscurity lies providence it-self (70), that Crusoe must leave his father in order to come to God the father. On the whole, this reading is to me far more sound than those that depend upon the view that the text altogether damns Crusoe's decision to leave, but here I think it worth noting that contra Fliegelman's claim that it is provi-dence that guides Crusoe and determines his decisions, Defoe never allows Crusoe to say as much; on the contrary, Crusoe characterizes his decision as a rejection of the "voice of Providence" (73). If what I have been suggesting is true, if Crusoe's decision to disobey his father puts him in a more positive relationship to providence, why would he continue to regard that decision as having been impious?

For Crusoe to acknowledge that his life is a particular concern of God's and that his decisions are thus made for him in advance would be to over-look the fact that (*a*) Crusoe must make the choice to leave even against his judgment and (*b*) Defoe takes great pains to open up a space of agency not unlike that created in his intimation that Noah also was not compelled by God to make the Ark, but merely given guidance. Thus, when Crusoe writes of his inclinations and notions, we must take him at his word; that is, he is signifying nothing more than a motivational *something* that is neither reason nor divine determining force. I would submit that in Crusoe's cryptic rendi-tion of his motives, he gives his reader a glimpse of the risk-taking subject, in which one's action is prompted by neither a selfish motive (seeking to conquer uncertainty) nor a guiding, divine presence (having no agency at all) but by a choice to place one's fate into the hands of something other.

This seems, in any event, to be closer to the way that Defoe's contemporary Penelope Aubin (1670?–1738) read it. Comparing her own novel with *Cru-soe*, she writes that in the latter "Divine Providence manifests it self in every Transaction," and adds, "Would Men trust in Providence, and act according to Reason and common Justice, they need not to fear any thing" (6–7). It is not that Crusoe is guided by providence; rather, he "trust[s] in Providence."

Sure, when Crusoe finds himself in situations of adversity, he seeks to secure himself, but this only further confirms the importance of his initial choice to leave home. He remains *responsible to* his decision to leave. As Baxter put it, "Should *Noah* have made the Ark his home, and have been loth to come forth when the waters were fal[len]?" (565). Crusoe must not bring destruction upon himself willingly; he must instead allow himself to be shaped by circumstance, and his destiny to be unfurled in an unprogrammed futurity. He will of course work to get his "daily bread," but beyond that everything remains, and ought to remain, obscure. When the father promises Crusoe that he will not need to struggle for his "daily bread" if he stays (and those are the exact words he uses), how can a reader in 1719 not be aware that a principal feature of fallen-ness is precisely the need to work for one's bread, or at least to eat it in the sweat of one's brow? When the father claims God in the curse that closes his admonitions, he reveals the impious secularism that has defined him all along, implying that fathers, not gods, have a monopoly on their sons' lives and that fathers, not gods, are to be trusted for "daily bread." Indeed, in acting as a guide who uses the name of God instrumentally to persuade his son, the father splits apart the very identity that had made Crusoe's father and God the Father political and spiritual equivalents.

This helps us, further, to read the meaning of the shipwreck itself. His father wishes that Crusoe would not work at all, would not have to "labour for [his] daily bread," a locution that gains in importance when Crusoe decides to make his new life in the Brazils "easy" by procuring new slaves. He is marooned on his island before this mission barely gets under way; thus the second major event in the novel conforms to the pattern set by the first—his decision to leave England—in which self-destructive or self-abnegating behavior meets with reward, while self-affirming, productive acts of consolidation and securitization of one's present state meet with disaster. Wishing to literally profit by the sweat of another man's brow (to procure African slaves), he finds his comfortable life in the Brazils, a life he expressly compares to the life his father had promised for him—"Had I continued in the station I was now in, I had room for all the happy things to have yet befallen me, for which my father so earnestly recommended a quiet retired life, and of which he had so sensibly described the middle station of life to be full of" (32)—interrupted by a violent and punitive interposition of providence. Defoe reminds his reader that Crusoe's life of ease in the Brazils has been achieved by way of his exploitation of labor, which at first was acceptable because unexpected; but now, because it has become programmatic, anticipated, expected, it requires disruption. Crusoe's attainment of "all the happy things" must be short-circuited, shipwrecked. Of course, the fact that he simply goes to sea from the Brazils to procure slaves does not mean that he has entered himself into a system of total risk. The sea only serves as a space of risk under certain conditions (such as at the beginning, where the alternative is to live in a state of ease in England). The space of true risk might entail, at this point in the novel, a variety of things, but buying up slaves to further secure his already dominant economic position in occupied territories does not a risky sea make.

Crusoe's rationale for making the journey, in other words, is to shore up gains already gotten. The sea is a shifter, so to speak, and its meaning changes with the circumstances of its narrative deployment. What originally presented itself as the space of risk—the sea—later becomes the means whereby Crusoe can further secure himself (i.e., a conduit for slaves). The decision to go to sea originally, therefore, is not the end of Crusoe's ethical life; it is merely the first of many ethical decisions he must make. As a recent theorist has put the problem, "The excess of decision in undecidability does not end once a decision is made, for as soon as a decision is made, it folds back into the aporia of future decisions" (Anker 45). The shipwreck serves to remind Crusoe that his attempt at totalization, at the completion of his own self in the Brazils through his dominance and ownership of territory, wealth, and the bodies of slaves, is an attempt to eat the bread of another's labor and an attempt to escape the uncertainties of life. It is therefore entirely unsurprising to see Crusoe finally get his "servant" Friday, not through an act of forcible conquest, but through a self-sacrificial act of rescue (160, 161). That today readers, myself included, find this interpretation of Crusoe's relation to native peoples historically naïve and somewhat difficult to stomach does nothing to change the world of probable death into which Crusoe plunges himself on Friday's behalf.

Crusoe's spiritual journey is far from complete when he makes the decision to leave, but the larger point is that that journey perpetually resists completion. This is why I balked earlier when speaking of a "conversion": conversion implies finitude, closure, and determinacy. There is no such thing as conversion in *Robinson Crusoe*; there is at best *converting*. Arriving at any putative state of spiritual finality would be as impious a determination as the belief that having a steady job and a roof over one's head means that one is truly "well."[28] But it does help us to reevaluate the question of the novel's formal realism in relation to the question of spiritual autobiography. The world Crusoe inhabits is not a figure for or sign of a purified or transcendent spiritual realm; it is the real world through which everyone must pass. Defoe had no need to reconcile the one to the other. Returning to Novak's remark: "However much his God may have remained hidden behind the physical nature through which He worked,

Defoe never appears to have doubted His continued presence" (*Daniel Defoe: Master of Fictions* 660). The question that this world poses is therefore an ethical one: shall one rest in it, or shall one pass through it as it was meant to be passed through? The goal is to avoid a state of rest; and the sequels or continuations to the first volume of the Crusoe series, however much they may have been written to satisfy audiences' appetite for them, are narratively possible because there is no closure, no completion, no finality to the world Defoe creates, just as he perceived no finality to his own, lived world (to say that death is a finality misses the point). If we wish to describe his novel as realist, then that is because the form assumed by reality in a condition of risk and open futures was constitutively process oriented, uncertain, and therefore opening onto the divine and the infinite. Similarly, if we wish to speak of the novel as a spiritual (auto)biography, then that is because the form assumed by the spirit in this world is that of a body traveling through it and suffering and sometimes experiencing pleasure. The narrative's very ability to go on and on—to encounter, for instance, wolves, in the novel's closing pages, just when we thought we were as far from danger as possible—illustrates the dynamic principles of Crusoe's world and the ever-present command to engage with it fully and fairly. If Crusoe leaves behind, in a passing sentence, his wife and children, this is because they too threaten to become that place of rest and ease that Crusoe's "secret over-ruling decree" tells him must be avoided.

This all leaves one crucial question unanswered: if Crusoe's decision to leave is to be read as his spiritual moment, why does Crusoe himself describe his disobedience as his "Original Sin," even after he is converted? Why does he not return to the site of his original temptation, when he might have obeyed his father's temptation to complacency, rest, and ease, and treat it for what it is, namely, encouragement toward slothful complacency? The simple answer is that Crusoe's experience, and how he describes his experience, is not the same thing as the novel *Robinson Crusoe*. There is a meaningful and important difference between what Crusoe does/says and what *Robinson Crusoe* does/says. But while there has never been doubt about Defoe's ability to ironize in his poetry and his essays, most notably his infamous *Shortest Way with the Dissenters*, with rare exception readers have approached *Robinson Crusoe* as conspicuously devoid of ironic potential.[29]

To understand one of the key ironies of *Robinson Crusoe*, it is helpful to first return to Weber. To illustrate the roots and nature of the "Spirit of Capitalism," Weber highlighted a series of remarks made by Benjamin Franklin, among them the following maxim: "He that idly loses five shillings' worth of time; loses five shillings, and might as prudently throw five shillings into the sea" (16). On the basis of such remarks, readers of Crusoe have been inclined to read his every action as directed ultimately toward acts of saving (he does, after all, get saved, at least from his island). On the Weberian reading, we must read Crusoe as fearful of losing every minute and every shilling, which naturally leads him to try to preserve himself. His is the life of the solitary individual, *homo economicus*, seeking, squirrel-like, to gather every nut and perfect his enclosure. On this reading, his choice to leave England, to reject a settled way of life, takes on the character of impudence, impetuosity, and imprudence. But Defoe, when contemplating the nature of savings and loss, may have been guided by another, somewhat more authoritative injunction than a deistical aphorism on shillings written by a lapsed Puritan decades after Defoe died. Here is how Baxter put it:

> *Then Jesus said to his Disciples, If any man will come after me, let him deny himself and take up his Cross, and follow me: For whosoever will save his life shall lose it, and whosoever will lose his life for my sake shall find it.* Me thinks a man that hath time, and strength, and money, should long to be disbursing all for God, that he might put it in the surest hands, and it may be out of danger; yea that it may be set to the most honest, and profitable usery. For when God hath it, from the dedication of an upright heart, it is sure. (*Directions and Perswasions* 319)

The only acceptable usury, in other words, is in guaranteeing return by *not guaranteeing* return and giving everything, including one's life, to God. Saving, in Franklin's sense, meant the exact opposite of this: usury in its bad sense, the securing of the worldly future, the avoidance of risk. I have been arguing that it is Crusoe's choice to *disobey* his father—who paints a picture of a future life defined by comfort and security—that brings about his eventual reward, but Crusoe of course never acknowledges that his choice to disobey is the *reason* for his wealth, nor does he assign any special significance to his choice to leave once he is rescued from the island. If we consider, though, the aporia generated by the ethical mandate in Baxter's text, Matthew 16:25, a very popular one for seventeenth- and eighteenth-century Protestant preachers and theologians—"whosoever will save his life shall lose it, and whosoever will lose his life for my sake shall find it"—it becomes apparent why Crusoe refrains, and why Defoe refrains, from reflecting on his choice to disobey as an ethical one.

To reflect on an act of disobedience toward the father—or any act at all involving his own agency, for that matter—as the proximate cause of his de-

liverance, salvation, or ethical merit would be to unwrite the ethical content
of the original act and thereby impose upon Crusoe a level of calculative reasoning respecting his salvation that is firmly at odds with the ethical logic
that can truly save him. Weber detects an anxiety in Calvinists regarding their
status as elect. How much more terrifying would it have been for a Calvinist
who believed that he or she was saved to reflect on the experience that first
suggested that he or she might be saved? Would not such reflection on having
been saved imply precisely that one was lost? In order to be "found," one must
lose oneself, and in finding oneself, one would become lost. This was precisely
the problem Baxter addressed in his attempt to prevent false, counterfeit, and
superficial conversions and to help honest converts realize that their work was
never done. Defoe capitalizes on his position as narrator to bridge the gap
between the impossible states of being lost/found and found/lost, concealing
from his reader Crusoe's original ethical moment through a kind of oblique,
coded, hidden, perhaps parodic version of satanic temptation in the form of
his father's pleas for Robinson to stay. At the risk of embarrassing his father
and affirming his own moral and spiritual superiority, Crusoe will not, and
cannot, reflect on his unnamable act of justice within the ethical moment. He
cannot point to his refusal of his father's affectionate and loving regard for
his son's well-being and say, "This! This is when I was saved!" Defoe, however,
helps him to do so, guiding him carefully in his narration of his father's address and concealing its shameful impieties even as it is busy exposing them.
If we find that Crusoe's decision to leave is not the origin of his Christianity—
though it is the first Christian moment in the text—we cannot say that it
positively takes place elsewhere. McKeon's sense of the importance of the iteration and reiteration of conversion, rather than a moment of conversion, is
an absolutely vital insight. Crusoe's conversion, by its very nature, resists the
finality and determination of a moment.

 While Crusoe in his choice to risk his life by heading out to sea resembles in certain ways the projecting Noah of the *Essay upon Projects*, Defoe's
attempt to "think with Noah" may be somewhat more complicated in *Robinson Crusoe*. In the formal arrangement of the novel, Crusoe attributes his
salvation to such things as the reading of the Bible, his dissociation from impious and wicked sailors, his praying, and so forth. But all of this is strictly at
odds with the ethical and salvational mandates that one not know or not say
what it is that saves; for in knowing and saying, one achieves a state of rest
and self-satisfaction that militates against the ethical and salvational. What
Crusoe must therefore do is know and not know, say and not say. This puts
him, as it turns out, in league not so much with the Noah of the Flood but

with Noah's good sons, Japheth and Shem, who cover their drunken father's shameful nakedness after Ham sees him in his tent and then spreads word of Noah's nudity. Knowing and then naming Noah's nakedness to his brothers, Ham does nothing more than expose sin, but this naming of sin of course is Ham's crime. Noah later curses Ham, and although Ham himself is not without a homeland, his descendants, the Canaanites, will be. In these respects, the disappearance of Crusoe's middle brother figures that of the symbolically exiled Ham, who by some accounts is himself a middle brother.

In the biblical story, Japheth and Shem walk into their father's tent backwards in order to blanket the exposed body of their father, Noah. I suggest that we can read Crusoe's religious talk—talk of prayer, talk of the Bible, talk of his dreams, talk of his wicked ways with sailors, and so forth—as performing a similar sort of blanketing action. A textual and talkative blanketing of the wicked life led by his father, in his self-satisfaction and goutiness, that Crusoe can reject but cannot, on pain of again being lost, bring himself to see or name. Manifest and performative religiosity—*talk* of what saves him—draws Crusoe's own and the reader's attention to something other than the original act of refusing his father's offer of love and support, an offer that Crusoe must resist in order to be saved. In fact, the character of Crusoe himself cannot see, or name, or even fully understand what it was, or what it meant for him, to trade a life of ease for one of risk. In order for his refusal to be ethical, it must be a secret even to himself; what directs his behavior is, in his words, a "secret over-ruling decree." Even as he speaks of religious practice and prayer, he does not reveal this fundamental secret, which even to him must remain something of a mystery and a secret. Thus he talks religion so as not to have to talk about the truly ethical choice to leave, which would expose his father's sin. "Speaking in order not to say anything is always the best technique for keeping a secret," writes Derrida with respect to Abraham's secret promise to God (*Gift of Death* 59). Transposed into the Christian, Protestant, Calvinist world, Crusoe cannot name the thing that saves him (his refusal of his father's care), and so the secret he keeps is not only with God but with himself, and therefore with the reader.

Defoe knew of and took great interest in this other Noah, perhaps just as much as the Noah whose courage and faith led him to sea in the Ark. He wrote about Noah's drunkenness in his *Essay upon Literature* (1726), where he speculated about what became of sins left unwritten: "How would *Noah's* Drunkenness, of which it pleases Heaven, by the help of Writing, to give us a Part, (at least) of the truer History, been abhorr'd and detested by the Ages following, and recorded to his Shame, if a true Account of it cou'd have been written down and preserved to Posterity?" (18).[30] In his *Compleat System of Magick* (1729) Defoe argued that Noah's "Defection of his own Morals" was the reason why his descendants tended toward sin: "What Regard would he obtain, when the debauch'd Instructor had expos'd himself by his Drunkenness to the Ridicule instead of the Reverence of his Posterity, and when the drunken Monitor by his own Practice had render'd his Instructions fruitless and ridiculous?" (14). Much as Defoe stressed Noah's own sin, he considered the "Banter and impious Jest of his Grandson *Ham*" equally significant in the story of Noah.

To avoid sinning in the manner of Ham, Crusoe, like Derrida's Abraham, must violate the terms of affirmative ethics—which demands that he speak, translate, and explain the motives behind what is finally a truly responsible act—and he does so not only in practice (by leaving England) but also by repackaging his father's sin as his own "Original Sin." Everything Crusoe writes tends toward marking his decision as abominable, and yet what is to be expected from a deferential subject of God but the immolation of one's reputation on the altar of one's own exquisite faith? Quoting Kierkegaard, Derrida reminds us that "Abraham *cannot* speak, because he cannot say that which would explain everything . . . that it is an ordeal such that, please note, the ethical is the temptation" (*Gift of Death* 61).[31] The same holds true for Crusoe, who cannot speak of his father's impieties, his father's dubious commercial certainties, tempting as it would be for him to do so and clear as it would make his decision to leave. Hence, he blankets his father's shamefulness. Crusoe walks into the tent—his father's "chamber"—backwards, by virtue of going back over the course of his life as it is narrated, and knowing now what he knows, covers over his father's sinful advocacy of prideful certainty by describing it in positive terms. By emphasizing that his father's speech is born of the most sincere affection, Crusoe appears to be wrong to leave England and seems to defy the words of his doting father and mother. Crusoe must suffer the fate of seeming evil, of seeming to have abdicated his duty, but the demands of worldly fathers and the infinite demands of God are not, in the end, the same (a point that Defoe, as an inveterate critic of divine right, often stressed). Like Abraham, Crusoe must turn his back on his family and his community, violate everything that is conventionally ethical—and must himself see his decision as unethical—in order to perform a more absolute ethical duty.

One last point: Derrida's formulation in *The Gift of Death* asks us to consider the performance of absolute duty as a commitment to "every other," which returns us ultimately to the stakes of *Robinson Crusoe* in the context of the commercial culture of Defoe's time. Crusoe, like his brother who died in the Low Countries, has made a sacrifice of himself. He would appear to believe that sacrifice is vitally important for his spiritual life and salvation, though again, to even speak of it as a belief instrumentalizes the practice of sacrifice and risk, thus undercutting their ethical meaning. But to risk a moment of bathos, is the salvation of Crusoe's eternal soul all that matters here? In the face of the changing economic times, we might also think of Crusoe's rejection of the ease and comforts of the middle state—in which gaining goods and maintaining security is regarded as the ultimate reward and reason for working—as an intervention in the political economy of his time, an intervention made on behalf of "every other." It does make some sense to think of Defoe as an advocate for a "middle state," since he seems to have fallen, at times, into something like a socioeconomic middle position, but I would argue that Defoe never set out to end up in the middle. Defoe, as a man of commerce, aimed high and fell very far at least three times. And as it happened, he ultimately settled somewhere in the middle. Does this necessarily mean that he advocated a world in which "middle states" were to be universally pursued? In offering readers a character who turns his back on the easy certainties of the middle state, Crusoe makes what can only be described as an irresponsible decision. This, however, may have been an irresponsibility with a higher purpose, an attempt by Defoe to reach out to readers and shift their emphasis away from the goal of being simply "well" or being in the "middle."

In seeking to carry out his promise to sacrifice his son and incur the hatred of others, Derrida writes, "Abraham is thus at the same time the most moral and most immoral, the most responsible and the most irresponsible of men, absolutely irresponsible because he is absolutely responsible, absolutely irresponsible in the face of men and his family, and in the face of the ethical, because he responds absolutely to absolute duty, disinterestedly and without hoping for a reward, without knowing why yet keeping it a secret" (72). We hear in Derrida's ethics the echo of early modern anti-finance. Abraham acts "disinterestedly, and without hoping for a reward"; these are the exact words that loomed large in commentary regarding usury. So too Crusoe: he must keep from his readers the secret of his sacrifice and his absolute commitment to a different commercial order of things. Of course, he cannot hope for a reward; hope of return is a modulation of the contract and thus a form of sin, as I sought to show in the previous chapter. The cost of Defoe's narrative strategy—and had there been no cost, the gambit would not have been a gambit—has been the tendency to take Crusoe at his word, to read the novel straight, to discount its ironies, and to mark his act of leaving as he himself marks it: as his "Original Sin." But we must remember that unlike Abraham, who could make his promise to an external God while keeping it secret vis-à-vis others in his community, Crusoe had to keep the secret from both readers and himself, which the loneliness of Calvinism, the immanence and interiority of the Protestant God, made absolutely necessary.

CHAPTER 4

Risk Aversion and the Economization of Prudence

Fielding, Gambling, Gifts

I F ANTI-FINANCE stresses the ethical value of an approach to the future as an open and indeterminate set of possibilities wherein the rationalized control or objectification of those possibilities constitutes an ethical failure and the bold and in some ways maddened dive into risk is regarded as being ethically necessary (as, in fact, the very substance of ethics as such), prudence, as Adam Smith puts it in his *Theory of Moral Sentiments* (1759), is what makes us "averse to expose our health, our fortune, our rank, or reputation, to any sort of hazard" (213). Frequently positioned in opposition to gambling, coded by Smith as "hazard," *prudence* in the eighteenth century increasingly served to name the part of the self that sought to avoid risk.[1] Thus the debate over prudence represents an extension of anxieties about the degree to which an individual ought to assume responsibility over future contingencies and to make certain that which ought to remain uncertain. After exploring this debate in more careful detail, showing how tightly interwoven the questions of prudence and economics were in the eighteenth century, I will turn my attention to Henry Fielding, who was implicitly involved in this debate as a gambler and whose writings explicitly addressed it.

Prior to the emergence of an autonomous economic sphere, the primary arenas for the development of prudence theory were those of statecraft on the one hand and moral judgment on the other. The most influential expositions of these were Niccolò Machiavelli's *The Prince* (pub. 1532) and Thomas Aquinas's *Summa Theologica* (1265–74), respectively.[2] The early lexicographer Robert Cawdry (b. 1537 or 1538?, d. 1604 or after), defined *prudence* as "wisedome, wittinesse" (n.p.). Edward Phillips (1630–ca. 1696) in his 1658 dictionary does not define the term except to say that it is a "Christian name of divers women, the signification well known"; not much help there, but he does use *prudence* in his definition of "Discretion," or, "how to make a right distinction of things" (n.p.). In the eighteenth century, however, prudence began to be discussed explicitly in relation to economics.[3] The pervasive association of the two in popular and literary discourses meant that by the nineteenth century the one could be defined in terms of the other.[4]

The first such recorded definitions appear in the *American Dictionary of the English Language* (1828), where Noah Webster defines *economize* as "To use with prudence." Under his third definition of *economy* he writes, "Economy includes also a prudent management of all the means by which property is saved or accumulated"; under his fourth definition of *prudent* he writes, "Frugal; economical"; and under his second definition of *prudently* he writes, "With frugality; economically; as income *prudently* expended." Webster's legacy is evident in the *Oxford English Dictionary*'s first definition of *prudence*, the "ability to recognize and follow the most suitable or sensible course of action; good sense in practical or financial affairs; discretion, circumspection, caution." That the conjunction *or* in the phrase "practical or financial affairs" strikes the modern eye as relatively unproblematic is the legacy of a specific struggle over the meaning of *prudence* in Fielding and Smith's time, one that reflected, much as did the discourse on projects, how dislocated the ethics of uncertainty had become by midcentury. As I observed earlier, in the seventeenth century the ethical critique of modern finance almost invariably depended upon the discourse of usury (usury marked the point at which finance became unethical, so to speak). But by the middle decades of the eighteenth century, with anti-usury sentiments now relegated to the medieval past, the war over financial rationality unfolded here, in the debate about the meaning and value of prudence, as well as in discussions regarding prudence's constant (antithetical) companion, gambling.

But prudence had not merely been imported from the discourses of Machiavellian politics and Christian morality for application to economic problems or situations, leaving its earlier forms fundamentally unchanged. In the eighteenth century, prudence began to assume a shape that was—and was criticized for being—formally economic. "There are those in the World," said the English divine Thomas Manningham (d. 1722), "who frame to themselves a Notion of Prudence, which has no dependence upon Religion; and practise it without any regard to the Laws of Justice" (2). This new prudence supposed that the world was a finite and, to some extent, predictable system that could, in some measure, be directed to produce desirable outcomes. Unlike Machiavellian *virtù*, which was locked in an endless battle with fortune, this newly conceived prudence in fact *presupposed* finitude, closure, and limits both spatial and temporal, since only within the confines of such limits could prudence be said to yield benefits. "We may study and observe those Laws of Motion which are imprinted on the Universe," Manningham urges, "but we must not exclude the First Mover." "We may likewise carry on our Publick Affairs and Private Business," but we must not do so without an appreciation of the "Providence of God" and a recognition of the "infinite," a word Manningham repeats throughout his criticism of this worldly, bounded form of prudence. Evidence of the infinite, and thus evidence of the inadequacy of this worldly business prudence, is revealed when attempts to control the world fail: "Tho' [business-prudent men] prosper in some few Attempts, yet their main Design miscarries; and ... their vain Projections are dash'd in pieces" (5). Manningham's critique of prudence here approaches Defoe's critique of modern projects in arguing that while human endeavors may proceed, their ultimate success "depends on Circumstances without his reach" (10). Manningham's sermon on prudence, delivered and published in 1693, the year after David Jones's sermon, at times appears to gesture directly toward the financial wiliness assailed by Jones: "If to avoid what one dislikes, and to obtain what one desires, by any means whatever, were all that were requir'd in Prudence, then *common Instinct* might serve the Turn as well as Reason; for that supplies some Creatures with Tricks and Shifts enough to compass and effect their little Ends" (7). What Manningham encourages his reader to think upon is what cannot be "compass[ed]" and the forces beyond human control that will blast the "vain Projections" of those who seek nothing but the attainment of one's "little Ends" (5, 7). Manningham described, much as Jones did, those "little Ends," pursued without an eye to bigger ends, as becoming a bigger part of daily life.

The discussion of and around prudence further helped to give form to the economic realm as such by providing that realm with a virtue whose presupposed terrain of exercise—a limited and closed time and space—could provide political economy with the object of its analysis. In other words, just as the emergence of an autonomous economic realm required a subject to suitably inhabit it—that is, the prudent individual, almost always figured as masculine—so did the development of the character of the prudent man help to delineate the nature of the economic world (or, rather, the world as seen through the lens of economics). As Manningham's contemporary, the mysterious "William de Britain," put it in his *Humane Prudence, or the Art by which a Man May Raise Himself and His Fortune to Grandeur*, a tract printed at least twenty-six times in Europe between its original publication in 1680 and the end of the eighteenth century, "If you will gain respect, turn Usurer, and make all Men enter into Obligations to you. The World is a Shop of Tools, of which the Wise Man only is the Master" (54).[5] While the connection between usury and prudent conduct here is interesting in its own right, de Britain captures what essentially connected the two by regarding the world as a "Shop of Tools," one capable of being mastered by the prudent man. Like the usurer, whose "Obligations" are enforced by the restrictive and regulatory powers that secure his loans' returns, and the shop master, who exercises complete control over the tools of his shop, the "Wise Man" relates to others in his world as so many objects susceptible to calculation, prediction, and manipulation.

Elsewhere, "Prudence is an Armory, wherein are as well defensive as offensive Weapons" (202); if this is so, then the entire world shrinks into a battle, with combatants and arms, winners and losers, a beginning and an ending. When considering how to gain preferment, de Britain imagines the court as a predictable circulation of celestial bodies that the prudent man, astronomer-like, must study (200). Similarly, de Britain advises, "In your address behave your self with Prudence (that's the Key to unlock Secrets, and unriddle Mysteries) otherwise you will have no good return" (190). While the promised "return" on investment again evokes the usurer's loans and repayments, more important in terms of the economizing of prudence is the idea that prudence functions as a key in a mechanical world of human secrets that is no more complicated than a lock. As in Machiavelli, prudence is self-serving, but in de Britain prudence works because the world it acts upon is structured, contained, calculable, machine-like; Fortuna is absent from de Britain's largely material order.

Contemporary with later printings of de Britain's delineation of "humane prudence" was Adam Smith's construction of the prudent man in his major works. In *The Theory of Moral Sentiments* and his later *Inquiry into the Nature and Causes of the Wealth of Nations* Smith, we must take note, was not simply *describing* an extant subjectivity when he wrote of "the prudent man" (*Theory* 212–17; *Wealth* 1:37, 456, 525). Smith was also *crafting* a figure that could occupy a reality that he understood, or wished to understand, in primarily economic terms. The passage in which Smith introduces this character in *The Theory of Moral Sentiments* reads, in fact, very much like de Britain's own character sketches. Regarding the prudent man's moral character, Smith writes that "the prudent man always studies seriously and earnestly to understand whatever he professes to understand" (*Theory* 213). Regarding his speech, "His conversation is simple and modest" (213). And regarding his relationships, "The prudent man . . . is always very capable of friendship" (214). Smith's "prudent man," like de Britain's, is the hero of reality narrated as an economy. Meanwhile, economy increasingly seems to mean the space occupied by prudent people, or, what amounts to the same thing, the space insufficiently, improperly, or inadequately occupied by *im*prudent people.[6] But whereas de Britain, still more or less in touch with matters of ethics and spirit, could qualify the extent of his prudent man's abilities—"that which is out of your power, let it out of your care. . . . Leave God to govern the World as himself pleaseth" (164)—there was no theoretical reason why Smith's prudent man should ever consider something "out of [his] power."

Perhaps because it was a matter of such great interest to the foundational economist Smith, the discipline of economics would go on to ground itself in the history and the analysis of prudence. Deirdre McCloskey, one of the most rigorous analysts of the methods and assumptions of Economics, succinctly puts it as follows: "Economics since its invention as a system of thought in the eighteenth century has been very largely about that third virtue of the seven virtues, prudence, an androgynous virtue counted good in both men and women stereotypically viewed. You can call it practical wisdom or *ratio* or know-how or self-interest or competence or rationality. The word 'prudence' is a useful, long-period compromise among the wisdom-words from *phronesis* in Aristotle to 'maximization' in the modern economists" (317–18).[7] McCloskey accurately depicts the centrality of prudence to the development of eighteenth-century economic thought, but her words also produce the sense that because prudence was always there, so too was economics itself always already there, as old as prudence itself, as a science in the making since Aristotelian *phronesis*.[8]

However, notwithstanding McCloskey's "long-period compromise," *prudence* was a highly contested term in the eighteenth century. The contest concerned whether prudence was or should be considered an "economic" virtue. The two sides of this contest are succinctly illustrated by the "prudence and discretion" of Samuel Richardson's supremely moral Pamela on the one hand and the "prudent" manipulations of Fielding's scheming Shamela on the other. Building upon this simple opposition, here I wish to read two other works by Fielding, with an eye not simply to Fielding's moral objections to Pamela but to the way in which he was engaging in the evolution of the meaning of *prudence* and to the impact of his intervention on both ethics and literary form. Looking to his early play, *The Modern Husband* (1732), I argue that Fielding presented his viewers with a sense that relationships between and among people ought to be mediated by gifts rather than loans. The gift economy he establishes, though, ends up looking conspicuously like a lottery, with the original gift coming to seem a sort of lottery ticket and the happy ending a grand prize. As evident as this similarity is, I argue, the play's internal treatment of gambling suggests that perhaps Fielding was not altogether comfortable with the economy of rewards and punishments that his play's lotterylike structure implied. There is a certain degree of discomfort with this kind of poetic justice, since it implies that ethical behavior might be performed with the intention of bringing about reward, that ethics might be subordinated to a logic of prudence. Turning my attention, therefore, to *The History of Tom Jones, a Foundling* (1749), I argue that Fielding appears to have recognized that not only did the increasingly economized virtue of prudence threaten to erode traditional ethical values but those traditional values too, particularly as they served to create the conditions of possibility for narrative fulfillment (i.e., poetic justice), were themselves susceptible to prudential management, thereby destabilizing their ethical quality altogether (turning them into a currency that buys happy endings). In the end, it is necessary for Fielding to, as it were, hang the hero he only half jestingly describes as having been born to be hanged: bestowing upon Tom the tainted virtue of prudence at his novel's end provides Fielding with a way out of all economistic ethical systems. By sacrificing Tom, Fielding suggests the possibility of an ethics without exchange.

Henry Fielding: Hazards and Systems

"I imagine wisdom," writes Fielding in 1739, "to be of very little consequence in the affairs of this world: human life appears to me to resemble the game of hazard, much more than that of chess; in which the latter, among good players, one false step must infallibly lose the game; whereas, in the former, the worst that can happen is to have the odds against you" (*Champion* 88). It is easy to see why these words have loomed large in discussions of Fielding's work: they seemingly represent a complete about-face by Fielding on the nature of the cosmos and the value of prudence within it. Although Fielding does not use the word *prudence*, his turn to Machiavelli in the ensuing paragraph suggests that by "wisdom" this is what he had in mind and what his readers would have taken him to mean. Martin Battestin considers this passage an occasional and strategic departure from a larger pattern in which Fielding celebrated "*prudential* or practical wisdom, chief of the cardinal virtues of antiquity—implying both a penetrating moral vision enabling us to distinguish truth from mere appearance, and the ability, through the proper exercise of the rational faculties of memory, judgement, and foresight, to make sound moral choices based on an awareness of the probable consequences of our present actions" (*Amelia* 15). W. B. Coley, however, has suggested that perhaps Fielding was undecided on the matter of prudence;[9] Oliver Elton considered Fielding's words the product of a passing "mood" possibly occasioned by misfortunes (188); though Jesse Molesworth, in an adroit reading of the openness and accidental character of *Amelia*, has also observed that the remark evidences "a much more complex, much more problematic, view of chance" than is sometimes implied by an emphasis on Fielding's providentialism (153).

I would like to observe that the thrust of Fielding's remark may have less to do with who or what is in control of the future—gods or men—and more to do with the form of the games mentioned in his analogy: chess and hazard. Confined by its limited number of spaces and pieces, chess is also, by its very logic, a circumscribed arena, each game having a beginning, a middle, and an end, at which point there is a winner and a loser. In hazard, however, as in its modern descendant, craps, the game never ends; it has the potential to unfold indefinitely. Win or lose, there is nothing to theoretically prevent a player from continuing to play. Bad luck now may be greeted with good fortune later, and vice versa. Fielding seems to register this difference in describing the game of chess as one that leads to a final win or loss, whereas his remark concerning hazard registers his awareness of the game's theoretical endlessness (one's odds simply change). Fielding places no emphasis—which is a kind of emphasis in its own right—on the "end" of hazard, because hazard, in principle, has no end. Oliver Cromwell's surprising rise to power—Fielding's concluding example in support of his metaphor of life as being more like hazard than chess—is evidence that people sometimes reap benefits in this world when they, at least in the case of Fielding's Cromwell, have absolutely no reason to deserve or expect them.

Fielding did very much believe in, at least for a time, the form of prudence described by Battestin, and he acknowledges, in some of his writings, the workings of some kind of higher power or logic that would reward the prudent individual, but his choice to compare life to a game of hazard is also consistent with the prudence that Battestin describes. This is because in hazard the reward of prudence is at best only probably winning, and even then one might later lose, however prudent one is in placing wagers. Because hazard offers no guarantees and no state of finality, prudence takes on a more indeterminate aspect than it does in chess, where the logic of the game is nothing more than to be more prudent, to have more foresight, than one's opponent. In Fielding's analogy, chess serves as a comparatively bad or limited example for "human life" because it implies that human life is a fully controllable thing. This was what the new, economic meaning of *prudence* implied, first, in its subordination of ethics to neutral rules concerning manipulable objects and people and, second, in its hubristic belief that the prudent individual could calculate, order, and guide those objects and people so as to maximize returns. Cromwell may or may not have been prudent (a good or bad chess player, so to speak), but it was his luck (his good fortune at hazard, to continue the analogy) that led him to greatness. Hazard, unlike chess but very much like human life, no matter how well played, always entails the possibility of unexpected results; there are forces that produce outcomes that frustrate even the most calculating of individuals. In other words, in this much-debated passage Fielding does not so much give up on prudence as acknowledge the faultiness of a certain modern conception of it, namely, the view that prudence, if properly exercised, would invariably yield returns and that imprudence would invariably yield losses.

There are other reasons to credit Fielding with a modicum of sincerity in his representation of human life as a game of hazard. Fielding, like his father, was an enthusiastic gambler and, also like his father, not a particularly good one (Battestin and Battestin 131, 146). In Martin and Ruth Battestins' biographical portrait, Fielding oscillates between diligent producer and imprudent man of passion and excess; his acts of positive self-affirmation are perpetually canceled out, in their view, by his self-destructive tendencies. One of these tendencies, they suggest, was gambling; this is in keeping with the Freudian reading of gambling generally as a form of self-destructive, wasteful, masturbatory behavior.[10] A different way of interpreting Fielding's attraction to gambling, a way that fully accepts the evidence presented by Battestin and Battestin, if not their conclusions, is to construe gambling not as self-destruction but as the destruction of a certain part of the self, to construe the act of gambling as completing, in a moment of glorious destruction, the gains of legitimate labor. Such an extravagant and improbable claim for the sinful practices of a conservative Whig author and judge must be tempered by many things, foremost being remarks made in "Inquiry into the Causes of the Late Increase of Robbers," wherein Fielding mercilessly indicts gambling culture, more or less directly stating that gambling leads to more serious acts of crime, such as theft. However, Fielding reserves for himself just enough space for play: "I must remind the reader, that I have only the inferior part of mankind under my consideration. I am not so ill-bred as to disturb the company at a polite assembly" ("Inquiry" 180). This would seem an ordinary act of deference to social codes and breeding, but by the phrase "company at a polite assembly" Fielding also implies that among individuals for whom the bare necessities of life have been provided, gambling is an acceptable pastime. Gambling is suitable for such company not because members are polite or more restrained in their passions but because by *polite* Fielding means a state of relative excess, one in which subsistence and survival are no longer meaningful worries or concerns. For those living in such a happy condition, gambling *deals* with the excess. It would be wrong, obviously, to say that Fielding was a great proponent of gambling, but it is undeniably right to say that he could at once lambaste gambling and comfortably engage in play himself.

One view of Fielding would have us believe that he was on the side of his doctrinally stated position against gambling and then go on to read his actual gambling as a departure from his doctrine (hypocrisy). I am merely reversing the terms, taking Fielding's lived attraction to gambling as his own (mostly) unwritten doctrine and his (occasional) printed resistance to that doctrine as an anxiety effect born of a more deeply rooted belief in the workings of providence, of whose wisdom and reality he often speaks, though his skepticism regarding evangelical religion and nearly all performances of religiosity makes such statements sometimes appear in code. To assume that Fielding's rational "interests" lead him to the right conclusions about gambling in the "Inquiry," while his "passions" led him astray in real life, is to reproduce in so many ways the very distinction that the eighteenth century appears to have produced or at least accepted from an earlier age. To provide one concrete example, is it not possible that Fielding, writing under the pseudonym Scriblerus Secondus, would have construed the popular success of his farce *The Lottery*—which, along with the less successful play *The Modern Husband*, procured him a "little less than a thousand Pounds" (Battestin and Battestin 131)—as a success in only the most tentative kind of way? Given Fielding's fictional experimentation with characters whose benevolent imprudence marks them as virtuous, is there a more fitting end to revenues generated by *The Lottery* than losing them all in a game of chance? If we are to credit Fielding with even the slightest sense of irony, is it not probable that he would have understood the surprise success of a farce about lotteries as itself in some way cosmically farcical and the squandering of his profits at cards or dice a case of cosmic justice reasserted?

To read Fielding in this way requires us to abandon orthodox assumptions about the economic—or, going on Webster's definitions, *prudent*—nature of the subject. It is a commonplace of modernity and narratives of modernity to assume that the primary objective of human behavior is to follow through with our destiny as "selfish individuals" and to perpetually accumulate more, to build up, to conserve, to produce, and to otherwise, as McCloskey put it, maximize. And the image of Fielding as characterized by "self-destructive recklessness" leads us to assume that what attracted Fielding to gambling in the first place was an ultimately rational desire to gain thwarted by irrational practices (Battestin and Battestin 131). So far as it conforms to a model of subjectivity that evolved in the later eighteenth and nineteenth centuries, there is certainly nothing incorrect about this characterization, but it does overlook the fact that Fielding was writing in the midst of this evolution, that he was himself witness to the consolidation of such a subjectivity, and that he may have been under the spell of different models of subjectivity than *homo economicus*. In other words, it overlooks Fielding's outsider status vis-à-vis the liberal economic individual that was taking shape in his own time. Here I would like to explore the possibility that Fielding's works testify to the allures of a form of subjectivity imagined or implied by anti-finance, one whose drive is not toward maximization, wherein gambling codes as a sickness, but toward self-abnegation, diminution, and vulnerability.

It is useful, therefore, in this particular instance to draw upon the work of someone who also occupied the position of outsider vis-à-vis the liberal economic individual, whose ability to look back upon nineteenth-century political economy from a later historical period in some ways mirrors Fielding's position in the 1730s and 1740s, before political economy had established itself as the most dominant analytic for the theorization and assessment of human behavior. Working against the dominant political economy of his day, Georges Bataille helps to illuminate the position that Fielding may have occupied in relation to the emerging economic realm.[11] Theorizing, contra liberal political economy, that subjectivity can also be viewed from the standpoint of the desire to sacrifice, lose, expend, waste, or destroy, Bataille observes that there is something unwholesome about holding on to an excess ("the accursed share" might be best defined as a savings account), which compels one to slough it off in nonproductive expenditure. Actually, one does not have the choice whether or not to slough it off; it will be spent in some way. The questions for Bataille are therefore ethical ones: Given that an excess will be spent, what is the best way to do so? In war or in charity? In further producing or in glorious destruction? Is war an instance of glorious destruction? If so, is this a good or bad form of destruction? Gambling, for Bataille, exemplified the inherent tendency of an excess to be unloaded. Although when discussing gambling Bataille typically emphasizes its vitiated modern form, in which one gambles for appearances (which simply reinserts gambling into the order of production, where the yield is symbolic rather than material), gambling in its pure form, like sacrifice, "destroys that which it consecrates. It does not have to destroy as fire does; only the tie that connected the offering to the world of profitable activity is severed" (*Accursed Share* 58).

That literary endeavors and gambling both, in their own ways, can count as such sloughing off makes Bataille's insight particularly interesting to consider in assessing Fielding's bifurcated life—or perhaps unified life—as both author and gambler. While Fielding surely wrote *The Lottery* with every intention of making a profit, he could not have seriously anticipated the "extraordinary Success" of it (*See and Seem Blind* 7–8, qtd. in Battestin and Battestin 131).[12] The excess revenue generated by *The Lottery*, a critique of the very incommensurability between the wealth that lotteries confer and the (in)ability of winners to spend it, must surely have entered Fielding's mind at some point. As an excessive form (farce) that appealed to and cashed in on the opportunities for wasting time and money at the theater, Fielding's "extraordinary" profits must have seemed to him, when viewed from the heights of Bataille's general economy, as nothing more than an accursed share. At the moment they are transformed into stakes, however, the profits from *The Lottery* and *The Modern Husband* assume the form of Bataille's sacrifice, because they can no longer be regarded in terms of the productive order that generated them in the first place (i.e., as profits). Gambling severs this tie whether Fielding wins or loses. It is the equivalent of setting money on fire—a common, pejorative idiom used in reference to gambling—but the important part is the symbolic removal of wealth from the domain of production.

That Fielding himself dolefully regarded his bouts of extravagant eating, gambling, drinking, and otherwise wasteful behavior does nothing to alter the fact that he did these things. It is in fact typical, writes Bataille, for the "miserable conception" of the complete primacy of utility to be regarded by modern individuals as the only acceptable way of relating to the world ("Notion of Expenditure" 168). Because gambling (and other forms of wasteful behavior) cannot be regarded as having any utility, even "the most lucid man will understand nothing" of his actions and will likely "imagine himself sick" (168). This is because "it does not occur to him that a human society can have, just as he does, an *interest* in considerable losses, in catastrophes that . . . provoke tumultuous depressions, crises of dread, and, in the final analysis, a certain orgiastic state" (168). Bataille helps us to understand Fielding's gambling and Fielding's reaction to his gambling, but Bataille's words also suggest that Fielding himself understood something of this. For if Fielding frowned upon

and regretted his moments of unproductive or wasteful behavior, he nevertheless demonstrates an awareness of the great potential of the "orgiastic state"
in his fictions, and not simply because he wrote about sex and food. It is also
because Fielding's writing often takes on an orgiastic form, one in which the
"production" of wise or virtuous readers is quite beside the point. Foremost
among such moments is that in which Molly Seagrim's confrontation with an
angry mob is extravagantly rendered by Fielding in a mock-epic "Homerican
Stile" (*Tom Jones* 159).

Bracketing these sweeping theoretical and philosophical matters for a moment, we must at least say that Fielding rarely, if ever, characterizes gambling
as itself an evil. The card-playing Mrs. Modern of *The Modern Husband*—a
play to which I will shortly turn—is generally vain, but she is not loathsome
in the way the villain Lord Richly is. If the force of Fielding's satirical portrait
of Mrs. Modern consists in her perpetual need to be gambling, she is somewhat excused by the fact that her pleasure is not simply financial. We might
laugh at her penchant for cards or even hold her in contempt for it, but we
could never call her evil for it. Similarly, when in *Jonathan Wild* (1743) Fielding writes of "that cursed Itch of Play" (33), he gestures toward the physio-
logical thrills—the sensation of scratching the itch—that are associated with
gambling and that have less to do with winning or losing than with gambling's
"elemental appeal," as Molesworth describes it (89). While Fielding's characterization of the "Itch" is obviously negative—it is "cursed," after all, as well
as a phrase that comes out of the villainous and untrustworthy Wild's own
mouth—the suggestion of its somatic origins prevents it from fully entering
the discursive domains of "vice" and "virtue," positioning it, therefore, closer
to uncontrollable sexual urges than to treachery, deceit, or cruelty. Fielding's
"Itch" announces an amoral remainder that appears once the desire for gain
is accounted for.

While the idea of a Fielding who gloried in waste may seem perverse, that
very theme runs through his fictional works in myriad ways. Paul Kelleher
persuasively argues that Fielding's idea of generosity is articulated in his representation of sexual, bodily, and passionate extravagance (188–89). Financial
promiscuity is equally central to the moral economy of his narratives. Tom
Jones's giving to George Seagrim's family the proceeds arising from the sale
of his horse and Bible (*Tom Jones* 131), the imprisoned Thomas Heartfree's
unwillingness to more aggressively pursue the repayment of money lent (*Jonathan Wild* 66–71), the destitute peddler's offer of his last "six shillings and
sixpence" to the cash-strapped Parson Adams and Joseph Andrews (*Joseph
Andrews* 220)—in each of these narratives, gifts end up being rewarded,

however indirectly, at the end of an improbable arc. Such instances to me reveal an author more convinced of the moral potential for loss than of the moral potential for gain, though each end does rebrand the loss as a form of gain, an incremental movement toward happiness.[13] In the space between the local celebrations of sacrificial loss and these narratives' implausible, happy resolutions—featuring, in *Tom Jones*, a "plot which depends for its complication and happy resolution upon a remarkable series of chance encounters and fortunate discoveries" (Battestin 150)—can be located a trace or remainder of the anti-usury position: providence asserts itself to finally reward local and momentary acts of sacrifice so long as the possible future reward or return is not anticipated at the time of the gift.[14] In Fielding's early play, the gift comes back only so long as it is not expected or sought out. But Fielding takes this logic one step higher in *Tom Jones*. By imbuing Tom with a virtue that implies economism, Fielding prevents his hero's fate from being read as his reward, as recompense in an equally facile economy of providential rewards and punishments. *Tom Jones*, in other words, turns anti-finance against itself, or, more specifically, turns the ethic of uncertainty against the providential foundations upon which earlier forms of anti-finance had rested. Aside from the obvious and incontrovertible fact that Fielding ultimately refuses his reader the assurance of a providential God, Fielding dares to imagine the value of an ethic of uncertainty rooted entirely in the human.[15]

Gambling and Gifting: *The Modern Husband*

A summary of the somewhat twisted plot—a "badly flawed" one, according to Robert Hume (*Henry Fielding and the London Theatre* 123)—of *The Modern Husband*, an understudied play in the Fielding canon, may be helpful for some readers. The play opens with the mercenary Mr. Modern attempting to persuade his wife, Mrs. Modern, to get caught in flagrante delicto with her wealthy lover, Lord Richly, so that Mr. Modern can sue Richly for damages. Mrs. Modern refuses her husband's plot on the grounds that her reputation would suffer, but she is happy to continue the affair with Richly in secret. She also, we learn, has been having an affair with Mr. Bellamant, who immediately prior to the story's commencement has lost a protracted lawsuit, leaving him with sufficient but not great wealth to support his family. The libertine Lord Richly, ever on the lookout for new paramours, sees Mr. Bellamant's financial misfortunes as an opportunity to seduce Mr. Bellamant's wife. Lord Richly eventually executes a plan to lose a small sum of money to Mrs. Bellamant at the game of piquet, leave her with a large banknote in trust until he can procure small change, hope that she spends the entirety of the banknote (she does not), and then extort sexual favors from her under the threat of prosecuting her for theft of the larger sum. When Richly attempts to collect those favors later by direct bribery instead, she defiantly refuses him. Mrs. Bellamant then discovers Mr. Bellamant's affair with Mrs. Modern, but after a very brief argument she forgives her husband for his infidelity.

Alongside these dramas, a younger generation of potential lovers woo and tease one another: Lord Richly's rakish but fundamentally good nephew, Gaywit, falls in love with the Bellamants' virtuous daughter, Emilia; meanwhile, the Bellamants' foppish son, Captain Bellamant, manages to successfully woo Richly's daughter (and Gaywit's cousin), Lady Charlotte. Both of these younger couples eventually marry, though it is the marriage of Emilia to Gaywit that properly marks the happiness of the ending, as their courtship has been modest, honest, and urbane, unlike the silly exchanges between Captain Bellamant and the impossibly stupid Lady Charlotte, which end in hasty but jolly nuptials.

With the Bellamants reconciled and his liaison with Mrs. Modern effectively at an end, Lord Richly settles on another scheme: he privately gives Gaywit, who is his ward, approval to marry Emilia, with the sinister intention of later publicly denying having done so. Because the entail to Gaywit's estate requires him to marry Lady Charlotte (whom Gaywit reasonably detests), should Gaywit marry Emilia without Richly's public approval, Gaywit's inheritance will revert to Richly. However, because Lady Charlotte herself marries Captain Bellamant all of a sudden (in the middle of act 5), Gaywit not only is free to marry Emilia but will collect his estate in its entirety. Richly and Mr. Modern are revealed as scoundrels, and the play comes to a close.

Given the obvious importance of marital and domestic affairs, which this summary only begins to capture, it is understandable that the play has been universally read as Fielding's satirical criticism of men who, in one way or another, attempt to profit from their wives' sexual liaisons, either by prostituting them directly or by attempting to catch them in flagrante with other men to extort or sue for payment. Robert Hume has classed the play among other instances of "marital discord comedies" (272).[16] Charles B. Woods's identification of a 1730 trial involving Lord Abergavenny's suit against one Richard Liddell (sometimes Lyddell) for having had criminal conversation with his wife, Lady Abergavenny, has provided the historical basis for this reading, and there remains little doubt that it influenced Fielding (364–67).[17] Alexander Pettit has convincingly argued that the marital themes and topics raised in

The Modern Husband and other such comedies helped to give form even to Fielding's fictionalized account of Jonathan Wild (24–25).

But if, following the lead of scholars who have highlighted the importance of object- or it-narratives in the mid-eighteenth century, we recount the plot of Fielding's comedy from the standpoint of a single hundred-pound banknote that circulates among many of the characters in the play, we may observe that *The Modern Husband,* like *Jonathan Wild,* is concerned with more than purely marital affairs: it reflects as well Fielding's wider concern with the strange forces that govern the movement and transferal of value.[18] Given what we know of the rise in it-narratives in the eighteenth century, it is even possible that Fielding structured his play with this object in mind rather than the thoughts and feelings of his human characters.[19] In fact, if we look at the plot from the standpoint of the banknote, the plot is not quite as flawed as it may at first appear. We can see how the subplots vitally feed back into the main storyline and even account for the otherwise rather unaccountable levee scene involving Captain Merit (who does not figure into the marital plots and hence does not appear in the summary of marital discord).

Early in the play, during a conversation with his wife, Mr. Bellamant receives a letter from his lover, Mrs. Modern, in which she pleads, "If you have, or ever had any value for me, send me a hundred pounds this morning" (2.1.72–73). Mr. Bellamant, a slave to her at this point, instructs his wife: "I gave you a bank note of a hundred yesterday. You must let me have it again" (2.1.61–62). She unhesitatingly obliges and gives him the note. Perhaps feeling guilty about his request, knowing of course that it will be given to his mistress, Mr. Bellamant replies to his wife that she "will be repaid in a day or two" (2.1.127).

In the following scene, Mrs. Modern receives the banknote from the hand of "a Servant," who has presumably received it from a courier sent by Mr. Bellamant (2.2.44–45). Although in the opening scene of the play we are made to understand that duns pursue her to collect on debts, we begin to learn here that her wish for the hundred pounds has more to do with her passion for gambling. She entices Richly, Lady Charlotte, and Captain Bellamant to a game of hazard, the first of several gambling scenes that take place offstage (a crucial staging decision, to which I will return). She reenters the stage with the others, boastfully proclaiming victory; she has, it seems, won big. Lady Charlotte is dismayed; Captain Bellamant is silent; Richly, however, knowing her weaknesses, lures Mrs. Modern into an after-game[20] of piquet, which also takes place entirely offstage. As Richly puts it to her, "To anyone who loves play as well as you, and plays as ill, the money we lose, by a surprising ill fortune, is only lent" (2.2.195–97).

Recasting Richly's role—as a lender rather than a gambler—gives us leave to consider the difference between the two. As a lender, Richly forecloses the possibility of ever losing; his talent at cards, which is figured in the play as of a piece with his sinister financial self, is associated with the temporal security generated from the loan contract. Risk is thus excluded entirely from his gambling practice—he never really expects any loss at all—and his villainy stems precisely from that fact. Unlike the Christian providential subject who puts himself or herself into a condition of sufficient ethical vulnerability, who would truly and fully take a gamble, Lord Richly occupies the moral space of the usurer.[21] Compared with gambling, lending as practiced by Richly stands as the play's true financial vice and is partly why gambling remains relatively untainted, ethically speaking, in the play.

The scene involving Captain Merit, which cannot be reconciled with the marital plots, builds toward the revelation of Richly's usurer identity. Surveying the room full of men seeking his assistance, among them the proud Captain Merit, who has been tragically reduced to supplication, Richly declares, "All gaping for favours, without the least capacity of making a return for them" (1.3.111–12). The levee, we now see, is really more of a bank, and Merit a disappointed applicant for a loan. The seeds of this association may be planted at the close of the preceding scene, when Merit complains that he, along with many others, is forced to "go to the feeding the vanity of that leviathan, one great rogue" (1.2.61–62). Fielding's play on words—a "levee-athan," which makes leviathans, levees, and banks akin to one another and thus makes Richly a sort of scheming banker—calls to mind the subject projected and imagined in Hobbes's famous work bearing that name in order to more convincingly draw together Richly, his levee, and new economic conceptions of a lending, rather than a giving, subject. That Merit does not appear again in the course of the play makes perfect sense: he has been denied entry into the circuits of wealth and thus cannot partake in the main plot, involving the note's circulation.[22] I say the main plot because unless we assume that it was the banknote, rather than the marital drama, that Fielding found most interesting and important, it would be unclear why Fielding continued to regard *The Modern Husband* as his finest dramatic work. Was it because he understood that its unity derived not from his rendition of marital dramas but from his adroit deployment and management of the banknote?

At the beginning of the following scene (3.1) we are greeted with the news that Lord Richly has turned the tables and stripped Mrs. Modern of everything. While the banknote is not mentioned specifically, we know that his spoils include it, for it appears in his possession in the immediately ensuing scene. Lord Richly entices Mrs. Bellamant to a game of piquet, much as he had enticed Mrs. Modern just moments earlier. She reluctantly agrees, and the scene ends, the gambling for a third time taking place between scenes and offstage. But when Richly and Mrs. Bellamant reappear, after their game has come to a close, we learn that Mrs. Bellamant has, surprisingly, won, though only an unspecified small sum. We do not know whether it was good luck or whether Richly let her win in order to encumber her in a new way. For Richly, it does not really matter: he offers Mrs. Bellamant the excessively large banknote he has just taken from Mrs. Modern, the same note that Mrs. Bellamant had given to her husband. Mrs. Bellamant at first dismisses the debt entirely, suggesting that the winnings do not at all matter to her. But Richly needs her to take the banknote because of his plan to later extort sexual favors from her. In response to his insistence that he is honorable and pays his debts—which the audience can obviously see through—she ends up taking the note and promises to return the difference to him as soon as she can change it for smaller notes or coin. There are no stage directions to guide us here, but she must pocket the note without even looking at it, for she does not acknowledge her perception of any of the signatures or script that might have enabled her to recognize it as the same one she had given to her husband earlier that day. The fact that she does not look at it closely suggests that she does not want it, which, ironically, proves that in a moral sense she is entitled to it. Her blindness to it reproduces the same form and spirit of disinterest that guided her when she initially gave it to her husband. Mrs. Bellamant's disregard for the money in fact means that she could, theoretically, continue to receive and regift the note an infinite number of times. It will continue to come back to her so long as she does not seek it, avow it as hers, or expect it to come back to her. It is in the logic of the note to return to its owner, so long as that owner continues to give it away.

While Mrs. Bellamant has been obliviously winning money and not caring about it, her husband has agreed to procure another hundred pounds for his mistress, Mrs. Modern. Repeating the sequence from the first act, he asks his wife for more money, and she agrees to give him the banknote she has just received from Richly, on the condition that he repay it soon (not because she wants it but because it is not hers to give). Again, presumably not looking too closely at it, she blithely passes it to her husband, and he elates. Until, that is, he recognizes it as the same note he had given Mrs. Modern earlier that day. He presses his wife to tell him how she came to possess it, not at all revealing to her why he wants to know. She resists telling him for fear that he will construe her having won the money from Richly as a sign of an affair between them. The irony, of course, is that the money is for the purposes of Mr. Bellamant's affair with Mrs. Modern.

Dissatisfied with his wife's answers, Mr. Bellamant leaves to ask Mrs. Modern how his wife came to possess the banknote he had given to Mrs. Modern earlier:

> *Mrs. Modern:* Then to introduce my explanation [of how Mrs. Bellamant got the banknote], the note you lent me, I lost at Piquet to Lord Richly.
> *Mr. Bellamant:* To Lord Richly!
> *Mrs. Modern:* Who perhaps might dispose of it to some who might lend it to others, who might give it to those who might lose it to your wife.
> *Mr. Bellamant:* I know not what to suppose.

Mrs. Modern mentions four forms of transferal: disposal, lending, giving, and losing. None of these terms have a decidedly positive or negative connotation as Mrs. Modern clinically states them. Mrs. Bellamant has truly "given" the money to her husband, but so might a libertine "give" money to a potential mark (as Richly does to Mrs. Bellamant); "losing" money might be bad, but in suggesting virtuous imprudence, it might be good to be a loser (the play's more moral characters profess disinterest or incompetence in gaming). Lending too might be good, as when Merit comes to seek assistance at the levee, unless it is money lent in the way that Lord Richly lends in order to collect the "mortgage" on his female victims (4.1.125–26). Mr. Bellamant, unable to assess the meaning of Mrs. Modern's proliferating ambiguities of exchange, "know[s] not what to suppose." What is interesting, though, is that Mrs. Modern quietly alludes to the possibility that she will later lose it again, and to none other than Mrs. Bellamant. To paraphrase her remark: Lord Richly has disposed of the note to Mrs. Bellamant; Mrs. Bellamant has lent it (back) to her husband; Mr. Bellamant might give it to me (Mrs. Modern); and, I (Mrs. Modern) might later lose it to Mrs. Bellamant ("your wife"). This final transferal, though, is not a rehearsal of the note's past; it is Mrs. Modern's utopian and in some ways unconscious sense of the note's future: its eventual progression back into the hands of the original giver, Mrs. Bellamant. What exhilarated Fielding, I suspect, and what gives form to his play is the tension between the different ways that money circulates, intentionally or unintentionally, predictably or chaotically. The play derides forms of transferal that are directed, calculated, and purposive (lending or cheating, where what goes out is certain to come back), while he praises those that are unintentional.

This helps to explain the play's title: much as the play may seem to be about marriage, the title might also refer to an overly zealous steward of resources or money. Thus, "modern husband" might refer not just to Mr. Modern but also to Richly, who must be countered by someone whose does not "husband" money so much as give it away without thinking about it. In this sense of *husband*, Richly's countervailing force is not Mr. Bellamant but Mrs. Bellamant, who does not need, in this sense, to be a man in order to be the better "husband" (even Mrs. Modern, in her willingness to cede control to the playing cards, is a morally superior sort of husband).

What Fielding needs at this point in the play is a way to get the note back into Mrs. Bellamant's possession, one in which money moves without needing to be "husbanded" in a "modern" sort of way. It is in this respect that gifts and gambling become images of one another: neither represent prudential strategies for husbanding one's resources. As de Britain put it in the shortest and most unequivocal chapter of *Humane Prudence:* "Avoid Gaming. . . . It's a Madness beyond the Cure of *Hellebore*, to cast a Dye [*sic*] whether your Estate shall be your own or not; if you have not a care, I can without an Augure [*sic*] tell what will be your fate, this, like a Quicksand, will swallow you up in a Moment; and Goods which are so gotten, are like Pyramids of Snow, which melt away, and are dissolved with the same ill Husbandry that did beget them" (134). Recommending prudent rather than "ill Husbandry," de Britain objects to gaming not simply because it will cause one to lose money; rather, gambling leads one to altogether forget the purpose of money: wealth becomes "Snow," which is inherently predisposed to melting. But for Fielding, gambling facilitates the process of circulation that gifting initially sets into motion. Thus, grudgingly, Mrs. Bellamant agrees to Lord Richly's invitation to gamble, and as a result of the game (as well as Richly's plan to entrap her), Mrs. Bellamant gets the note back. Displaying her "ill Husbandry," she regards it, literally, as no more than a scrap of paper when she casually stuffs it into her pocket. It is this very action that precipitates, however unintentionally, the resolution of the affairs. After the affair between Mr. Bellamant and Mrs. Modern ends— which comes about because he realizes Richly's plans in the wake of Mrs. Modern's comments about the note—a resulting schism between Mr. Bellamant and Mrs. Bellamant is quickly healed. Mr. Bellamant confronts Lord Richly and returns the banknote to him (along with a threat intended to keep Richly away from his wife).

Thus begins the final phase of the play, which only seems disconnected from the plot if we regard the marital problems of the Bellamants and the Moderns as Fielding's primary concern. Richly now commences with his attempt to secure Gaywit's fortune. As noted above, because Lady Charlotte precipitously marries Mr. Bellamant's son, Gaywit is free to marry whomever he chooses, and that happens to be the Bellamant daughter, Emilia. Although this final series of marital actions may *seem* divorced from the main plot, they are the precondition for the banknote's final, triumphant return to the hands of Mrs. Bellamant. With the Bellamant children now married or engaged to the heirs of the Richly fortune, it can be gathered that the banknote, which has most recently passed back into the hands of Richly via Mr. Bellamant, will, at some point and in some form, return to the hands of Mr. Bellamant, who, as the patriarch, is both metaphor and metonymy for the Bellamant family at large. And we may further presume that Mr. Bellamant will therefore be able to give the note, as he had done just prior to the commencement of the play's action, back to Mrs. Bellamant. In fact, the note has in reality lost all of its materiality and is now merely a part of Richly's vast estate; its fungibility guarantees its absorption into a much larger mass of undifferentiated wealth. The note no longer has any determinate status, which in its own way protects the Bellamants from imputations of pettiness. The note comes back, but magnified and glorified, by virtue of the ethical actions and virtuous love that animates the play.

Patrick Reilly has similarly remarked of *Tom Jones* that "the bread cast by Tom on the waters comes back a hundredfold, but the thrower must throw without wanting or even thinking of a return" (113). Such a reading works even better for *The Modern Husband*. For just as the radical, honest gambler—here figured by Mrs. Bellamant, with her disregard for wealth and future wealth— represents entry into a system of risk, so does the world of play seem structured like a lottery (scatter a little and reap a hundredfold), the subject of Fielding's next dramatic production, *The Lottery*.[23] Albert J. Rivero rightly notes *The Modern Husband's* "deep ludic structure," where human actions "are reduced to, and interpreted as, games" ("Politics" 11). But there are more reasons for the aptness of this description. Just as a lottery winner gets back the money used to buy the original ticket *only in a sense* (that is, the specific, material coin or specie used to physically purchase the initial ticket is not itself returned), so do we find in *The Modern Husband* that the Bellamants get back the original banknote, but *only in a sense*. In place of the note itself, we are, at the end, presented with a picture of the Bellamant family's future financial wholeness that swamps the single note by fully reversing the financial ruin that had been brought about by the lawsuit. Putting the note into circulation also makes it somewhat like the lottery tickets that circulated between and among London citizens, often through brokers. We are given examples of such circulation in *The Lottery*'s "Mr. Stocks" (2) and in the story of Mr. Wilson in *Joseph Andrews* (273).

Although Mrs. Bellamant's blind act of giving the hundred-pound note may seem only a contrivance to set the play in motion, it fits within a larger tradition of associating charitable giving with great and unexpected returns and reveals the latently economic character of even the Christian ethic of uncertainty, which I will shortly argue Fielding resists in *Tom Jones*. The seventeenth-century Protestant theologian and preacher Anthony Horneck, for example, the same preacher who spoke of wealth stealing unexpectedly on good Christians (114–15), explains that charitable giving can be understood as a kind of investment, one that is the "readiest way to prosper in [one's] secular Concerns" (154–55). In a fascinating and highly revealing comparison of charity and usury, he adds that those "men"

> who by consecrating a great part of their Estate and Incomes to pious and charitable Uses, have enlarged their Fortunes, and by casting their Bread upon the Water, have found it again with Interest after many days; who have denied themselves in their superfluities, and yet are grown rich; given away, and yet got more than they had in times past. This would lead them into the pleasant Field of God's Providence, and shew them how that wise and gracious God wheels and turns things about for the good of those that dare trust him for a Recompence, and makes that Money which was laid out for the use of the Needy, return with advantage and usury. (155)

Fielding's moral heroine, Mrs. Bellamant, has, through an initial act of gifting the sum to her husband, led the entire Bellamant family to financial success. Crucially, though, this is all an accidental and unplanned gain. The twists and turns of the plot are dexterously managed by an author who brings his characters to the brink of destruction, only to save them as a reward for this original moment of selfless gifting. In Mrs. Bellamant's having truly given something to her husband, the arc of justice that is the plot of Fielding's play manages to imply that risky behavior is the best kind because it is wholly unlike the guaranteed returns of Richly's "loans."

That the gift comes back, magnified, confirms what James Thompson has written regarding Fielding's "comic rule of conservation, under which it is finally impossible to lose anything" (113). But this does present one problem. If Mrs. Bellamant, within the play, relates to the object that is the note in a manner that enables a transcendent power to return it to her through mysterious and uncertain channels of causation, including both gifting and gambling, Fielding, by contrast, exercises a rigorous form of control over the note such that its destination is the farthest thing from uncertain. Perhaps this very tension explains why Fielding, on three separate occasions, depends upon gambling to energize the moral flow of the banknote but places the actual scene of gambling offstage.[24] The staging of actual, honest gambling—such as that which we must assume would be practiced by Mrs. Bellamant—is problematic for Fielding because its plausibility depends upon the possibility that a vicious character might receive the benefit of his or her risk; equally troubling, it would require him to acknowledge that virtuous characters sometimes sustain losses. Fielding could just rig the game, of course, to make the virtuous win and the vicious lose; however, that would reveal the man behind the curtain to be a cheat and threaten to expose the arc of his plot as a grand contrivance.

Which, of course, it is. While the gifts of Mrs. Bellamant resemble gambles, the plot of *The Modern Husband* is a rigged game, one in which the virtuous always win and the vicious always lose. Gambling serves to correct the course of money that is otherwise lodged in the hands of all-too-human beings, who have motives, plots, intentions, and desires. But the play's critique of such baseness, which consists in the vicious ultimately being punished, requires motives, intentions, and, well, a plot. Where gambling seems to resemble the unstated, unconscious paradigm upon which Fielding's larger vision of a just order is in fact truly based, plots defiantly resist such openness. Because actual gambling or hazard is constitutively open ended, as Fielding observes in his analogy in *The Champion*, it cannot be fully accommodated within the bounded, chesslike world of comedy. Even in nondramatic works, where it presumably would be easier to narrate the progress of dice or cards (one thinks of the game of ombre in Pope's *Rape of the Lock*), Fielding does not render gambling in terms of the real riskiness that defines it. Count La Ruse, in *Jonathan Wild*, for example, often plays cards, but he cannot by any means be said to take risks, stacking the deck as he does. As Molesworth puts it, in that satire "card play is hardly card play. Rather, it is taken up as a natural extension of the career of a criminal by the cads, nicks, vultures, bites, and cheats confined within Mr. Snap's sponging house" (155). It is not just that Fielding was interested in playfully satirizing vice; gambling, real gambling, literally has no place in a narrative whose rules are decided in advance and whose outcome must be made certain. In *Tom Jones's* terminal ambivalence Fielding presents his readers with a less certain outcome.

The Taint of Prudence: *The History of Tom Jones, a Foundling*

Tom Jones is structured by an opposition between a villain who, with the assistance of a lawyer, makes strategic use of insider knowledge to sharp and trick others—including the novel's readers—in order to gain wealth and power and a hero who, though not lacking in desire, nevertheless seems chronically unable or unwilling to expect returns for his good deeds. That these two characters' distinguishing moral traits, conniving and generosity, are by the narrator either equated with or eventually accommodated to, specifically, "Prudence" shows that Fielding's novel was meaningfully involved in that term's semantic transition, which, as Webster's 1828 definitions begin to suggest, and McCloskey's more recent remarks confirm, was also a transition in how economic subjectivity was understood. If Fielding's comic plots show that gifts ultimately pay off in accordance with a providential but invisible economy of punishments and rewards and that selfishly prudential actions will be punished in the end, *Tom Jones* incorporates the ethics of uncertainty into the form of the novel itself, leaving its reader with a terminal unease that suggests that Fielding wished to cede control over his hero's fate to his reader. By turning anti-finance on ethics itself, *Tom Jones* liberates ethics from the tacitly economic form it had earlier assumed in the providential economy of *The Modern Husband.* Reading *Tom Jones* anti-financially—with an eye to uncertainty—helps to account for the problem of how (and why) the good, generous, charitable, and otherwise ethical Tom who has been gradually revealed to readers over the course of several hundred pages can, in the space of a single, brief sentence in the penultimate paragraph of Fielding's novel, be said to have acquired prudence, a "virtue" that the narrator routinely attributes to Tom's vile nemesis, Blifil, and that has marked everything contrary to what readers have, up to that point, come to associate with Tom's ethical conduct. Engaging in a public, popular, and complicated struggle over the meaning of prudence—and its attendant implications that the world is a predictable system and can therefore be manipulated to produce certain future outcomes— and its relation to ethical practice, Fielding transformed the ethics of uncertainty into the uncertainty of ethics. It is not that Fielding or his novel is uncertain about ethics; rather, they claim that for ethics to exist, it must itself remain uncertain about the truth and permanence of its own propositions.

There is no better testimony to Fielding's success in this endeavor than the ongoing and likely eternal debate about the where-ness of goodness in *Tom Jones*. Just where, in other words, does Tom's goodness come from? Critical approaches to this question and their limits will be addressed in due course, but it is important to explain first how prudence bears on it. Martin Battestin has provided the most convincing case for the ultimate harmony of Fielding's ethical vision and Tom's acquisition of prudence, arguing that "the meaning of *Tom Jones* turns upon the presentation of two major and complementary themes: these are the doctrines of Providence with respect to the macrocosm and of Prudence, the analogous rational virtue within the microcosm, man. Together with charity and good-nature, always the essential and indispensable qualifications of Fielding's moral men, Providence and Prudence define the specific ethos of *Tom Jones*" (142–43). According to Battestin, Fielding regarded prudence and providence as obedient to the same logic; but if they are analogous, and providence is infallible and omnipotent, what need is there for a modification—"together with charity and good-nature"—in the case of the microcosmic prudence? Whereas the goodness of providence consists in its simply being providence, the wisdom and power of God, the goodness of prudence would appear to consist in something outside of it, and writers of the eighteenth century worried about this very problem. Worries over the lack of emphasis on the infinite in popular conceptions of prudence and concerns that prudence might spin out of control unless it was checked by a countervailing moral virtue complicate the analogy between prudence and providence.[25]

Prudence was, for many, not a mirror of providence but a distortion of it, as is perhaps evidenced by a passing remark made by de Britain in a chapter recommending the avoidance of luxury in eating: he prudently pays so little regard to food that he would "without any disgust eat Man's Flesh" (120). An extraordinarily unique remark for its time—for any time in Western European culture, really—de Britain's casual acceptance of cannibalism under the justifying rhetoric of frugality suggests that prudence was, potentially and really, so fundamentally unhinged from anything resembling orthodox ethical sentiment that a companion virtue like "good-nature" could only be a laughable afterthought to its exercise. It was not simply a matter of prudence needing to be paired with an ameliorating, companion virtue but a matter of prudence quite literally rattling the most basic assumptions about the meaning of "good-nature." This is, of course, quite apart from whether *we* can conceive of the eating of human flesh as possibly good-natured. De Britain's acceptance of cannibalism under the banner of prudence implies the rejection of then current aesthetic (to the extent that aesthetics could be conceptualized apart from ethics), legal, political, and religious codes as well. There-fore Battestin's qualification of prudence—"together with charity and good-nature"—overlooks the difficulties that writers on prudence faced in trying to keep all these things all together. "Prudence with charity and good nature" was, given the context Glenn Hatfield has described, as sound a formulation, or at least as likely a one, as "prudence and not-prudence" (20, 30–32). This was not simply because prudence could be employed as a tool or device to bring about immoral ends. It was because the notion of a tool or device being used to bring about any ends reflected belief in the world as a self-contained system or economy of objects that could be subjected to the manipulation of an individual and that was therefore beyond the pale of even so foundational a prohibition as that concerning the human consumption of other human beings. Whatever Fielding wanted it to mean, prudence referenced not only secular but profane space (and was damned for doing so), while adherents to this profane virtue were therefore no longer encumbered by an ethic of un-certainty whose authority consisted ultimately in the rectifying force of God. The debate over prudence was not, therefore, so easily resolved by assertions of an analogy between it and providence, since material forces were producing the sense that the one had no need of the other. Fielding knew these argu-ments, and he understood them, incorporated them, and, as he was wont to do, imagined his engagement with them as meaningful on more than purely metaphysical grounds.

Some have suggested that in *Tom Jones* Fielding was aiming not for the kind of metaphysical reconciliation suggested by Battestin but for the more attainable reality of happiness, which might require the sort of prudence Field-ing ultimately confers upon his hero. Though he ultimately stresses Fielding's relentlessly ironical perspective on the world, Nicholas Hudson writes that

> *Tom Jones* portrays a world in which happiness depends far more on obedience to external rules, a respect for appearance, and the appropri-ate "dress" of social decorum, than on our desire to do good to others. It is precisely this consideration that withholds Tom from the sexual seduction of Sophia that he is repeatedly given the opportunity to undertake. Similarly, while engaging in drunken fisticuffs with his tutor, or revealing his love for a gentleman's daughter to an itinerant barber, does not undermine our sense of Tom's basic decency, these and other largely unreflective misdemeanors contravene a code of genteel conduct that the novel finally affirms to be necessary to social rehabilitation. (89)

Hudson repeats the point concerning Sophia a few lines later—"Tom does respect these limits [of "respectable or 'wise' behavior"] in certain cases, particularly that of Sophia, and he becomes a legitimate member of the novel's ruling class only by virtue of his deepened respect for the world's judgements" (89)—so it is worth considering this particular choice made by Tom. In refraining from seducing or molesting Sophia, he certainly does conform to the dominant codes of moral conduct, in which seducing innocent young women is considered vicious. And his "unreflective misdemeanors" do "contravene a code of genteel conduct." This qualification notwithstanding, Tom's conformity with or contravention of code seems to have little to do with his actions. Tom may conform to the code in refusing to seduce Sophia, but Hudson surely does not mean that the novel suggests that it is Tom's desire to remain in conformity to code that "withholds" him at such moments. Obviously, were the narrator to state that Tom's reason for letting Sophia alone is his desire to adhere to a code of sexual conduct—rather than, say, his love and respect for her desires—not only would Tom come off as positively monstrous for cloaking his desire to ruin a woman under the veil of social conventionalism but he would appear, as Blifil often does, impotent to the extent that his primary virility could be checked by evanescent rules of propriety. It is important to distinguish, that is, between the "code-ness" of the code and the code itself. Mrs. Western appreciates the code-ness of codes, because it enhances, at least in her mind, her public reputation. Tom, on the other hand, merely finds himself sometimes in step with the code. On such occasions, however, the basis of readerly interest in Tom is not this accidental syncopation. Even if Fielding's novel may be read as every bit as orderly and structured as a code, Fielding himself would have us approach his text as a "History" rather than as a "System" (*Tom Jones* 573).

The larger and more complicated question Hudson raises, that concerning Tom's gentility, might be answered in much the same way. Hudson writes that Tom must end up following a "code of genteel conduct that the novel finally affirms to be necessary to social rehabilitation." Again, though, a "code of genteel conduct" seems to me not at all necessary for Tom's "social rehabilitation." Tom has always been socially able, even, and perhaps especially, when most overtly defying society's "codes." His sociability is established early and often, in his ability to make friends across the social spectrum—from Squire Allworthy to Squire Western to the treacherous Black George and the party of soldiers he meets shortly after leaving Allworthy's estate. His estrangement from one impudent member among the soldiers, Northerton, in no way affects others' fondness for him; on the contrary, the other soldiers rally to

Tom's defense. If Tom does receive abuse for failing to behave in a "gentle" manner, a reader of the novel inclined to sympathize with Fielding's project is more likely to accuse the abusers than to accuse Tom, for the reader knows that there are often good reasons why Tom contravenes the code (as in the case of his drunkenness after Allworthy's unexpected recovery from illness). In other words, Tom needs no rehabilitation in the eyes of the sympathetic reader; if anything, Tom is necessary for the rehabilitation of society! For by the same logic that makes Tom sociable, each society is materially improved by his presence within it, directly or indirectly, as bon vivant, tenderhearted listener, moral counselor, or exposer and purgative of society's hidden crimes and vices.[26] This includes the gentility as well, which until Tom's ascendancy to it does not have a single unequivocally healthy or virtuous member. Comprising, with the possible exception of Allworthy, either upstart pretenders to it or the dessicated remains of the ancien régime, the gentility in Fielding's novel requires Tom's salubrious ethical presence.

In order to establish Tom as ethical, for the better part of the novel Fielding fixes his sights on the dangers of prudence and offers Tom as an alternative. Rather well trodden critical territory, the opposition of a dangerous, calculative prudence and what is frequently called Tom's "impulsiveness" has come to define, in one manner or another, many readings of Fielding's characterizations.[27] William Empson was unequivocal on the matter: "Tom is a hero because he is born with good impulses" (40). It may come as something of a surprise to learn, however, that neither the word *impulsiveness* nor *impulsive* appears anywhere in Fielding's novel. The word *impulse* appears precious few times. Once, it is in the narrator's insistence that Sophia was *not* emotionally moved by the "supernatural Impulse" that is "Cupid" (321); another time, when the narrator derides judgments of the heart, which he claims, as typically being the result of an "inward Impulse," are therefore usually wrong (542); once, perhaps surprisingly, the term is used in reference to the perfidious lawyer, Dowling (582); another time, when the narrator does seem to praise, although still somewhat ironically, the "honest Impulses of Nature" that justify the occasional lie (646); and finally, when the narrator describes, by way of a metaphor of a shocked man surprised at his trial, how a "violent Impulse on the Blood" contorts Blifil's face after he is asked about Dowling's complicity in Tom's imprisonment (828). (*Pulse* appears exclusively in the context of doctors and phlebotomy.) The "impulsiveness" of Tom is not typically given much thought, the word used more as shorthand than anything else, but it is, strictly speaking, wrong. So what do we mean when we say that Tom is impulsive? And how does describing him as impulsive affect our understanding of Fielding's ethics? For it is in this impulsiveness that much of Tom's goodness is presumed to consist, and it is against it that the diabolical prudence of Blifil is positioned.

It seems to me that by *impulsive* readers tend to mean that Tom does not think, more specifically that he does not think things through, that his actions are directly connected to his nature, or, put another way, that his nature is connected to his actions without the mediating interference of calculative reasoning or prudence, that he is a corpuscle rather than a complex human organism. In narrative terms, this means rendering character and action without an intervening exposition of thought. This being said, however, none would suggest that Tom is unintelligent, dense, stupid, dull, vulgar, or even simple. At times Tom demonstrates an unusual capacity for understanding and the calculation of consequences. Consider, for example, the scene in which Jones revolves in his own mind the possible consequences of abandoning Molly and debauching or eloping with Sophia. He considers the wrath of Western, the scorn of Allworthy, and the body—and soul—of an abandoned Molly left as prey for her envious sisters and subject to the tyranny of her neighbors: "How ready they would all be to tear her to Pieces" (197). Tom considers Molly not only in terms of the pain and suffering that he might be made to feel but also in terms of how she would feel if placed under such pressure. Fielding does hint that Tom may be thinking of Molly's body in a more earthly way, but this only goes to show that Tom is not a theologian, constitutionally predisposed to suppress the reality of embodiment, and that his sexual appetites inform his reasoning to the extent that he is an embodied being. What this does not mean is that his reasoning is the product or superficial expression of his appetites. The narrator explicitly distinguishes the two, and it is only a wish to see impulse that might lead a reader to conclude that Tom's moral thought reduces to sexual desire in this instance at least. This all being said, while there is nothing at all impulsive in Tom's reasoning, he arrives at a conclusion—to stay beside Molly—that is good to the same degree that his "unthinking" acts of charity and "impulsive" acts of self-sacrifice are good. One might say that in this passage Fielding sets up a "thinking" Tom so that Tom's other unreasoning moments bear trace remainders of the forms of ethical thought represented in moments such as this one regarding Molly. That Tom is ultimately wrong in trusting Molly's fidelity is quite beside the point; based on what he does know, he is right.

If Fielding does give us a moral, thinking Tom, whence, then, does the ascription of impulsiveness come? One factor is Fielding's efforts, in his characterization of Tom, to collapse the time between input and output, to shrink the time between Tom's initial perception of circumstances requiring his attention and his reaction to those circumstances. I have emphasized some key terms with italics: hearing Sophia's name raised in public by a boy, he *"started from his chair"* and *"immediately"* retires to another room with him (573); discovering that he might catch up to Sophia, Tom does not patiently mount, but *"directly leapt* into the side saddle" (575); arriving at an inn, still in pursuit of Sophia, he *"immediately* [bespeaks] post horses" (576). The immediacy that marks Tom's decisions here, taken from one randomly chosen chapter, runs throughout the novel. In the scene that introduces us to the Man of the Hill, the narrator piles immediate reactions on top of one another: "Jones ... *snatching* an old Broad-sword which hung in the Room, he *instantly sallied out.* ... Jones *asked no questions,* but fell *so briskly* to work with his Broadsword, that the Fellows *immediately* quitted their hold; and without offering to attack our Heroe, betook themselves to their Heels" (392, my emphasis). Similarly, in the scene involving the puppeteer and the Merry Andrew, in which the former attacks the latter, Jones *"instantly* interposed on Behalf of the Suffering Party" (571, my emphasis). And a bit later, when Jones rescues Nightingale from the belligerent footman in the house of Mrs. Miller, we learn that after hearing the commotion below, *"Jones,* who was never backward on any Occasion to help the distressed, *immediately* ran down Stairs" and after an equally brief and equally decisive scuffle triumphs over Nightingale's irascible servant (616, my emphasis). At nearly every opportunity, Fielding works to collapse the time between input and output; the effect of Fielding's almost complete excision of any suggestion of mental processing or calculation is read as his investment in a moral impulse.

And it is not just calculation that Fielding shies away from in his depiction of Tom. For if he wishes to bury any sense of calculation in the interest of demonstrating Tom's unmediated connection to justice, there are points at which Fielding would have his hero just as blind as the legendary figure of Justice. If *prudence* on the one hand refers to calculative reasoning, it is also inextricably bound up with vision (*pro-videre,* lit. "to see ahead," or "foresight"). Tom's charitable acts, for instance, are spurred an unusual number of times by nonvisual cues: "a most violent noise" causes Tom to rescue the Merry Andrew (571); Tom "heard at a Distance the most violent Screams of a Woman" (433); "more than one Voice was heard" threatening the Man of the Hill, prompting Tom to dash out to rescue him (392). Tom hears from a serving woman her verbal report of the abuses being inflicted on the Man of the Hill, and it is Mrs. Miller who informs Tom, at two removes from the actual spectacle of desolation, of the woes Nightingale has brought upon Nancy. Whereas aural and verbal information is to an extent directional, it does not assume the definite shape of visual phenomena, and thus Tom's reactions in these cases appear less motivated than they would be were Tom given the opportunity to visually process the scene of violence or suffering. By eliminating the visual experience, Fielding makes Tom seem one with the set of circumstances that call upon him.

The blindness of Tom Jones is manifested in two other ways. First, regarding Sophia's physical beauty, Jones remarks to Nightingale "that though she is never from my thoughts, I scarce ever think of her beauty, but when I see it" (678). Jones's gradual progression toward her must be figured in nonvisual terms; should he see her, he will delight in her beauty—as he memorably does with the aid of a mirror in the meeting prior to their marriage (866)—but the lack of a visual imagination prevents his quest from being tainted by the comparative, objectifying, and calculative judgments that sight enables. That Tom's ultimate testament of his affections for Sophia is his presentation of a mirror rather than an encomium to her physical beauty (which amounts to the same thing insofar as it is her beauty that is re-presented to her) further shows Tom's simultaneous ability to see and inability to avow the act of seeing.[28] At a different level of analysis, Fielding makes the broader insinuation that Tom does not see where he is going, specifically that he does not look in the direction he needs to be going. After rescuing the Man of the Hill, Tom and he ascend the fictitious "Mazard Hill"—one that Wilbur Cross located in the Malvern Hills (182–83)—to survey the landscape. Tom looks to the south (Gloucester, where Sophia is), and then he moves to "that Part of the Hill which looks to the North-West" (433), but not, it seems, to the east, where his future, Upton and London, in fact is (433). He sees the landscape behind him, but just when he begins to turn his gaze in a direction that he might go—and indeed does go—in the future, Tom is interrupted by the screams of Mrs. Waters, which precipitate another round of temporal compressions and elisions of thought and deliberation: Tom "listened a *Moment*, and then, *without saying a Word* to his Companion (for indeed the Occasion seemed sufficiently pressing) *ran, or rather slid*, down the Hill, and *without the least Apprehension or Concern* for his own Safety, made *directly* to the Thicket whence the Sound had issued" (433, my emphasis). Denying us the chance to see Tom behold his future course, Fielding plunges his hero back into the brush and down the hill, where he defeats Northerton and thus begins a new phase of his adventure.

In Fielding's compression of time, in the intimation that Tom is activated not by visual but by aural and secondhand verbal cues, and in the generally uneasy stance Tom takes toward the future, it is easy to see why readers have elected to describe Tom as impulsive: his actions seem unmotivated, untainted by a calculative reasoning that the ironic voice of the narrator often associates with prudence. Prudence thus comes to seem a relatively tainted virtue insofar as it works against the unthinking, unseeing instinct or impulse that directs Tom in his many virtuous performances. So, if we accept that this distinction or binary structures the novel, readers are presented with two versions of Tom: the thinking Tom, who ponders the rightness of his choices, and the unthinking Tom, who acts immediately, or more specifically, without the medium of prudence. Ascribing to Tom impulsiveness seems to me an insightful but ultimately flawed attempt to describe what connects Tom's character to Tom's ethical acts, which Fielding constantly overwrites with words like *instantly* and *immediately*. It is insightful because it captures Fielding's collapsing of time at moments of decision and because it speaks to the motif of blindness that Fielding enlists to render Tom's character at both micro and macro levels. It is flawed, however, because Fielding refuses to fully ground ethical action in what Terry Eagleton, in his critique of moral-sense philosophy, called "the stubborn self-evidence of the gut" (38). Fielding provides the reader with not only a moral, thinking Tom at times (times the impulse thesis must overlook) but also, as the aforementioned examples of Fielding's use of the word *impulse* begin to illustrate, a consistently critical perspective on the goodness of impulses. *Impulse*, in other words, gets us close, but it does not get us close enough; and in getting as close as it does, it has made readers somewhat complacent about what Fielding is really up to in mixing forms of moral thought with forms of unthinking moral action. Fielding may have at times believed in the inherent moral goodness of (some) bodies, but there is a way of understanding Fielding's wish to disappear the moment between input and output that takes into account intimations of, if not explicit testaments to, Tom's ability contemplate consequences.

One way to reconcile calculation with ethics, which would help to naturalize the prudential change we encounter in Tom at the end, is to say that Fielding opposed the Machiavellian understanding of prudence and preferred instead the Aquinian understanding of prudence as moral judgment or as the ability to discriminate between good and evil. This would certainly help to account for those too often overlooked moments in which Tom carefully considers the moral implications of his actions, but it does less well in accounting for Tom's ethical behavior when he finds himself without any time to think (the "impulsive" moments), which, it might be added, greatly exceed in number and swamp in overall effect the tiny handful of instances in which Fielding presents his reader with a picture of Tom engaged in thoughtful deliberation. The argument that Fielding was attempting to rescue prudence from the process of its economization by recourse to the Aquinian tradition suffers, in other words, from the opposite problem raised by Tom's impulsiveness. It must bracket or exclude an array of scenes in which Tom is presented as ethical precisely because he does not think. Even if Tom, for example, were to decide that it would be right for him to give Mrs. Miller as much money as she deems fit to help Nancy, and followed through with doing so, would anything be more absurdly out of ethical character than for him to retire to his chamber in order to ponder the implications of doing so on account of his charity's potential encouragement of vice? This is precisely what Allworthy earnestly recommends to Tom with regard to Black George toward the end of the novel. But because Tom's virtue is so closely linked to his inability and unwillingness to think through the consequences of his actions, such moral calculations do not square with Tom's character. Finally, it is worth mentioning that when Fielding seems most inclined to praise prudence unironically, it is consequentialist reasoning, and not moral judgment, that he encourages.

The truth is that by the time we reach the end of the novel, prudence has become as much of a mess as the sometimes prudent, sometimes imprudent Tom Jones. The narrator recommends it as a "Maxim" (128), but Fielding then sends up Mrs. Western for attempting to teach "Maxims of Prudence" to Sophia (287); Fielding has the venerable Allworthy speak on prudence's behalf (217), only to then make it fall from the mouth of Partridge to cover for his cowardice (386); he assigns it to the gentleman farmer who is the father of the Man of the Hill (396), to the villainous Blifil (131, 149), and, elsewhere, to the heroine Sophia via Allworthy (847); Fielding references it in chapter titles, twice, in reference to Captain Blifil, who would have Allworthy die so that he can inherit his estate (63, 96), only to finally leave the reader with a prudent Tom (874). Whatever Fielding may have meant by *prudence*, it is impossible to overlook the tortures to which Fielding subjects the term in the course of his novel. This semantic torture mirrors at the level of theme the dramatic and psychological ups and downs of the novel's principal character, Tom.

One way to make sense of this semantic instability, to untangle this knotty virtue, which aims to stabilize our sense of who Tom is at the end, is to isolate the moments in which Fielding was being satirical about prudence, exclude them, and see what remains of the concept in order to sound the depths of Fielding's real view; or, put otherwise, to say that Fielding encountered a term, *prudence,* which had been corrupted through a series of nonserious or satirical usages, and exaggerated its corruption in order to bring the reader back around to the proper meaning of *prudence*. This strategy, however, faces two problems. First, it divorces the matter of prudence from the substance of the novel. Treating prudence as a theme, as Glenn Hatfield has done, gives us insight into Fielding's attitude toward the meanings of words but tells us little about *Tom Jones* other than that it differs from *Pamela* in its more complex and ambivalent presentation of prudence (Hatfield 31–32), leaving us rather where we started as far as the proper meaning of *prudence* is concerned.[29] More significant as a problem, an attempt to read Fielding's ironies as inverted clues to Fielding's real, underlying meaning of *prudence* discounts the ironies in *Tom Jones* and, by pinning the text's presentation of prudence on something radically exterior to it, forgets that the instability of prudence in *Tom Jones* may itself be meaningful. That Fielding elected to provide his readers a final image of Tom as in some ways against himself—as gaining prudence in spite of, rather than because of, his "lively Parts"—troubles attempts to read Fielding as simply sarcastic, especially since the prudential transformation of Tom happens so late, and so abruptly, as to suggest that Fielding may have been aiming all along to leave his readers with a terminal sense of unease. However Fielding may have accounted for prudence himself, in other words, the text does less to settle prudence than to further unsettle it. And if prudence was already highly unstable when Fielding arrived on the scene, there is absolutely no evidence that his novel had any impact on righting things, as Hatfield himself notes at the end of his article on the subject (32).

The terminal unease of Fielding's novel on the matter of prudence—that virtue central to bourgeois conceptions of self and ethics—has been registered in a final set of critical preoccupations: the attempt to accommodate Fielding's apparent contradictoriness about prudence, among other things, to his "comic perception" of the world, that is, the effort to reconcile the vagaries of the novel's morality by highlighting the inherently comic, contradictory, and bizarre world that he narrates. As Charles Knight writes, "The silence of the talky narrator about ultimate moral judgements, especially moral judgements of attractive characters, shifts the function of the novel away from exemplary moral instruction and towards the comic perception of human complexity and contradiction. Fielding was, of course, deeply concerned about moral behavior, but the comic epic he developed freed the novel both to consider moral issues more openly and to withhold moral judgement. He freed the novel from being the servant of conventional morality" (187). A fair enough point, to be sure, it nevertheless begs the question how Fielding could at once be "deeply concerned about moral behavior" and simply comic about it. I say simply, because Knight resists offering, perhaps in the spirit of the subject about whom he writes, any sense of where to go from there.

While Knight portrays Fielding's comic turn as in some ways intentional, Hudson has read it more as a gesture of resignation: "Humour and irony seemed to Fielding the only responses that possessed the subtlety to bridge the old and new [versions of] an England in the midst of social transition and the upheaval of received values" (92). One might say in response that all writers write in times of transition of some form or another and that many of them relate to such transitions in comical ways—Dickens, for example—but aside from that, it seems to me that Hudson here projects onto Fielding what is ultimately a historiographic narrative of shift in order to account for what he perceives to be an otherwise incoherent ethical stance within the novel. On this reading, according to which Fielding's novel is the articulation or expression of historical forces that are in some measure beyond Fielding's grasp, it is not possible to credit Fielding with the insight Hudson has, which is to say, it is not possible for Fielding to have comprehended for himself and *then made use of* the contradictions that Hudson perceptively intuits to be at work in *Tom Jones*. Hudson's "humour" and Knight's "comic perception" both, I think, capture the fundamental dynamic at work in the novel, but at the cost of underestimating Fielding's radicalism. This is not to say that Fielding did not recognize the power of laughter as an ethical disposition or act, simply that there is a certain danger in leaving it at that.[30] One might say that Fielding's novel may treat the pretenses of poor people as amusing, but it does not treat beggars as comic. Recognizable ethical boundaries surround Fielding's comic perception, limits that neither exuberant nor despairing laughter dares cross.

The great virtue of the "humour and irony" thesis, on the other hand, is that it recognizes the terminal unease with which readers are left when Tom turns prudent, and it situates that mystery, rightly, at the center of readings of the novel. Both Hudson and Knight are therefore correct in their sense that the novel rejects "conventional morality," but just how unconventional is the novel's morality? In *The Modern Husband*, the formulation seems to be something along these lines: the giving of a gift that is not seen as a gift and is therefore truly risked because it has not been recognized as having been given gives the giver an even greater gift in the end. In the closing pages of his essay, Hudson writes that the novel's tension between "spontaneous goodness and prudence" might allow us to "approach conclusions that might satisfy even post-structuralists, with the value they place on paradox and *aporia*" (89). It is not entirely clear whether Hudson means to deride poststructuralism tout court or to demonstrate Fielding's prescient insights into modernity. Whatever the case may be, Hudson rightly estimates the poststructural *potentialities* of *Tom Jones*, potentialities that seem to reach beyond the outwardly providential form of a narrative such as that presented in *The Modern Husband*. Instead of settling on Fielding's resignation to a sad humor, however, it is worth considering the extent to which one of poststructuralism's most valuable ethical categories—the gift—works itself out in *Tom Jones*.

If the new, modern order dictates that gifts be given for reasons of expediency or utility (to receive a return) and the old order gives gifts in accordance with codes (to live up to one's state), these orders nevertheless share an underlying economic attitude toward ethics, and so each has its own prudent adherents. Members of the new order make decisions with an eye to the future improvement or betterment of the self, while members of the older order do so in the hopes of further consolidating and cementing the order that places them in positions of wealth and power. But this is only half the story, for this merely emphasizes the ethical *failures* of the old and the new. The older order also has its real gifts, its noblesse oblige, which, although at times virtuous in the past, was no longer appropriate for the world. As Rawson has shown, Fielding may have been nostalgic, but he was not atavistic. What, then, serves as the story's comparably virtuous modern gift? At a glance, one might say there is no such thing, that in the modern order there is only the diabolical gift, the gift that is given with the full expectation of repayment, Richly's loans, for example, or Blifil's outwardly moral behavior—his gift of liberty to Sophia's bird, for example (*Tom Jones* 145), which conceals a more wicked intention. But this is not right; for these gifts are not really gifts but acts that are in essence no different from other expressions of cunning and calculation. They are loans, and full repayment is expected in such cases, and there is no suggestion of any virtue in them. So where, then, if Fielding was attempting to locate an ethical moment in his modernity, do we look for such a thing?

I argued earlier that in *The Modern Husband* Fielding alerts us to the fact that in order for the gift to reap the giver rewards, the giver must exhibit a certain blindness toward his or her gifts. Tom exhibits this blindness often, and he does, to be sure, reap great rewards. But this is too obviously economic a formulation, and had Fielding continued to write comedy, he might not have pushed things much farther than this. Even so, in Fielding's insistence upon Tom's lack of awareness at the time of his gifts, he continued to express a faith in the basic idea that the gift had to be misrecognized or unrecognized at the time of its being given in order for it to truly attain the status of a freely given gift. Tom gives instantly and immediately. From the vantage point of the reader, this imparts Tom with an extraordinary, even superlative ethical character, the origins of which readers disinclined to read him merely as a nostalgic remnant of the past have been inclined to locate in Tom's body, specifically in his impulses. I think that in providing us as well with a Tom who at other points exhibits a remarkable intellectual adroitness when considering ethical matters, Fielding wishes to resist precisely such readerly surmises and that he understood that Tom must be read not as a subject in the world that corresponded in all respects to his reader, or his ideal reader, but as a composite narrative entity who could (who *should*) only be evaluated from the standpoint of his total narrative representation. Which is why nothing Tom does, thinks, or says can (or, again, *should*) be evaluated until we read Fielding's final words about him, which Fielding reserves for the final sentence of the penultimate paragraph of his novel: "He hath also, by Reflexion on his past Follies, acquired a Discretion and Prudence very uncommon in one of his lively Parts" (874). The impact of these words is not to make Tom less ethical but to undermine the idea that Tom has arrived at his present state of happiness as a result of having been impulsively, transcendently ethical. It tells us less about who Tom will be than what he has been all along: a textual framework capable of accommodating attributes more complex than those envisioned in Christian moral discourse. More simply stated, because Tom can ultimately be reconciled to a potentially devious prudence that excludes ethics, it becomes apparent that Tom's character does not depend upon the providential framework of God for its ethical significance.[31]

As far as communicating to his reader the value of prudence, nothing forces Fielding (or the narrator) to write his final sentence on Tom. It cannot be that Fielding wished to simply praise a noneconomistic, moral form of prudence; he had already done so, at least three times, and without much hint of irony in any of them: when Allworthy provides his judicious words on the necessity of prudence (217) and when the narrator twice encourages its practice (128, 154). Had Fielding, on the other hand, simply wished to reconcile Tom to some truly moral form of prudence, he might have done so mere pages before this, in Allworthy's speech to Tom concerning the forgiving of Black George, which takes place almost as late in the novel. There, Fielding might have naturally introduced Tom to the prudent order; instead, Fielding sends Tom into the next room to dress for the arrival of Sophia: "This was spoke with so stern a Voice, that *Jones* did not think proper to make any Reply: Besides, the Hour appointed by Mr. *Western* now drew so near, that he had barely Time left to dress himself" (863). One might say that the narrator's excusal of Tom ostentatiously denies Fielding's hero the chance to come to rational terms with prudence, whatever the stamp. When has Tom, on the pretense of needing to "dress himself" or anything of the sort, declined discourse with Allworthy? Notwithstanding, that is, Allworthy's and the narrator's unironical praise for prudent conduct in life, Tom is never moved by it, and however much the reader might politely nod to the "Maxim" of prudence recommended by the narrator (128), that same reader has been conditioned to more fervently applaud Tom's acts in defiance of it.

Similarly, the guinea bestowed by Tom upon the beggar bearing Sophia's pocketbook may be in defiance of one of the narrator's definitions of "good" prudence—"not to buy at too dear a Price" (251)—but readers would hardly expect Tom to haggle. When Tom does haggle with the "Serjeant" who offers to sell him a sword for "twenty guineas," he is not haggling so much as righting an ethical balance that had been tilted by the Serjeant himself, who had sought to take advantage of Tom's presumed delirium following his altercation with Northerton (343). Fielding's choice to impart to his hero, at the last possible moment, the virtue of prudence therefore appears to be a *violent* resolution to a conflict—between goodness and prudence—that the story has thus far suggested cannot end. Rawson characterizes it as a "convenient tidying up," which is a less dramatic of way of saying that Tom's prudential conversion is more forced than earned ("Henry Fielding" 141). I think Rawson is right in regarding it as a strategic move on Fielding's part, not because it serves as an expedient "tidying up" but because it messes everything up: it denies Tom that otherworldly goodness that in Christian moral discourse, and comedic plot, would necessarily end in happiness and salvation.

The issue Fielding faces with Tom at the end of the novel is not how to get Tom to be less instinctual and more prudent, for Tom has achieved everything, it would seem, by being nothing but instinctually ethical. The issue is, how does Fielding refuse Tom credit for his ethical actions? Or rather, how does Fielding deny his reader the uncomplicated satisfaction of treating Tom's situation at the end of the novel *as credit* for the gifts that Tom has given? Tom's virtuous deeds have been so much the product of something other than himself, an ethical energy, an impulse, a good heart, an instinctual deference to code—call it what you will—that Fielding's challenge at the end of his novel is not to resolve the tension between ethics and prudence but to intensify that tension and thereby rewrite the "History" of Tom Jones as something other than "System," as something other than an economy of rewards and punishments. Tom lives up to the early prophecy that he was born to be hanged: to save ethics from a mandate the comic plot seems predestined to follow (reward for the good), in the end Fielding is forced to hang Tom Jones, or rather, to hang an unalloyed, ethically pure (and Puritanical) version of Tom Jones (*Tom Jones* 109).

Of what he calls the gift, or the impossible gift, Derrida writes that in order for a gift to be a true gift, "the death of the donor agency" is required. Death is "the fatality that destines a gift *not to return* to the donor agency" (*Given Time* 102). Agency, for Derrida, introduces into the gift relation an element of ethical satisfaction, a sense of having done well, that delivers returns in a "closed circle of exchangist rationality" (47).[32] In the case of *Tom Jones*, a novel written before the discourse of economic rationality had come to dominate individual decision making and to determine standards against which decisions would be judged or measured, before *prudence* meant "economical," we are presented with the same problem, but the terms are reversed: Tom has been "dead" to his gifts all along, a stranger to them, so utterly unaware of the benefits he confers upon the great mass of humanity that he can be said to have, for the majority of the novel, only given gifts by not giving them in a determinate sense of the term. Tom has, like a good Christian, cast his bread on the water, and it "comes back a hundredfold" precisely because he does not "sit by the tide in eager expectation" of returns (Reilly 114). Tom, in other words, has thus far been the ideal subject of early modern anti-finance, embodying the "Christian paradox" of giving and not giving at the same time (Reilly 114).

But the elaboration of that subject, however paradoxical it may appear, itself presents a new kind of problem, namely, the lurking economism hidden within the paradigm of the Protestant ethic of uncertainty. The problem with Tom's gifts is that they are the kinds of gifts, and represent the kind of goodness, that in accordance with the (older) ethics of uncertainty *pay off* in a larger, more ideal economy of providential rewards and punishments. And it is here that Fielding's narrator as a figure for providence therefore poses the greatest problem for ethics: how can the narrator leave Tom with happiness without making it seem as though he is being rewarded for goodness? As I have said, if we approach Fielding with an eye to his resistance to the economic rationalization of the world, rather than to his confirmation of it, it becomes possible to read the imposition of prudential rationality on Tom not as acquiescence to it or as an exasperated narratorial shrug but as a higher-order critique of the tacitly economic rationality of the early modern ethic of uncertainty, a recognition of something sinisterly economic in the providential form that Fielding's comedies assume and that *Tom Jones* is in danger of assuming as well. Thus, Fielding must unwrite Tom's "deadness" to his gifts by imposing prudence upon him in the most spectacular-because-unspectacular manner possible: after nearly a thousand pages of narrative, unfolding the mystery and progress of Tom's almost otherworldly communion with moral goodness, Tom is made prudent in a swift, authoritative, final but intensely ambiguous single sentence.

Fielding thus one-ups that strain of anti-finance that taught that to disregard the future and to leave one's well-being in the hands of a rewarding providence was the highest of ethical aspirations. Rather than delivering ethics in the form of the gift that does not expect a return, as he had in *The Modern Husband*, Fielding leaves his reader with the caution that even that which does not expect a return—which in his time was an *ethical* uncertainty to the extent that it meant handing power to the divine—bore a trace of economism or exchangism. This trace economism becomes particularly evident when manifested in the form of narrative deliverance. Imparting to Tom prudence, Fielding denies us the comfort of knowing that the happy felicity that Tom presently enjoys is intelligible only as God's reward for his earlier gifts. Empson perceived that there may have been a connection between Fielding's novel and Calvin's doctrine that "no action could deserve heaven which was done in order to get to heaven." *Tom Jones* turns this logic back onto itself and raises the question whether Tom's apparent generosity, his "non-egoist" gifts, might, by virtue of Tom's fortunate happiness at the end, be too easily read as conducive to a heavenly state (Empson 39). So the prudence Tom gains is not just a "good" prudence that confirms his imprudent good deeds but a messy admixture of prudential forms that includes economistic prudence, discretion, Allworthy's recommended virtue, Blifil's signal vice, as well as the semi-ironical prudential maxim "not to buy at too dear a Price." It is also "the Principle" that sits "on its Throne in the Mind" (154) to guide moral choices, or perhaps it is "the great, useful, and uncommon Doctrine which it is the Purpose of this whole Work to inculcate" (574). Likely contenders these last two, but Fielding does not use the word *prudence* in either case. That it is not *simply* discretion that Fielding has in mind when he writes the sentence at the end is signaled by the fact that Fielding specifically notes that Tom gains both "Discretion *and Prudence*."

It is the semantic leakiness of *prudence* that therefore plays the vital role in delineating Tom's character and in opening up the possibility that Tom's acts of goodness come not from a space that is uniquely his (his soul, his body, or his impulses) but from a space to which anyone potentially has access. It is not that in sorting through the great pile of meanings Fielding has bestowed upon *prudence* we might discover one that can be comfortably situated within Tom's capacious moral frame; it is that Fielding denies his reader the comfort of knowing precisely which prudence it is that Tom acquires. All we know for sure is that Tom's ethics have been in some way compromised, for better or worse. Having alienated Tom from himself, Fielding denies his readers the comfort of knowing that pure, Christian selflessness is the source of his elevation; and Fielding denies himself the satisfaction of such an end. It cannot be emphasized enough how parallel are Tom's introduction to and exit from the narrative—introduced with his eyes closed, a "sleeping infant" (40), Tom at the end is presented as prudent, possessed of the ability to see (*pro-videre*). To describe this as tidying up is to ignore what Fielding has been preparing us for all along: a perfect inversion of the blessed child who cannot but be good, but whose good must therefore be unmade in order for goodness to remain *in* the world.

What Fielding thus points his reader toward is a move from the ethics of uncertainty, which had been elaborated in primarily Christian terms, to a more solidly earthly form of justice. Tom is no longer the ethical being we took him to be, with every other he encounters indistinguishable from every other other. George Seagrim, the Merry Andrew, Mrs. Waters, Nightingale and Nancy, the highwayman, and even Blifil—presenting a potentially infinite series of opportunities for Tom to be selfless, these figures serve only to show how little Tom is transformed by each, that he will conduct himself in the exact same way each and every time. Now, however, Tom must be responsible to others, and to them as particular others with distinct faces; he must weigh and consider the competing needs of his community and consider himself as bound to and into community. "The responsibility for the other is an immediacy," writes Levinas, but this immediacy is interrupted and problematized "when a third party enters" (157). The introduction of such a party raises the possibility, though not the guarantee, of justice: "comparison, coexistence, contemporaneousness, assembling, order, thematization, the visibility of faces, and thus intentionality and the intellect, and in intentionality and the intellect, the intelligibility of a system, and thence also a copresence on an equal footing as before a court of justice" (157). It is no wonder, then, that Fielding's last words say nothing of Tom as a moral being but rather how he is perceived by friends, relations, neighbors, tenants, and servants (875). The (Christian) ethic of uncertainty had traded risk in exchange for heavenly reward but had had little to do with fathers, mothers, wives, friends, or the earthly community in general. Pushing Tom toward a form of justice whose only determinate content or rule is regard for third parties, Fielding resists an older formula in which gifts were exchanged for salvation and denies his readers the comforting solace of both ethical and narrative elegancies.[33]

Conclusion

John Ruskin and the Ghost of David Jones

O F T H E sin of usury, David Jones bids his auditor/reader to remember that "all those Trifling and Shuffling Distinctions, that Covetous Usures [*sic*] have invented, shall never be able to excuse your Damnation" (29). Over the course of this volume I have discussed the importance of the occlusive distinction-making Jones attacks and suggested that such continuous occlusions of the usurer's true identity—a manipulator or shifter of risk who is bent upon the attainment of certainties—meant that the terms used to resist usury also had to undergo change. I have focused on two figures who mediate the progress of the usurer into the eighteenth century—the projector and the prudent individual—and on occasion I have highlighted these figures' connections to other, related figures, such as the stockjobber (not a seller of stocks but a rumormonger, who trades on the basis of secret price manipulation) and the gambler (not simply a player of cards or dice but a deck-stacking, dice-rigging cheat). All these figures have more in common with the figure of the usurer than with bankers or moneylenders, but they potentially share with bankers and moneylenders—as well as monopolists, engrossers of commodities, certain monarchs and ministers, and others—a common interest in foreclosing the possibility of a truly open and uncertain future. In attempting to show that *usury* meant the calculated avoidance of risk, I have attempted to highlight links between these figures and demonstrate an important continuity between the premodern and modern economic orders.

Over time, interest became acceptable, which at first glance suggests a discontinuity in the history of economics, and to an extent this is certainly the case. But the ethic of uncertainty, which had grounded the original ethical prohibition on contractual delimitations of future possibility, which for some included the contracted money loan, nevertheless remained fully in play even after lending for interest was legally acknowledged. In fact, I have argued that it was the primacy of the ethics of uncertainty that made it possible for individuals to lend money in ethically circumscribed ways (according to "equity") and enabled writers, incidentally, to praise the idea of a bank while worrying that it might become tainted by the "Spirit of Usury" (e.g., Chamillart). This is a complicated story to tell because anti-usury of the early modern period was in some ways set against itself. By promoting risk opportunities, sometimes tacitly but often explicitly, and challenging a system in which a select few achieved great gains by shifting risk onto helpless and ignorant others, anti-usury discourse gave birth to systems of finance and credit that other aspects of anti-usury discourse considered sinful (i.e., interest). In this sense, the financial revolution happened not in spite of anti-usury opinion but because of it.

The myth that the reverse was the case arises from the assumption that anti-usury was a monolith. Quite the contrary, there was the legal prohibition on interest, based largely on Old Testament texts, and the ethical recommendation to lend without expectation of return, based primarily on Luke 6:34–35. I have assigned the term *ethics* or *ethic of uncertainty* to the latter of these two forms of anti-usury, since the early modern period did not always appreciate that these two lines of thought, deriving from two different sources, were distinct and even potentially at odds with each other. In light of recent events, when finance seems so utterly detached from ethical considerations, it may seem somewhat strange to think—though it is more necessary today than ever before—that financial revolution might have arisen from an ethical call in the first place, from that other aspect of anti-usury, from the ethic of uncertainty, from the belief that the only fair system of commerce is one in which outcomes remain radically uncertain, and thus the measure of an economic or commercial act consists not in the potential for profit—the material index of an outcome's success or failure—but in the ethical character of the investment act. It is for this reason that I have been cautious in my use of the phrase *financial revolution* throughout my analysis. Viewed from the standpoint of anti-usury of this second type, the events following the Stop of the Exchequer, such as the founding of the Bank of England and the Million Lottery, may also be understood as an anti-financial revolution, if what we mean when we use the phrase *financial revolution* is the rejection or transcendence of older values regarding lending, for it was more than that.[1] It has been the goal of the preceding chapters to show some of the ways in which the estrangement of finance and ethics took place and to suggest that if the story of usury abruptly ends in the 1690s, it is all the more important for us to scrutinize the literature of the ensuing decades with an eye to its traces and mediations.

The shifting terrain of financial experience—what has been called *financial revolution*—was not itself solely to blame for the mediations of the ethic of uncertainty in the eighteenth century, in other words. More directly responsible was the medievalizing of the discourse of usury itself, effected principally, though not exclusively, in writings by founding figures in the growing discipline of political economy. Many of these figures sought to make the history of usury into the history of attitudes toward interest and to discredit all objections to emergent financial forms and economic practices by making them seem a reflection more of a medieval than of a modern frame of mind. Because political economists such as Dugald Stewart and Jeremy Bentham, for instance, understood and represented usury exclusively in terms of Deuteronomic law and the Aristotelian hypothesis (interest, money making money), both they and their readers lost sight of the unbroken albeit distorted progress of the ethics of uncertainty into their own century. The representations of usury by political economists like Stewart and Bentham were not without a reasonable foundation; these writers were not merely pawns instructed to pervert historical reality. They based their characterizations of usury upon earlier interpretations of usury as interest, forgetting only that usury also meant that certainties, when attained in commerce, were constitutively illegitimate.

The truth is that while the political economists *exploited* the narrow meaning of *usury* to discredit stances against finance altogether (throwing the baby out with the bathwater, as it were), this narrow meaning had long been accepted as an important meaning, if not always the fundamental one (for Luther, interest was subordinate to certainties, which was why he, for instance, regarded monopolies and extortion as forms of usury). Casually, confusedly, and sloppily employing *usury* as a term merely signifying "interest," political economists like Stewart and Bentham—and later, Mill, Lecky, and countless other historians, economists, and economic historians—tactically, if not maliciously, rerouted this signification to imply that there was *no* solid ethical basis for a critique of emergent financial capitalism, thus further disembedding economic life from a more complete spiritual and ethical framework. Of equal importance in the mutations of the ethics of uncertainty were writers who positioned themselves against financial innovation, who were unable or unwilling to perceive the deeper connections between their criticisms of projects, prudence, stockjobbing, cheating, and so on, and older ethical criticisms of usury. These writers elaborated a series of new figures and saw themselves as formulating new strategies for resistance that appeared to them as suited to unique and heretofore unseen events, identities, and practices, rather than as part of the longer tradition sketched in chapter 2.

The fate of the ethics of uncertainty thus resembles that of David Jones, whom we might be tempted hold up as the last earnest, public opponent of usury were it not for the fact that Jones's intolerant and extravagant damnation of his parishioners was partly the reason why the critique of usury per se came to seem so alien to modern observers. As he became a byword for futility, so did his doctrine itself come to seem increasingly futile, a living body of ethics tragically drowned by the sinking body of Jones, to which it had been too tightly bound. Hence, Jones's demise was not symptomatic of an ineluctable historical tide (i.e., financial revolution); Jones's demise and the concomitant discrediting of anti-usury opinion helped to provide the narrative of financial revolution with one of its critical points of origin: the death of moral concerns about usury. After Jones, and partly because of Jones's tactics, the voicing of moral concerns about finance would be increasingly regarded as instances of raving. But when we sift through the literature and extract from early modern anti-usury literature its vital principles concerning risk and then track those principles into the eighteenth century, it becomes evident that the major change with regard to usury between 1500 (roughly) and 1750 (to mark the endpoint of this study) was the terms employed to describe it.

This is not to discount the importance of those terminological changes, however, but rather to emphasize the impact of terminological change on our sense of the cultural forces that drive our understanding of economic history. One of the most important implications of the terminological shift away from the discourse on usury toward more localized and historically immediate critiques of projects or prudence or stockjobbing was the loss of a robust spiritual framework in which to interpret economic experience. Within the context of the ethics of uncertainty, understood specifically as the Christian ethical prescription to remain uncertain with respect to future returns, it was impossible to conceive of economic space or experience as meaningfully distinct from other spaces and experiences, since an underlying providential layer supported it all. Jeake's casual movement from lotteries to broken legs to dead fathers illustrates his sense of this layer. Because the discourse of usury was fundamentally a Judeo-Christian discourse, elaborated by preachers, bishops, and other ecclesiastical personages, once usury was considered no longer relevant to commercial affairs—by those who, in associating it strictly with interest on loans, rendered it unsuitable for a world of banks and credit—it became increasingly difficult to ethically ground objections to finance. Those that did so openly were pegged as superstitious and religious in a bad way, whether their focus was on interest or certainties.

For example, in the criticism of projects as being godless we see how the earlier ethic of uncertainty continued to inform opinion; but *the ethic of uncertainty* has merely been an abstraction and a trope that enables us to see certain structural similarities between arguments about projects and earlier arguments about usury and risk. The important point, therefore, is that eighteenth-century writers and thinkers were bereft of such a term or phrase. Since they lacked an awareness of the ties between their misgivings about projects (or prudence), on the one hand, and earlier Christian writing on usury (in its broad sense), on the other, eighteenth-century writers' perspectives could have only so much impact, appearing more as local, tactical responses to cultural events than as expressions of an established and authoritative ethical tradition. In other words, without the ethical support provided by the Bible and its exegesis, it was difficult to find a legitimate basis for the rejection of new financial formations. (De Britain's casual admission of cannibalism into the sphere of prudent conduct is merely one indication of this difficulty; the atrocities committed today by people and corporations on the basis of finance's having nothing to do with ethics are the sad legacy of this difficulty.) As soon as the faith-based rejection of finance became branded as irrational dogmatism in the face of the practical necessities of financial modernity, *usury* could no longer legitimate any ethical critique of finance, leaving opponents of the turning tide, religious or not, without a basis for resistance and with no language to articulate that resistance.

Put simply, if finance could not be critiqued from the standpoint of divine law and justice, from whence could it be critiqued? Defoe sensed that the projectors of his age, having lost their sense of God, had begun to cheat and trick their contemporaries into sponsoring projects that could never be completed. In *Robinson Crusoe* he illustrated that a life of true risking really meant refusing any arrangement in which one's bread was assured or made certain (first by his father, later by slaves). But in Defoe such risks were undertaken in the complete knowledge of a rewarding providence. Fielding, I have suggested, may have been seeking ways to ground the ethic of uncertainty in this world, to envision a way of thinking about ethical action without the stabilizing presence of God. He structured his early work *The Modern Husband* like a lottery and in doing so expressed his commitment to an economy of punishments and rewards. Pushing that economy to the side, in *Tom Jones* he imposes that evolving, often diabolical "virtue" of prudence on a hero whose goodness otherwise seems both otherworldly and singular, thereby raising the possibility of being both worldly (prudent) and good (ethical). How successful he was in doing so in *Tom Jones* is unclear. The novel was as often accused of being impious as it was considered an ethically refreshing step away from Richardson's providentially rewarded virtue. What is more interesting about *Tom Jones* than its indebtedness to providentialism is that it demonstrates how compelling an ethic of uncertainty can be even when the presence of an organizing and underlying deity cannot be confirmed.

Risk served to express one's willingness to subordinate economic outcomes to realms of pure uncertainty, realms beyond calculation and management, in which individual agency was sacrificed as part of a commitment to something higher than the human. To call this a religious view is to repeat the error, however, for the splitting of the religious and the economic was not comprehensible for writers such as David Jones, Samuel Jeake, or Daniel Defoe. Lady Credit gave incipient rhetorical form to a realm of paper value, yes, but she also reproduced in key ways the image of the economy as it had been elaborated by religious writers such as Malynes, the beautiful but unstable system that could not but reflect the ethics of the people that made up that system.

By the end of the eighteenth century, a once vibrant anti-usury ethical discourse had fully lost its force and coherency, not because the core values that discourse espoused were abandoned but because those values were increasingly expressed in realms far afield from the comparatively narrow realms of money and banking. And when that discourse was turned back toward those narrower realms, it was seen as evoking an outmoded worldview, a medieval worldview, an irrational worldview, a religious worldview, further enabling English men and women to think through economic problems independent of the restrictive and constraining traditional parameters that had formerly been in place. The discipline of political economy, whenever it may have been invented, created and promoted a myth of an autonomous domain of economic experience in the lives of the subjects the discipline called into being to study. Scholars in the field would discover that subjects' "true" nature was to be selfish, which in turn meant that economic decisions would always have to be primary for those subjects, while forms of experience or belief that challenged the prioritization of the economic were to be regarded as both unnatural and irrational.

But if the political economists were responsible for sinking the critique of usury along with its pundit David Jones, neither disappeared altogether. I would like to turn my attention here, in closing, to one later testimonial concerning usury, risk, and the ethics of uncertainty as a way of illuminating the dangers of allowing political economy's version of events to dictate the course taken by opponents of economic injustice. Directing his intellectual energies toward the political economies of David Ricardo (1772–1823) and John Stuart Mill, the Victorian cultural sage John Ruskin found a reason to restore David Jones to life in the "Notes and Correspondences" to letter 53 (March 1875) of his monumental series *Fors Clavigera: Letters to the Workmen and Labourers of Great Britain* (published between 1871 and 1884). To highlight the significance of Ruskin's invocation of David Jones's name, it is necessary to explain the circumstances surrounding it. Ruskin's letters, begun in the early 1870s and continuing into and far beyond the short-lived but tremendously influential Paris Commune, offer a bewildering array of observations, recommendations, and satires concerning the moral, aesthetic, political, religious, and economic affairs of modernity. To many of his letters he attached additional commentaries, received correspondence, further reflections on the topic of the main letter, and assorted other paratextual material. In the body of letter 53, Ruskin attacks the inability of modern capitalists to conform to the laws of God. They had abandoned their spiritual commitments and thus their ethical obligations to other people, Ruskin proclaimed, and replaced the godhead with wealth: "Behold, *this* is your God, you modern Israel, which has brought you up out of the land of Egypt in which your fathers toiled for bread with their not abortive hands; and set your feet in the large room, of Usury, and in the broad road to Death!" (*Fors Clavigera* 321). Much as Jones had imagined himself as battling the implacable usurers of his parish, Ruskin goes on to assert that "Mammon" insinuates himself into the ears of the once innocent and makes it so that they "become literally deaf to the teaching of true and noble men" (321).

In the "Notes and Correspondences" appended to this letter, Ruskin offers his reader, first, a brief missive from an unnamed correspondent who exhibits, in Ruskin's view, a modern, economistic way of thinking that Ruskin wishes to challenge. Arguing that lending money for interest is acceptable, and apparently unaware of the tradition of anti-usury writing, the missive's author challenges Ruskin: "You ought to ask your bishop, or the whole bench of them, to find a place, in their cart-loads of sermons, for one on 'usury,' as condemned by the Psalmist and enjoined by Christ" (337). Eagerly accepting the challenge, Ruskin comments, "When the Christian Church was living, there was no lack of [sermons against usury]" (340), and then makes good on his claim

by providing excerpts of anti-usury sermons from both Bishop John Jewel
and David Jones.

Ruskin provides the following heading for his excerpt from Jones's sermon: "Extract from the Farewell Sermon preached in the Church of St. Mary
Woolnoth, Lombard Street, by the Rev. David Jones, *when the present system was in its infancy*" (341, my emphasis). Those last words, the ones I have
italicized, put a fine point on much of what I have been arguing. In the first
place, by the closing decades of the nineteenth century Ruskin's treatment
of Jones required a frame of mind so evangelical and a course of reading so
vast in scope that David Jones, at best a byword for futility and at worst a
joke about a madman, could not be regarded with anything more than contempt. (Pitt's poem was still being reprinted in Ruskin's time in anthologies by
Charles Dickens's acquaintance Henry Morley and by the popular Anglican
preacher J. C. M. Bellew.)[2] But even with the benefit of such reading and mental habits, the power of Whiggish stories of the 1690s—stories of banking's
triumph that, I have suggested, were important to the rise of political economy itself—had taken hold of even someone so defiantly opposed to political
economy's version of events as Ruskin, who was otherwise known for seeing
through the ideological fictions of capitalism. But in his claim that the "system
was in its infancy" in the 1690s, Ruskin reveals how much even he had been
influenced by Whig historiography concerning the 1690s, a historiography
that taught that anti-usury meant nothing more than being against interest
on loans. That Ruskin makes this error is all the more surprising given his
intimate familiarity with the wide range of anti-usury arguments that had
been presented in Blaxton's *English Usurer*, a text Ruskin once extravagantly
described as being worth more than "its weight in gold."[3] More importantly, in
electing to excerpt only those passages in which Jewel and Jones discuss lending money for interest specifically, Ruskin shows himself to have been blind to
usury's other meanings, so much so that even while he would go on to situate
his critique of economistic understandings of the human at the center of his
more systematic and equally trenchant critique of political economy, *Unto This
Last* (1860), he appears not to have appreciated the ethic of uncertainty as it
pertained to usury.[4] Thus, Ruskin is forced—how much he resisted is another
question—to characterize his very own views as out of joint with time and to
thus come off as once again merely raving at usurers in Lombard Street.

Even though Ruskin saw the economistic understanding of reality as an
ethical scandal and at times could frame the problem of political economy
in ethical terms, when it came to the history of usury, he drew upon early
modern critique only for its Deuteronomic, legal claims regarding interest on

loans. His insistence upon law rather than ethics pushes him ever closer to a position of extreme religiosity suffused with intolerance: letter 53 begins with a paean to the glories of living under God's laws and swiftly becomes rabid with damnation, fire, the devil, and all manner of threats. Although every-thing Ruskin has to say regarding lending and political economy as a science gestures toward a possible recognition of the ethic of uncertainty as it was developed in anti-usury literature and elaborated in later writings on proj-ects, credit, stockjobbing, cheating, and prudence, he could only conceptualize his relation to the pre-financial-revolution moment of the sixteenth and early seventeenth centuries in terms of a shared, antiquated, and obsolete hostility to interest on loans and interest. Ruskin, in other words, had fallen prey to political economy's version of events—the medievalizing of usury critique— which compelled him to perversely and masochistically align himself, not with a living tradition of anti-finance, but with a dead, premodern past, with a time when "the Christian Church was living."[5] Ruskin purports to be a living reminder of such times, but the violence and terror he inflicts on his audience show him instead to be dead alive, cut off from his historical present and thus unable to speak legibly to the problems of finance and economics that works such as *Fors Clavigera*, *Unto This Last*, and *Munera Pulveris* demonstrate were central to him, especially in the latter half of his writing career.

    In attempting to reanimate the dessicated remnants of Old Testament legal prohibitions on lending to respond to the challenges of his time, Ruskin sealed his own fate: "The impractical nature of some of Mr. Ruskin's teach-ings, especially in Political Economy, his startling assertions and vigorous protests against received opinions, and his apparently eccentric criticism have, in times past, been often the cause of regret to his friends and . . . have even provoked ridicule and supercilious banter" (Kaufmann 21). Even men of the cloth considered his views impracticable (Kaufmann 25). Before the end of the century, Ruskin's views on political economy would appear to some as nothing more than "the ravings of a lunatic," notwithstanding the fact that his "ethical theory of Political Economy" was regarded as being both incisive and sound (Kaufmann 25, 26). Writing about a series of exchanges with the bishop of Manchester on the legitimacy of usury, a writer for the *Saturday Re-view* in 1880 described Ruskin's discussion of "Mosaic law" as inaccurate and characterized his argument against the bishop as "very discursive, occasionally apocalyptic, and not unfrequently rude" ("What Is Usury?" 179). As a result, the *Review* contributor added, if a reader of this debate were personally im-plicated in some kind of usurious arrangement, Ruskin's argument "will not" confirm or remove "his doubts" about the legality of such arrangements (179).

In short, Ruskin "lost his opportunity," because while the bishop was busy "arguing from the point of view of the state of England, Mr. Ruskin [argued] from the point of view of the state of Utopia" (179).[6]

This view was widely held. Ruskin's "sweeping moral judgments," wrote the clergyman George Bigg, failed to appreciate changing historical circumstances: few believed that "every old lady who lives harmlessly on her railway dividends ought to be excommunicated, or with the general principle implied in this opinion, that every prohibition in the Old Testament is still as valid as ever under social circumstances altogether different" (135). However substantial Ruskin's impact on social and economic policy may have been in the long run, it is impossible to ignore the fact that in electing to align himself with the figure of Jones in Pitt's poem (a raving preacher) rather than with that of Jones himself, who took aim at the changes he perceived happening in his historical moment, Ruskin perpetuates the idea that the only position one might take against finance is an extreme one that is always already out of date, impractical, or utopian. "There is a time for fierce language," adds Bigg, "but it does not often come" (136).

Recent financial crises at the individual, family, community, state, and global levels once again raise questions regarding the ethics of finance, while the shape assumed by those seeking answers is only the most recent manifestation of a centuries-old doctrine concerning usury. Presenting themselves as the 99 percent against the 1 percent, Occupy Wall Street protestors—and the various movements that they spawned around the world—rearticulate for a new moment the ethic of uncertainty, the view that risk must be borne equally by all in order for commerce to pretend to any degree of legitimacy. But it might be said that those who attempt to seriously ask or answer questions about ethics and finance, or the ethics of finance, once again find themselves far too frequently marginalized, branded as raving lunatics, in ways that Ruskin's eventual disaccreditation, and Jones's before him, would seem to have anticipated and thus might have served as warning. The connection might have been easily drawn, for Jones, like the Occupy Wall Street protesters, also defined himself and was defined by others in terms of the urban geography of finance. For, as much as Occupy's moment is new, it is also vitally bound to, and thus might draw sustenance from, not Luke 6:34–35—which is merely an accidental manifestation of the ethic of uncertainty—but what is best understood as an ethical tradition that spans the premodern and the modern, the religious and the secular, a tradition that was only arguably interrupted in the decades of financial revolution.

To recognize Occupy's place in this tradition, or to speak to future articulations of this tradition, it is worth noting in closing that the ethic I have aimed to describe is complicated in the way that a fallen tree is complicated. Trees do not die in the way that animals do; parts of them continue living, and new trees may grow even from matter that is itself in a state of dying or in a condition of death. The dying tree becomes ground for—and thus newly grounds—new ethics and new forms of resistance. At points throughout this book I have looked to the theory of the gift—announced by Derrida and others as a challenge to economistic models and assumptions—to help illuminate what it might have been like to experience the financial before financial experience was understood as such.[7] The gift, it seems to me, is a new tree growing on old grounds and is thus in many respects less theoretical than it is political, a concrete idea appropriate for a specific set of late-twentieth- and early-twenty-first-century concerns about the ethics of finance. My purpose in turning to the gift has not been to wantonly or recklessly theorize the cultural history of the eighteenth century, or to imagine that the eighteenth century might be submitted to present forms of knowledge or ways of knowing, but to narrate a history in which the gift is not so much that story's end but a leitmotif and permanent potential energy within history.

Notes

Introduction

1. I use *early modern* to refer to the period between the Reformation and the onset of the financial revolution, which is typically located in the mid- to late seventeenth or early eighteenth century. I will be arguing that the distinction between the early modern and the modern when it comes to attitudes toward finance is problematic, in any case. I rely on Kerridge's account of the distinction between interest and usury, which is distributed throughout the first three chapters of his *Usury, Interest, and the Reformation*.

2. Norman Jones's more thorough discussion of usury dates the demise of serious concerns about usury to the early seventeenth century. See *God and the Moneylenders* 34–40. Cunningham provides an even earlier date for the obviation of public concerns about moneylending: "It appears that by this time [ca. 1600] the revolution in public opinion was complete, and that the practice of lending money for moderate interest was at length regarded as entirely reputable" (59).

For a recent version of this argument, see Persky 229–30. For Persky, as for Norman Jones, the moral issue of usury declines in importance and is gradually replaced by concerns with the proper or best rate cap/allowance. In these versions of the story of the legitimation of usury, John Locke's disregard for the usury prohibition serves as the critical piece of evidence. Exemplifying this mode of thinking, Persky writes that "by the late eighteenth century, virtually all economic commentators in Britain and many on the continent asserted the usefulness and accepted the legitimacy of interest payments in commerce and finance" (230). The story of anti-usury's decline gets reproduced widely in popular histories of business and economics, which is how this story is transmitted to the masses. See, e.g., Means 40–43.

Valeri suggests that the market increasingly seemed to incarnate a providential order, though he reads this as a departure from early modern anti-usury ethics. See esp. "William Petty" 578–79; and *Heavenly Merchandize* 58–59.

3. Nelson's focus is on the Deuteronomic prohibition of lending, not New Testament–based ethical objections to finance, even though early modern anti-usury sentiment is frequently articulated in terms of the latter of these two.

4. For the limits of Marxist analysis with respect to anti-capitalist discourse of the early modern period, see Hawkes 15–16. Although the gift does not feature in Hawkes's

analysis of idolatry, I am sympathetic to his efforts to read economies before theories of the economy were available and conscious of the challenges one faces in attempting to do so. Although he draws on Jean-Joseph Goux, Michel Foucault, and Jacques Derrida for other reasons, the theoretical method of Hawkes's *Idols of the Marketplace* is entirely *sui generis*, and in the best possible way.

5. Brantlinger, also keenly aware of the non-autonomy of economics in the first half of the eighteenth century, defines *economism* as "the reification of economic practices and theories as a realm of seemingly natural 'laws,' more or less divorced from the processes of political criticism, decision making, and reform or revolution that could change those practices and theories" (125).

6. Pocock, *Machiavellian Moment* 423 (hereafter cited in text and notes as *MM*).

7. Pocock describes Harrington as "the pioneer theorist of English republicanism" ("Post-Puritan England" 94).

8. For two excellent historical accounts of the relation between Puritanism and economics that refuse to presuppose the triumph of secular economics, see Valeri, *Heavenly Merchandize*; and Hawkes. Although Valeri's focus is on New England, his critique of historians' downplaying of providence in economic thought is every bit as applicable to the English context (*Heavenly Merchandize* 5–10). Likewise, Hawkes sees the Protestant, and often Puritan, condemnation of idols as bridging the spiritual and the secular. In "post-Reformation England," Hawkes argues, idolatry was an act "of *objectification*" (25, Hawkes's emphasis).

9. For an excellent discussion of morality, Christianity, and the early credit market, see Muldrew, ch. 5, esp. 128–32.

10. Later, Pocock observes that "Augustan political economics mark the moment when the trader—and, still more pressingly, the financier—was challenged to prove that he could display civic virtue in the sense that the landed man could" (*MM* 445). It is worth adding, however, that while it may be true that traders needed to assert the sort of civic virtue that neo-Harringtonianism demanded, merchants and traders had long been considered potentially, if not necessarily, virtuous in a Protestant, Christian sense.

11. For Pocock's most in-depth analysis of Lady Credit, see *MM* 436–61. It is worth remarking how sparsely annotated Pocock's volume is once he turns to Defoe's and Addison's essays (see, e.g., 456–61); in the face of their moral defense of credit, Pocock continues to assert that "the Augustan mind" was still primarily determined by its relation to land and mobile property (458). Mulcaire has been one of the few scholars to call the epistemological function of Lady Credit into question (see esp. 1029–36).

12. On the ambivalence of Lady Meed, for example, see Galloway 217–25.

13. Pocock, *MM* 436–61; Wennerlind, ch. 5, esp. 172–95.

14. For more on Defoe's positive characterization of credit's instability, see Wennerlind 182–84.

15. That Malynes intended the dragon to represent usury is further evidenced by the biblical passages he cites as cursing it and its followers. See esp. 65.

16. Wennerlind's penetrating analysis of the debate between the neo-Aristotelians of the seventeenth century omits consideration of the many professions of faith scat-

tered throughout texts by Malynes, Thomas Mun (1571–1641), and Edward Misselden (1608–1654). Relatedly, Jonathan Gil Harris, in his reading of Malynes in *Sick Economies*, acknowledges that Malynes "attributes the doctrine of cosmopolitan economy to God," but he insists that because Malynes relied upon the "Roman jurists'" concept of *lex*, or customary law, he helped to produce "a new object of knowledge: an orderly, systematic sphere of transnational commerce whose workings could be ascertained through empirical observation" (7). While one cannot deny the secular *potential* of Malynes's works, as Wennerlind's and Harris's readings illustrate, it is only by omitting consideration of his forceful, often creative, and pervasive devotional language that one can affirm Malynes's status as harbinger of secular political economy. More interesting to me is how, given his expressed dependence upon an array of Christian ethical values in his delineation of the commercial world, Malynes would or could come to be seen as a secularizing figure.

17. In the key to the allegory, which opens the text, Malynes writes that the "virgin is the kings treasure," which his tract shows is itself a figure for the whole economic life of the realm ("To the Reader," n.p.).

18. Michel Foucault is right in arguing that it is important to "avoid a retrospective reading of these things that would merely endow the Classical analysis of wealth with the ulterior unity of a political economy in the tentative process of constituting itself. Yet it is in this way that historians of ideas do go about their reconstructions of the enigmatic birth of this knowledge, which, according to them, sprang up in Western thought, fully armed and already full of danger, at the time of Ricardo and J-B. Say. They presuppose that a scientific economics had for long been rendered impossible by a purely moral problematics of profit and income. . . . In fact, the concepts of money, price, value, circulation, and market were not regarded, in the seventeenth and eighteenth centuries, in terms of a shadowy future, but as part of a rigorous and general epistemological arrangement" (166–68). I would submit that this "rigorous and general epistemological arrangement" includes, in the English context, Protestant and especially Puritan understandings of the relation between the individual and providence. Cf. Taylor 175–85.

19. For further discussion of the new economic criticism's treatment of the mediation of economic problems in imaginative writing, see S. Moore 10–13.

20. Sherman argues that Roxana's wish to change her "Figure and Circumstances in one day" delivers her "to the discourse of credit: Lady Credit, Air-Money, the Funds" (165). Poovey contends that the form of fiction offered up by Defoe in the 1720s was part of a larger cultural search, in the wake of the South Sea Bubble, for a way for readers and writers to jointly "explore uncomfortable cultural anxieties without suffering their consequences" (113). More specifically, *Roxana* "precisely (and accurately) detail[s] the way money could be transferred from country to country in the early eighteenth century, the way compound interest worked, or the way that mortgages could function as modes of investment," none of which, Poovey adds, feature in Richardson's *Clarissa* (1747–49).

The mediation of credit in imaginative literature during the financial revolution period has, more broadly speaking, been one of the most productive areas of recent research and is pursued in such works as Bellamy's *Commerce, Morality, and the Eighteenth-Century Novel*; Laura Brown's *Fables of Modernity*; Ingrassia's *Authorship*,

Commerce, and Gender in Early Eighteenth-Century England; Jenkins's "Defoe's Trinkets"; Sean Moore's *Swift, the Book, and the Irish Financial Revolution;* Nicholson's *Writing and the Rise of Finance;* Mitchell's *Sympathy and the State in the Romantic Era;* and Thompson's *Models of Value.*

21. Carruthers argues that financial markets of the later seventeenth century were "embedded in noneconomic social structures" (26) and that they "were not populated solely by *homines economici*" but included agents whose concerns were political first and only secondarily economic (21). At times, my sense of ethical commitments overlaps with Carruthers's claims about political commitments; at other times, however, the political infighting and posturing for control—over the chartered companies, for example— that his book charts in careful detail suggest a form of subjectivity that is fundamentally *economic,* in the sense that his subjects seek mastery, security, and maximization of power, if not of profit per se, and thus differs from the self-abnegating subjectivity I aim to explore here. Even so, I agree with Carruthers's view that it is important to stress the primacy of noneconomic motivations in the development of English capital markets.

22. Poovey locates an origin for the genre of political economy in Sir James Steuart's (1713–1780) *Principles of Political Economy* and other political economic tracts of the later eighteenth century but stresses that economics distinguished itself as such in the nineteenth century. Poovey tracks this process throughout her volume, but for a condensed account of important phases in this process, see 30–33, 64, 76–77. Foucault points out that the emergence of political economy was a discontinuous and interruptive process that found its completion not in any objective property of the science but in the retrospective identification of Adam Smith as its founder (167).

23. Worldliness features in virtually all omnibus moral and spiritual tracts of this period as a figure for material and earthly life, but only in retrospect does it appear to designate what will later be called the economic sphere (property, wealth, prosperity, goods, possessions, etc.). The theological attack on worldliness was closely connected to the attack on idolatry, which Hawkes convincingly reads as a critique of commodity fetishism (both entail a misrecognition of the telos of the sign). On Luther's connection of idolatry to the world of flesh and matter, see Hawkes 68–69.

24. I do not mean to imply that this totality was in any way ideal; thus it might be better to describe it as a totality relative to the later separated form it assumed. The analysis provided in this book aims to loosely approximate that used by Michael McKeon in *The Secret History of Domesticity: Public, Private, and the Division of Knowledge,* wherein the public and private come to be divided from one another through a series of "separations out" of one or the other from an antecedent totality that encompassed both. In terms of its content, however, this book is perhaps more greatly indebted to Talal Asad's *Formations of the Secular: Christianity, Islam, Modernity* insofar as Asad presents his work as "a counter to the triumphalist history of the secular" and I offer the present book as a counter to the triumphalist history of finance, a history that chapters 1 and 2 argue is in many ways a history of a break with the premodern and religious (Asad 25).

25. The story of the triumph of capitalism, understood as either a normative or a historical one, is hegemonic in that it is "especially alert and responsive to the alternatives

and opposition which question or threaten its dominance" (Williams 113). The narrative does not simply, or "passively[,] dominate," but "has continually to be renewed, recreated, defended, and modified" (112–13).

26. As Hayden White puts it, "There are always more facts in the record than the historian can possibly include in his narrative representation of a given segment of the historical process. And so the historian must 'interpret' his data by excluding certain facts from his account as irrelevant to his narrative purpose. On the other hand, in his efforts to reconstruct 'what happened' in a given period of history, the historian inevitably must include in his narrative an account of some event or complex of events for which the facts that would permit a plausible explanation of its occurrence are lacking" (51).

27. Anker's brief but powerful book *The Ethics of Uncertainty: Aporetic Openings* (2009) was unknown to me until late in the process of writing this book, but his placement of uncertainty at the center of the ethics of Jacques Derrida, Jean-Luc Nancy, and other poststructuralist theorists of ethics overlaps with my understanding of uncertainty as (1) a historical problematic germane to the history of usury, (2) a key term in the historical separation of ethical from economic life, and (3) an analytic that helps to account for ethical energies evident in a variety of eighteenth-century texts that has no place within economistic accounts of eighteenth-century literature and culture.

1. Raving at Usurers

1. Jones's death is reported as having occurred "about ten days" prior to the printing of the 11–13 August 1724 edition of the *Evening Post* (2). The death notice mentions nothing of Jones's life other than the sermon preached against usury at St. Mary's. The same notice, with the same details about the sermon against usury, was also printed in the *Original London Post, or Heathcote's Intelligencer* on 14 August; the *Universal Journal* and the *Weekly Journal or British Gazetteer* on 15 August; and the *Newcastle Courant* on 22 August.

2. For more information on St. Mary Woolnoth's history, see Brooke and Hallen; Godwin; and Noorthouck.

3. A text that exemplifies the sort of distinction making that Jones criticizes is a 1710 work whose title explains its purpose: *A Common Law Treatise of Usury, and Usurious Contracts: Wherein is set forth, The Nature of Usury, and what Contracts are said Usurious in our LAW*. The author states in the preface that his "Design is to instruct and inform *Lawyers, Conveyancers,* and other Gentlemen how they may secure their own or other Persons Monies (with which they are intrusted) with safety, and not be obnoxious to the severe Penalties of the several Statutes against Usury, which are indeed very Penal, and without being liable to the Vexations of greedy *Informers*" (xvii). The author goes on to unfold dozens of cases of possible usury—from "Bottomree" contracts to annuities to mortgages for lands—and by making fine and subtle distinctions excuses many of them from charges of being usurious.

4. See Dickson. Dickson's decision to begin the revolution in this decade suggests that the Whiggish narrative of liberation from the shackles of feudal institutions

continues to have a powerful influence on historiography. Cf., e.g., Macaulay, *History* 487–508. Others date the financial revolution's beginning at different times. Neal, for instance, sees it as beginning during the Civil War period. Although Arrighi sees the rise of English financial power as taking place toward the end of the eighteenth century, with the 1690s dominated primarily by the Dutch, he also acknowledges the importance of the early part of the century to Britain's commercial growth (203–4).

5. See North and Weingast. See also North 156–57; and Fratianni and Spinelli, esp. 4–5.

6. A few short paragraphs can only scratch the surface of political economy's complexity in the 1690s, but Steven Pincus's *1688: The First Modern Revolution* corrects the view that the financial revolution was born of Whig belief in "amoral, profit-seeking individualism" (398). For his treatment of the matter of political economy in the 1690s, which takes Pocock into account, see 366–400.

7. Godwin 2. Viner was interred in St. Mary Woolnoth on his death in 1688.

8. In 1665 Pepys watched the funeral procession for Viner's uncle from the balcony of St. Mary Woolnoth. See D. Clark 22.

9. The note is dated September 1727, well after Tenison's death, so the reason for its being among his papers must have had to do with the simple fact of Viner's importance when St. Mary Woolnoth was being improved in the seventeenth century.

10. Clark has shown that after the fire, Viner's house adjoined St. Mary Woolnoth. That Viner went so far as to cover the church in tributary "vines" suggests that he may have felt a degree of ownership of the church. See D. Clark 27–31.

11. That Jones was already planning to leave when he delivered the sermon—rather than its merely having been retroactively titled a "farewell"—is clearly evident from remarks internal to the text. See David Jones, esp. 2. The final paragraph, to provide further evidence, begins "And what I am to tell you from God at my going away from this place is . . ." (35). Given the numerous references to his impending departure and the shape assumed by the entire sermon—he responds systematically to ten separate objections to his style of preaching—it is probable that Tawney did not read the sermon. Tawney's apparent error is repeated by Needham (167). In any event, it is likely that Jones had been chastising the "usurers" of his parish prior to the sermon, in informal contexts and/or in unpublished sermons. For language suggesting this, see David Jones 33–34.

12. It is impossible to disagree with Brod's portrait. By all accounts, Jones was irascible, unbending, and often plainly disliked. For example, Narcissus Luttrell (1657–1732) reported that he was once "committed to the castle of Oxon by the vicechancellor of that university" for, it seems, having "reproved [a man] for mowing on a Sunday" (644). Even so, it would be a mistake to confuse Jones's singularity with that of his opinions on usury, particularly if one considers the popular discussion his sermon provoked.

13. For a slightly different perspective on the end of the usury problem, see Nelson. Nelson appears to recognize that the usury issue was not settled by 1700, but he does see post-1700 anxieties about it as antiquated at the time of their pronouncement.

14. Thompson Cooper (d. 1904), the prolific nineteenth-century contributor to

the *Dictionary of National Biography*, offers nothing more than this in his discussion of Huddleston's tract. It does not appear, however, that there was ever a "treatise" concerning usury by anyone named James Smith. As for the James Smith who was the vicar apostolic of the Northern District beginning in 1687, the only published work to which his name is attached, according to the English Short Title Catalogue, is *A Pastoral Letter from the Four Catholic Bishops to the Lay-Catholics of England* (1688).

15. See Jewel: "Tell me, thou wretched wight of the world, thou unkind creature, which art past all sense and feeling of God, which knowest the will of God, and doest the contrary, how darest thou come unto the church? It is the church of that God which hath said, Thou shalt take no usury; and thou knowest he hath so said. How darest thou read or hear the word of God? It is the word of God who condemneth usury; and thou knowest he doth condemn it. How darest thou come into the company of thy brethren?" (144).

16. For more on the disorienting effects of the new finance on ordinary subjects and the inability to grasp or name them, see Kramnick 39–40.

17. It would be absurd to dive into a debate here about whether a practice can exist before it has a name, but it is worth saying that financial practices often begin as ad hoc investments or contract structures, only to gradually morph into a nameable class of investment vehicles or instruments. To take a modern example, this process more or less describes the emergence of *collateralized debt obligations*, a term that came to describe instruments in a secondary market of repackaged risk exposure only after the practice had proceeded in widespread and somewhat anarchic fashion between firms and traders.

18. Summarizing the Calvinist anti-usury writer Robert Bolton, Charles George observes that anti-usury writers found the problem to be usury's real sinfulness, as well as language's ability to conceal it and thereby palliate the usurer's conscience. For Bolton, George writes, "worldlings may find loopholes in God's Law: the Christian conscience can never condone the exploitation of such corrupting cleverness" (468). He also quotes Thomas Adams (1583–1653), who had, in a manner anticipating Jones's "Trifling and Shuffling Distinctions," accused financiers of the tendency to "spinne *Usurie* into such fine threads of distinction that . . . they conceive [it] a toothless practice" (468). George's essay "English Calvinist Opinion on Usury, 1600–1640," written in 1957, is worth reviving generally for this vitally important insight into seventeenth-century thought.

19. Jelinger had published a more concise treatise, *The Usurer Cast*, three years earlier.

20. "Don't Lend the King *upon* Usury, but Lend him *Freely*. Let it be your Free-will Offering. Let it be your Voluntary Oblation. You can never Lend it better. You lend it to fight the Lord's Battles against the Mighty. . . . Is it not enough for him [the King] to *Hazard his Life* [in war], but must he also *Pay Usury for your Deliverance?*" (*Mr. David Jones's Vindication* 7).

21. Although the term *financialization* has a distinct meaning in the present—the shifting of the center of economic power from industrial to financial sectors—the debate around usury in the 1690s anticipates this shift and thus seems useful for describing the broader process attacked by Jones. For some discussion of this term and its present uses, see Preda 5.

22. I was unable to discover just how many guineas were paid to Jones for the sermon.

23. It seems that Dunton's attempt to discredit Jones with the answer was not immediately successful, for on 26 March the *Athenian Mercury* was forced to answer another question: "Whether is it [*sic*] not a sure sign that David Jones is a good Preacher, since the People follow him so?" (111). Dunton dismissively replies that popularity is no indicator of quality.

24. Thomas Brown, in a series of mock predictions, anticipated that on "*Sunday* [November] 17. . . . The Bankers in *Lombard-street* want David Jones to put 'em in mind of their Sins" ("Comical View" 128). In *The Rambling Rakes*, Ward remarked, in passing, of the Jones incident: "Having Anatomiz'd the Carcase of a cold Fowl, and wring'd a Lemon as hard as *David Iones* once did the *Bankers* Consciences; We took leave of his *Holiness*" (6).

25. Suggesting their cultural importance, the specific lines concerning Jones were included as well in an excerpt of the poem in the *Gentlemen's Monthly Intelligencer* in February 1749 (90).

26. See esp. the preface to Crouch.

27. For more on the inability of eighteenth-century writers to express the economic, see Poovey, ch. 2, esp. 95–100.

28. For Macaulay's views on the national debt and the Bank of England, see Macaulay, *History* 487–508. For Macaulay's contribution to the wedding of finance and modernity, see Poovey 76–77.

29. Lecky celebrates the pro-usury jurist Noodt as "one of the principal assailants of the theological superstitions about usury" (218).

30. Although Newell's research focuses on the founding of the American republic, her claim here applies more broadly to the Anglo-American Atlantic commercial world.

2. Hazarding All for God

1. As Giacomo Todeschini argues, even in the late medieval period usury had less to do with naming any particular economic practice and more to do with its strategic deployment. It was a "linguistic elaboration" that helped those in power differentiate between those who were considered a part of the "sacred social Body" of the church and those who were not (130).

2. For more on Portia's mercy speech and chivalric codes, see Meron 132–33.

3. While the risk criterion can be located in the medieval, early modern, and modern periods, there is much that distinguishes the medieval view of usury from later epochs' views. The most complete treatments of medieval usury theory are to be found in Noonan's *The Scholastic Analysis of Usury* and Langholm's *The Aristotelian Analysis of Usury*.

4. Luther surely knew the dictum, but there is no evidence that he accepted it in the way that Brandt implies. In a note to Luther's remark that "you cannot make money just with money," Brandt writes that Aristotle's formulation is "one of the two great pillars of usury theory" and that Luther subscribed to both. It is plain, given the full context,

however, that Luther is making a claim not about the so-called sterility of money but about the need to expose oneself to the dangers of the world when attempting to make money. For Luther, there were not two pillars of the anti-usury position, but one: the risk criterion. If anything, Luther invokes the Aristotelian claim to illustrate its subordinate position in the more fundamental doctrine concerning risk. See *Trade and Usury* 299–300.

5. See, e.g., Nelson 73–82.

6. Appleby writes, "The unrevolutionary pace of English economic change required persisting influences effective through many generations, but religion had spent its force in England before the modern restructuring was half complete" (14).

7. I see the persistence of the critique of usury—from Calvin and elsewhere—as further evidence for the existence of what Scott Paul Gordon has referred to as the "passivity trope" (e.g., 48–51). Such a trope privileges not the self-fashioning subject but a passive subject, respondent to the actions, words, and deeds of another. See S. Gordon, esp. 21–53.

8. Of note are Halpern 20–21; Laqueur 231–32; and Partridge 274. While writers such as Shakespeare clearly exploited to great poetic effect the sexualized dimensions of usury, Protestant theologians were disinclined to develop this ultimately scholastic argument. See Hawkes, ch. 4, esp. 97–101.

9. Benjamin Franklin may have been teasing those who unthinkingly embraced the maxim when, on the first page of his "Advice to a Young Tradesman," he defiantly advised the tradesman, "Remember that money is of a prolific, generating nature. Money can beget money, and its offspring can beget more, and so on" (52). Franklin completely inverts the Aristotelian formula while relying on its central terms (*generating, nature, beget*), playfully spins out the metaphor to later generations ("its offspring can beget more, and so on"), and asks his advisee to "remember" a fact about the nature of money that Franklin surely knew had been a matter of contestation until quite recently. These words may be considered a part of a tradition of mocking the sterility hypothesis, one that extends back to at least the early eighteenth century. Compare Bentham's mockery of the Aristotelian position in *Defence of Usury*, letter X, x.4–x.5.

10. Samuel Shaw considered work-as-labor and work-as-risk to be of a piece: "To be content our Neighbor should be subjected to all Casualties, and to take no further care but to secure our own profit, is filthily selfish, and somewhat like the ill condition'd Generation, of whom Christ Jesus complain'd; who laid great and heavy burdens upon the backs of others, which they themselves refus'd to touch with the least of their Fingers" (354–55).

11. See the entirety of Sanderson, "III. Ad Populum. 4" in *Ten Sermons Preached*, esp. 408–9 and 439–43.

12. Usury and failing to honor the Sabbath continued to march hand in hand for the reasons discussed. Interestingly, David Jones was once committed to a detention center at Oxford for having upbraided a menial laborer for mowing on the Sabbath.

13. Lazzarato, quoting Jacques le Goff, observes the medieval concern about interest generated at night (when one should be at rest): "[Usurers] sell nothing other than the

expectation of money, that is to say, time, they sell days and nights. But the day is the time of clarity, and the night is the time for repose. Consequently, they sell light and repose. It is, therefore, not just for them to receive eternal light and eternal rest" (48). I am indebted to Jacob Emery, of Indiana University, for bringing this reference to my attention.

14. Ceri Sullivan has argued expertly for the importance of risk in the early modern period, writing that the merchant's ethical need for risk at times brought him close to the figure of the aristocrat.

15. Mosse was a Church of England clergyman, but given his Cambridge education and his intimacy with some who were regarded as "closet Presbyterians," it is hard to think that he was anything less than a Calvinist. Further, he worked under John Knewstub, a principal figure in the development of Calvinist thought in England, and he "maintained a close connection with such Cambridge Puritans as Laurence Chaderton" (Bremer, n.p.).

16. Cf. Blaxton: It is not usury "when the borrower finding himself much benefited by the lenders curtesie, doth of his owne accord in testimony of his thankefulnesse, freely give to the lender, who neyther intended when he lent, nor expected whiles he forebore [waited for repayment], any gaine; and much less covenanted for it" (9).

17. One exception to this statement appears to be the defense of usury when it was practiced by widows or unmarried women who would otherwise have no income at all. Even in these contexts, however, it is seen as a necessary evil, not a positive good. See Korda 134–35. Bolton argues, in fact, that those who claim that widows and orphans are entitled to the profits of usury tacitly assume that widows and orphans are beyond the reach of God. "Let them," he writes, "imploy their goods in some honest Trade . . . wherein they have as good cause to expect a blessing from God, as any other. . . . And let not children bee tainted and maintained with the contagious, and insinuating sinne of Usury" (50).

18. For more on the history of aleatory contracts and the extension of this logic of risk distribution into the eighteenth century, see Daston.

19. Compare Blaxton's comments about the unequal distribution of risk with recent remarks made by Mike Konczal, a fellow at the Roosevelt Institute, on the subject of the post-financial-crisis banking situation: "Much of the capital in the economy is sitting on the balance sheets of banks and large corporations. These profits are based off milking the bad debts of the housing and credit bubbles while Americans struggl[e] under a crushing debt load. *Instead of sharing the losses, the financial sector has locked itself into the profit stream and left the real economy to deal with the mess*" (my emphasis).

20. As brilliant and thorough a study as Norman Jones's is, this particular aspect of the usury debates does not receive a full treatment. See, e.g., Lord Treasurer Burghley's position as articulated by Jones (*God and the Moneylenders* 39). Also, Jones's initial definition notes the centrality of risk, but his study does not trace the history of this part of the debate (4). This objection to usury, I would argue, was never entirely resolved, though it was displaced, and so does not entirely fit within the complex negotiation that his book traces.

21. Writing in 1678–79, nearly a century after Mosse's polemical *Arraignment and Conviction*, Jelinger admiringly referred to "Mr. Mose" as "a most able and learned Author" (*Usury Stated Overthrown* 6).

22. For an interesting eighteenth-century point of comparison, see Kadane. Kadane observes the deep ethical and spiritual tensions that arose for the Protestant clothier Joseph Ryder (1695–1768) when he was confronted with the threatening prospect of material success and abundance (see esp. 7–8, 101–8).

23. Similarly, Skip Worden writes that in certain ways "Calvin is more restrictive [regarding usury] than Aquinas," while in other ways he was "more progressive than the medievals" (181).

24. Carruthers states that the order to stop payment was issued on 2 January 1672 (62); Roseveare observes that the order was first formally given in December 1671.

25. For further reading on the impact of this event, see Dickson 43–45; Roseveare 21–26; and Scott 287–91.

26. See also Lawson 197–200; Sinclair 315; and Wennerlind 103–4.

27. On the sentimentalism surrounding orphans affected by the Stop of the Exchequer, see, e.g., *Memoirs relating to the impeachment of Thomas, Earl of Danby* 7.

28. For more on Backwell's finances, see "Hearth Tax."

29. According to Roseveare, "By [1677], a series of prosperous years . . . had enabled Charles to fund an annuity of £140,000 p.a. on the bankers' debt. This they were required to re-allocate to their depositors in the form of 6% annuities, drawn up and witnessed in the Exchequer, authorised under the Great Seal and registered on the securest portion of the royal revenues—the hereditary Excise" (22).

30. The "royal revenues" to which Roseveare alludes were composed primarily of what Michael Braddick calls "demesne revenues," or those monies the Crown accrued as a direct or indirect result of inheritance. These would include land rents coming from tenants upon royal lands, as well as "all revenues arising from a personal right belonging to the monarch," ranging from wardship fees to forest fines (Braddick 12–14).

31. For more on this condition of uncertainty and its relation to royal prerogative, see North.

32. The key taxes were the excise tax (on domestic manufactures and luxury goods), the customs tax (on imports), and the hearth tax (on the number of hearths per home). The last of these was abolished in 1688 by an act of Parliament because it constituted a "badge of slavery" for landowners. The land tax was imposed in its stead (Brewer 92).

33. Aids had been imposed by parliamentary acts in 1665 and 1685, although their importance for financing the national debt was not fully realized until William's reign (Roy 18).

34. Braddick remarks that the development of a system of public debt in which parliamentary taxation would play a larger role ensured that the monarchy would lose its "personal influence over . . . borrowings" (41).

35. The remarkable increase in government revenues in the 1680s and 1690s has been a frequent subject of inquiry for economic historians. Braddick remarks that "the

proportion of revenue derived from taxation climbed again, reaching 80 per cent by the 1630s and mounting steadily to over 90 per cent by the 1680s and 1690s. . . . In this respect the significance of taxation lies in its contribution to increases to total revenue" (9).

36. Extensive research in recent years has demonstrated the importance of the state's military expenditures to financial developments in England in the late seventeenth and eighteenth centuries. While there was no outstanding government debt when William and Mary took the throne in 1689, by the end of the Nine Years War the state owed nearly £17 million to various creditors whose money had assisted in the transportation, equipage, and wages of as many as 116,666 men in the army and the navy. The debt was more than twice that figure—£36.2 million—by the end of the War of the Spanish Succession in 1713. In a vacuum these figures have little meaning, but when one considers that the average annual total tax revenue for the period 1689–97 was £3.6 million and that the average annual military expenditure alone for the same period was roughly £5.5 million, it is easy to see the extent to which England's martial agenda dominated state financing decisions. To get a sense of the size of the loans the government was taking out to meet expenses, one should consider that from 1574 to 1603 the English state borrowed a meager £461,000 (Braddick 20).

37. Murphy emphasizes that the lottery provided an opportunity to test new forms of rationality, which differs from my argument in that I would emphasize the attractions of the lottery's randomness. There is little evidence that either motivation was primary, but we must remember that those who engaged in the lottery for its randomness— rather than as a rational investment option—would also have been those least likely to justify their actions in economic terms, or to justify them at all. Acknowledging that "the desire to take risk drives investment and provides the economy with funds that might otherwise lie dormant," Murphy writes of a "gambling instinct" at the root of capitalism ("Lotteries" 245). I would concede the existence of such an instinct, but I would place rather stronger emphasis on the taste for randomness such an instinct implies than on a desire for sudden gain, which many thinkers, from Sigmund Freud on have considered anathema to real gambling. For a useful survey of social scientific research into the desire for the randomness itself, see Mazur 183–201.

38. Phillips also shows that attitudes toward women in commerce were more complex than many have allowed (N. Phillips 186–94).

39. For Defoe's account of Rye's decay, see *Tour Thro' the Whole Island* 173–75.

40. Holloway reports that a petition of 1618 stated that the harbor was so decayed that trade had nearly ceased (337).

41. For a discussion of Jeake's diary in the context of the sixteenth- and seventeenth-century astrological almanac genre and the diary's emphasis on specificity of place and time in the casting of horoscopes, see Chapman 1261, 1264.

42. Although Grassby fully recognizes and helpfully explains the profoundly risky atmosphere of seventeenth-century business culture, he is too dismissive of the religious piety that may have been precisely what impelled investors to take such risks. For example, he writes that "Providence *was always on the lips* of merchants, because fortunes

gyrated wildly and bad luck could ruin the ablest and richest" (98, my emphasis). For Grassby, wealth is real, and providence therefore merely a verbal matter.

43. On Gataker's sympathy toward lotteries on the grounds of their providential character, see Daston 155.

44. Bolton was one of the loudest voices of the Puritan anti-usury camp, and given Jeake's investigation of the theological opinion concerning lots elsewhere in the diary, it is reasonable to assume that he would have been familiar with Elizabethan and Jacobean writings on usury as well. For an assessment of Bolton's role in this period, see George 463–67.

45. An example of treating Jeake's economic life without due attention to his religious life is Anne Murphy's assessment of Jeake's papers and his attitude toward the public funds. In the Diary Jeake mentions that his reasons for investing are connected both to providence and to his belief in the importance of supporting the nation (making no mention of profit considerations). Further, he openly admits that his justification for investing in the lottery derives from his reflections after reading theologians' works on the subject. Murphy, however, makes no mention of Jeake's devotional activities, his references to providence, or the fact that Jeake was an astrologer. These moments might productively complicate her claim that Jeake's "investment choices reflected his cautious attempts to create a secure income flow" ("Dealing with Uncertainty" 206). Similarly, in order to accommodate Jeake to an economistic portrait of seventeenth-century commercial culture, Grassby arguably mischaracterizes Jeake's horoscopes as economic tools. As the editors of Jeake's diary observe, however, Jeake knew that the instrumental use of horoscopes was dubious at best, and if he did make such use of them, it was not unproblematic for him (13). Grassby, writing that Jeake cast his horoscopes "to help him decide when to speculate in futures and when to build a new storehouse" (278), fails to mention that Jeake casts horoscopes for a wide array of reasons, which makes it appear as though Jeake's horoscopes are primarily economic and only secondarily religious or spiritual.

46. For evidence that Jeake's political opponents regarded him as a usurer, see Hunter et al. xx. When Jeake did feel as though his commercial self outstripped his Christian self, he made voluntary restitution (Muldrew 129).

3. Risk and Adventure in the Age of Projects

1. Novak writes in Daniel Defoe: Master of Fictions that "Defoe must have found the life of a student at Charles Morton's academy too remote from what must have seemed a world of excitement," and this is likely the case. It may well be true, too, that the lessons Defoe imbibed there and elsewhere led him to regard the "world of excitement" as an opportunity to test his spiritual commitment (52).

2. That Defoe attempted to avoid risk by cheating others is suggested as well by Backscheider, who importantly adds, however, that he likely felt intense guilt because of such crimes (52–53, 58, 60).

3. Defoe, like Morton, was a Presbyterian; Miles Mosse, as a Cambridge-educated young man of the later sixteenth century, is believed to have been one as well. See Wallace.

4. It was not uncommon in early modern anti-usury literature to clear space for "Spirituall usurers," for those who expected "God himself [to] pay usury" in exchange for showing "pitty and compassion [for] our neighbours" (Malynes 80).

5. See, e.g., Lodge 14.

6. For a later, similar account of the connection between projects and providence, see Dorman 8.

7. To illustrate that the projector and the jobber were of the same sort, one might compare the "Legerdemain" of Defoe's projector with George White's "Trick" of running stocks up and down by the "*Legerdemain* [of] a strange sort of *Insects* called Stock-Jobbers, who devour men on our *Exchange*, as the *Locusts* of old did the Herbage of *Egypt*" (5).

8. While the eighteenth-century division of public and private is the subject of much debate, the distinction between the selfish private enterprise and the public project was operative by the 1690s. The author of an account of Dr. William Assheton's (1641–1711) proposal for a system of annuities for the widows of deceased clergymen writes that "Dr. Assheton did not Project this Proposal for his own Private Advantage, but doth sincerely design a Publick Good," and that, regarding another project, "the Worthy Members of the *Mercers* Company have undertaken to Manage [another] *Proposal*, not from any Prospect of Advantage to their own private Persons, but only . . . *To Establish and Manage Publick Charities*: And thereby to enlarge their Capacity of Doing Good" (*Full Account* 1).

9. Pincus concentrates on the modern origins of projects, but for someone such as Defoe, Noah helped to speak to the truth of the project, historical or otherwise. As Preus puts it, "In Puritan *use*, the line between biblical 'similitudes' (or parables) and 'histories' was irrelevant, because the critical issue for religious use of a story was not its truth as *historicity* at all, but spiritual authority for the present, divinatory application" (456).

10. On Noah as "Shipwright," see Defoe, *Plan of the English Commerce* 8.

11. Defoe returned to and elaborates on the direction given to Noah by God in *A Compleat System of Magick* 298–99.

12. Defoe, *Protestant Jesuit Unmask't*. For commentary on this text's relationship to Leslie, see Novak, *Daniel Defoe* 241–42.

13. "If one was to define an *English-man* in particular, especially since the miraculous Rise of Stocks, I do not know how it could be done better than by calling him, A *Projecting Animal*" (T. Gordon 32–33).

14. Poovey explores Defoe's fiction as a response to the South Sea Bubble and argues that it helped to ameliorate the distress of risk the bubble precipitated: "Through the medium of fiction, a writer might teach a reader to believe once more in possibilities that could not be proved; in so doing, a writer could encourage readers to accept the deferral that was essential to credit, both private and public, without feeling imperiled by risk" (113). Noah and the Flood may have provided Defoe with a biblical reference point for understanding the earthly upheavals of the South Sea bubble, one that Defoe incorpo-

rated back into his fiction through the figure of the uncertain sea traveled by Crusoe and others.

15. Advertisements also appear in both the third edition (after 364) and the fourth (after 364). All were printed by Taylor in 1719.

16. Fiona Stafford has considered Crusoe as a last man, a tradition in which Noah obviously figures prominently.

17. Damrosch has suggested that the island is more of an Eden (193) and that Crusoe would have continued his solitude were it not for the arrival of others (191). Crusoe does at times rest content with his lot; there are also, however, numerous attempts to escape and an obvious desire to return home or otherwise forge a bond with humanity. The world of *Robinson Crusoe* could never be Edenic, for the reasons discussed in my reading of Weber's mischaracterization of Calvinist "work."

18. See, e.g., Stafford.

19. See, e.g., McInelly.

20. Crusoe's status as *homo economicus* has been argued for by many scholars who see in him a money-oriented, time-conscious, laboring, counting, accounting, calculative, writing, utilitarian protocapitalist (or protomercantilist). Others have replied to this reading of the novel by arguing that Crusoe's dependency on products from England (collected from the ship), on the gifts and charity of others, and on others' labor short-circuits this interpretation and that the novel in fact counts as a sustained critique of the possessive individualism at the core of *homo economicus* (see, e.g., Hymer).

21. For more on the cultural and historical construction of Crusoe as a selfish individual, see M. White; and Kern. White shows that a calculating Robinson Crusoe was born around the middle of the nineteenth century. Kern points out that this reading depends upon our taking Crusoe to be recognizably economic, when in fact early economists such as Smith could only conceive of economy in terms of collectives. The eventual transformation of Crusoe into a model of the economic self depended upon a later neoclassical economic paradigm's need for an archetypal solitary individual. For Kern, Crusoe fit that bill: "The shift in focus to the problems of microallocation characteristic of neoclassicism opened up significant opportunities to employ Crusoe. Because microeconomics focuses on the analysis of decisions made by individual consumers, workers, employers and business firms with given preferences and resources, Crusoe's setting becomes an ideal context in which to analyze these decisions" (65).

22. Although the two strands of possible thinking at play in Baxter are here separated from the question of justification by works, they may be related to it. Bataille writes in the first volume of *The Accursed Share* that "if the faithful's salvation is the reward for his merits, if he can achieve it by his deeds, then he has simply brought more closely into the domain of religion that concatenation that makes useful work wretched in his eyes. Hence those *deeds* by which a Christian tries to win his salvation can be considered profanations. Even the mere fact of choosing salvation as a goal appears contrary to the truth of grace. Grace alone brings about an accord with the divinity, which cannot be subjected to casual series as *things* can. The gift that divinity makes of itself to the

faithful soul cannot be paid for" (120–21). Defoe felt something of this as well, which may account for his resistance to the logic of justification by works, which is at one level of analysis a more explicit and more crassly utilitarian variation of the Weberian interpretation of Calvinism's promotion of the work ethic (i.e., time must be devoted to or paid to God). It is worth adding that Bataille accepts Weber's reading of Calvinism and as a result fails to observe the more radical critique of finance expressed in English Protestant writings of the sixteenth and seventeenth centuries. Of all people, Bataille should have had the wisdom to consult the resources from which Tawney and Weber derived their understanding of Calvinism, but he relies upon their version of events. Bataille, in fact, exaggerates Tawney's idea that Calvinism demands productive labor above all other things: "The reformed Christian had to be humble, saving, hard-working (he had to bring the greatest zeal to his profession, be it in commerce, industry or whatever)" (123).

23. A 1758 version of Baxter's *Saints Everlasting Rest* abridged by Benjamin Fawcett begins this passage with the following more stark proclamation (not in Baxter's original): "So, if the Lord see you begin to settle in the world, and say, 'Here I will rest,' no wonder if he soon, in his jealousy, unsettle you" (n.p.).

24. That work-as-production had no particular importance to Baxter in terms of its spiritual significance is attested by his equation of it with other bodily acts. One is just as liable to temptation while "eating, drinking, working, or what ever" one is doing (*Saints* [1750] 396). Working might produce a state of contentment that makes the sinner vulnerable to Satan (396).

25. Gregg has recently provided an alternative explanation for Defoe's interest in and apparent valuing of discontented states. For Gregg, Defoe was attracted to an older, heroic model of masculinity, one exemplified by men such as Drake and Raleigh (61–62).

26. For readings of *Robinson Crusoe* as a story of a "fortunate fall," see Barney 236–38; and Fliegelman 70–76.

27. Here is Defoe's depiction of that figure, one who resides, as the Crusoe family does, in a "Country Town": "The Man was bred to business, drove a great Trade, and grew Rich apace; he was an honest sober Man, and had the Reputation of a very fair Dealer, the Credit of what we call a good Man, that would do no body any Wrong; but as to Religion, he made no great Stir about that, he served God on *a Sundays* as other People did, and troubled his Head very little with any thing that was Religious all the Week after; indeed, he liv'd in a constant hurry of Business, so that he had really no time to think of, or to spare about Religious affairs" (*Family Instructor* 174–75).

28. As the Puritan Jonathan Edwards would put matters regarding his own conversion, "The very thought of any joy arising in me, on any consideration of my own amiableness, performances, or experiences, or any goodness of heart or life, is nauseous and detestable to me" (23).

29. A notable recent exception is Seidel.

30. Defoe's point, rather fancifully argued, is not that the scene should be rendered more vividly but that the Bible ought to have included a story of Japheth and Shem later going on to encourage Noah to repent. That Crusoe returns too late to help his father

do so means that exposing his father's sin would make him (and Defoe) no different from Ham.

31. Here, Derrida's use of the word *ethical* refers to the comparatively *less* ethical option available to Abraham, namely, of speaking the truth and behaving in conformity with ethical conventions. Abraham, for Derrida, *is* ethical in a more fundamental sense: he resists those conventions in favor of an anti-conventional but purer, self-sacrificial gesture. This is also true of Crusoe. There is a *lightly* ethical temptation to obey his father's words (which conventional ethics dictates he should do) but a *heavily* ethical need to reject them (which the ethic of uncertainty dictates he should do).

4. Risk Aversion and the Economization of Prudence

1. It is because of the tradition I highlight here that *prudence* appears, or its cognates appear, in the names of many financial service companies, most notably Prudential Financial, Inc.

2. For an exemplary seventeenth-century revival of Machiavellian prudence, see Reinking. The author's name is a pseudonym for the Scottish royalist Patrick Ker (fl. 1684–91). Ker advises his reader to contrive, discover secrets, counterfeit, wheedle, dissemble, pretend, falsely accuse, feign ignorance, speak under the cover of rhetorical figures, flatter, and attain one's ends through indirect courses (5–9, 15, 30–33, 39). Models of conduct include the Roman emperor Nero (48, 73), a Jew who disowns his faith when interrogated by a Turkish emperor about religion (55–57), an adulterous woman (67–68), and an array of lesser lights in the history of skullduggery. Written in the tradition of Machiavelli's *The Prince*, Ker's "Demonstrations of unparalleled Prudence" (title page) do not so much make prudence into a vice but call into question whether there can be any such thing as virtue. Information pertaining to Ker is from Dunnigan.

3. Interestingly, Samuel Johnson does not connect prudence to the economic sphere in his definitions of it or any of its cognates, even though he clearly knew of the association, as evidenced by his frequent use of the term in his account of the life of Richard Savage to describe what Savage, it is well known, was utterly lacking (*Account of the Life* 15, 84, 180).

4. The connection between prudence and economy was not by any means limited to political economic tracts; it can be found in virtually every conceivable part of eighteenth-century print culture, and in varying grammatical and poetic forms. Lawrence Whyte, for example, writing of "pious *Vesta*," remarks that she "in her Sphere with prudence doth preside, / Good Life her Care, Oeconomy her Pride" (188). The father of Hermann Boerhaave was described as "no less remarkable for his frankness and candour in general, than for the prudence of his economy" (Burton 3). In his novel *The Adventures of Mr. George Edwards, A Creole*, John Hill describes his hero's uncle Jeremy, happy with the inexpensive lodgings he has procured, as a "Man of great Prudence and Oeconomy" (3). William Thornton recommended emulating the "Prudence and Oeconomy" of France in forming a militia (47); William Douglass admired the "prudence and oeconomy" of Connecticut Congregationalists (149); Tobias Smollett found remarkable the

"prudence and oeconomy" of an Englishman who avoided the extortionate innkeepers of coastal Italy by sleeping on board his ship (154). Nathaniel Smith, off-and-on director of the East India Company between 1774 and 1794, described shipping with too few vessels during wartime as "inconsistent with prudence or true oeconomy" (72).

A number of scholars have noted the connection between prudence and economy. On James Boswell's use of these terms, Weed observes that the "man of economy" (225) holds to "an ethic of prudence, which is capable of mutating into avarice" (230). On the early American novelist Hannah Foster's linking of prudence to economy, see Hoeller 24–25, 34–37. Randall forges, in effect, a link between amoral or immoral Machiavellian prudence and economic interest via the mediating eighteenth-century category of "private interest." See Randall 209–11. Pesciarelli notes that it is in the midst of his analysis of the "psychological factors involved in the exercise of economic activity" that Adam Smith "introduces the figure of the prudent man" (532). Vivienne Brown, by contrast, contends that in Smith's *Theory of Moral Sentiments* "prudence cannot be deemed a specifically 'economic' virtue, as it is no more associated with commerce, manufacturing or any of the other activities that have since come to be identified with economic behaviour, than it is with a general solicitous care for the matters which tend to the self-preservation of a person in his 'best and most perfect state'" (97). I agree with Brown's view that Smith did not conceptualize prudence in strictly economic terms and in fact had a much more subtle understanding of prudence than is often allowed him.

5. Seager draws attention to the problematical identity of "William de Britain" (360–61), provides a more complete textual history of *Humane Prudence* (359–62), and shows that it was in any case a major source for continuations of Defoe's *Roxana*.

6. Manningham accurately anticipates this when he observes that for sinners "there is no true Prudence" except "that which tends to make Men Rich and Great" and, conversely, that those who lack a "Knowledge of Men and Business" are regarded by the false prophets of economic prudence as being "very Imprudent" (13). But why, he goes on to ask, "should the heaping up of Riches be look'd upon as the main Evidence and mark of Mens Prudence?" (14).

7. McCloskey continues, "The way most economists do their job is to ask, Where's the prudence?" (318). Garon has more fully documented the centrality of prudence to the discipline of economics, providing a useful discussion of how the prudential ethic of nineteenth-century Great Britain grew out of Thomas Malthus's writings: "A common sight in Victorian Britain was the allegorical statue of Thrift or Prudence" (50). Notwithstanding the contingent cultural factors involved in the economization of prudence discussed by Garon, many economists hold that prudence was always an economic matter. For Robert Hariman, however, prudence in this sense is really just a "shadow of its former self," for it fails to appreciate the extent to which prudence in the classical tradition entailed "habits of deliberation" and the attaining of a "good life in general," and not simply the ability to discern and carry out, as realists would have it, the most expedient means for the accomplishment of selfish ends ("Theory without Modernity" 15).

8. Amartya Sen similarly envisions economics as having always already been there, to be found in Aristotle and brought into the full light in Smith's theorization of prudence

(2–7). Sen, however, recognizes that Smith does not provide a fully ringing endorsement of prudence (22–28).

9. See Coley's note in Fielding, *True Patriot* 161n2.

10. For Freud's account of gambling and masochism, see "Dostoyevsky and Parricide" 235–36, 248–49, 254.

11. At the opening to his first volume of *The Accursed Share*, Bataille writes: "For some years, being obliged on occasion to answer the question 'What are you working on?' I was embarrassed to have to say, 'A book of political economy.' Coming from me, this venture was disconcerting, at least to those who did not know me well. (The interest that is usually conferred on my books is of a literary sort and this was doubtless to be expected . . .). . . . I had to add that the book I was writing (which I am now publishing) did not consider the facts the way qualified economists do" (9).

12. For more on the "extraordinary success" of the play, see Hume, who argues that while a thousand pounds seems high, six or seven hundred pounds seems likely (*Henry Fielding and the London Theatre* 126).

13. For an insightful (and skeptical) reading of the connection between financial generosity and the culture of sensibility, see Skinner.

14. Battestin summarizes the findings of his study as follows: "As the great world was characterized not only by Energy, but by Order, so too, the little world of man should reflect those essential aspects of creation in an active benevolence and a wise self-control—prudence and providence being regarded as the analogous attributes of order in microcosm and macrocosm" (271). I would add, however, that the relation between "benevolence and a wise self-control," or prudence, is precisely the problem Fielding must confront, for the two are often at odds with each other, and as the examples I have offered suggest, what Fielding often seems to mean by *benevolence* is an unwise and self-destructive generosity. This seems particularly true in the case of the peddler, who literally lives on charity but is himself charitable even to the point of potentially starving himself.

15. On the absence of God in *Tom Jones*, see Rosengarten 126; on the coded presence of God in *Tom Jones*, see Reilly 120–34.

16. Robert D. Hume considers the "realistic optimism" of *The Modern Husband* in relation to a longer tradition of "marital discord comedies" ("Marital Discord" 272). Building on Hume's and Woods's articles, Earla A. Wilputte provides a more detailed historical account of wife pandering and regards "the motif of wife selling used earlier by Behn and Haywood" as central to Fielding's play but also sees that Fielding's target goes beyond the family to the "profit-oriented fever and immorality" of "society" (461–62).

17. As far as I can tell, the Abergavenny link to Fielding's play first appeared in Woods's article. If it had been noted earlier, Woods, in any case, did not know as much. In his introduction to the play, Lockwood wisely notes that we have no proof that the trial was Fielding's source for the play.

18. Although the list of scholars working in this field is large and growing, works of note include Mark Blackwell's edited collection of essays, *The Secret Life of Things: Animals, Objects, and It-Narratives in Eighteenth-Century England*; Jonathan Lamb's *The*

Things Things Say; and Ileana Baird and Christina Ionescu's *Eighteenth-Century Thing Theory in a Global Context.*

19. Although the heyday of it-narratives—in the 1760s and 1770s and beyond, according to Liz Bellamy ("It-Narrators")—was yet to come when Fielding wrote his play, there were precedents for such a focus in, for example, Charles Gildon's *Golden Spy.*

20. An after-game, according to Ingrassia, is a "second game played in order to reverse or improve the issues of the first; hence, as Samuel Johnson describes it, 'The scheme which may be laid or the expedients which are practised after the original game has miscarried; methods taken after the first turn of affairs'" (Haywood and Fielding 126n2).

21. For an interesting discussion of Richly as a "Machiavel," see Keymer 65.

22. Tiffany Potter insightfully remarks that Richly's "distasteful economic metaphors" bring to mind "piracy in trade" (65).

23. Fielding appears to have finished *The Modern Husband* before the 1731 state lottery was held, so there is no reason to believe that the resemblance between the fortune of the banknote and a winning lottery ticket is intentional. But in evaluating the cultural force of Fielding's treatment of gambling and risk, it is worth noting that *The Modern Husband* and his farce *The Lottery* were staged within two months of each other (14 February 1732 and 1 January 1732, respectively). See Lockwood, "*The Lottery*: Introduction" 129–30; and Lockwood, "*The Modern Husband*: Introduction" 195.

24. For a discussion of the extent of indirect representation in *The Modern Husband* in relation to Fielding's other early plays, see Goggin 774.

25. For Manningham, prudence required a simultaneous attention to justice. Edmund Calamy (1671–1732), recommending that his parishioners be, as the title of one of his sermons (taken from Matthew 10:16) reads, as "prudent as the serpent and innocent as the dove," went on to illustrate in the course of his sermon just how diabolical prudence could be without the ameliorating effects of a dovelike moral innocence. For de Britain, "Policy and Religion, as they do well together, so they do as ill asunder; the one being too cunning to be good, the other too simple to be false; therefore some few scruples of the Wisdom of the Serpent, mixt with the Innocency of the Dove, will be an excellent Ingredient in all your Actions" (202).

26. Geoffrey Sill has pointed to the way in which Tom acts as moral physician, particularly with respect to Nightingale (162–65).

27. Tom's "impulsiveness" is such common critical shorthand that it hardly needs evidencing, and it may seem somewhat petty to do so. It is employed by some of Fielding's finest readers. In addition to Empson, Bartolomeo, in a wider context, writes to this effect in observing that "Tom's good-hearted actions sometimes seem impulsive and self-indulgent, and need, the narrator argues, to be tempered by prudence" (263). Poovey writes that Tom "is represented as honourable but imprudent, generous but impulsive," her parallel structure implying a harmony between imprudence and impulse (132). The rhetoric of impulse in conversations pertaining to *Tom Jones* is more critical shorthand than argument at this point; my point is to call into question that shorthand, not the substance of these scholars' readings.

28. We see a similar kind of disavowal of ekphrasis of the female form toward the end of *Joseph Andrews*, where the narrator more or less asks his reader to simply imagine something beautiful in order to understand the appearance of Fanny: "To comprehend her entirely, conceive youth, health, bloom, beauty, neatness, and innocence in her bridal-bed; conceive all these in their utmost perfection, and you may place the charming Fanny's picture before your eyes" (406). Resisting his own scopic presence, the narrator of *Joseph Andrews* simply calls upon his reader to imagine.

29. For a more recent approach to Fielding's attempt to arrest and fix meanings through satirical inversion and his evident failures to do so, see Bogel 158–67.

30. For a perspective on the radical, ethical possibilities of laughter, see Critchley 77–83, which offers humor as a corrective to the prudential considerations of the ego.

31. And it is this departure from the providential framework that I consider significant, though Sandra Macpherson seems to me absolutely right in saying that the novel does not live up to the ethical standard she sets for it (or asks whether it meets). Fielding does endorse "a humanist ethic predicated on fellow feeling" rather than an ethic that recognizes the importance of ties between those who are not nor could be comprehended as fellows (132).

32. It is on the basis of his treatment of the gift in an "exchangist" context that Derrida critiques Mauss (*Given Time* 37–50). Derrida rightly sees Mauss as analyzing the gift from the standpoint of "economic rationality" rather than "the reverse," that is, analyzing "economic rationality" from the standpoint of the gift (44). Mauss's move is the same one readers make when approaching Fielding's gambling from the standpoint of economic rationality; I read Fielding's gambling as a critique of economic rationality. For further consideration of the tacit exchangism in approaches to gifts and sacrifice, see Marion 74–75.

33. Fielding's resistance to system is what spurs Hudson to remark on Fielding's "comic wisdom" (90), and there is certainly a comic aspect to the undecidable conclusion. The ending also looks forward to an idea of ethics as formally undecidable. One might well say of Fielding's novel what Derrida says of Levinas's ethics when he writes that Levinas "does not seek to propose . . . moral rules, does not seek to determine *a* morality, but rather the essence of the ethical relation in general" (*Writing and Difference* 111). For further consideration of the relation between the determinacy of law and the idea of justice, see Derrida, *Acts of Religion* 241–58. Justice arises from the ethical relation but leaves in its wake the unmediated experience of proximity that characterizes the solely ethical relation to the other, since it necessarily deals with "a third party" (Levinas 157). As Peter Jowers puts it in his excellent reading of the relationship of risk to justice in Levinas's ethics, the "entry of another on the scene perturbs the one-way relation from the self to the Other," and "paying attention, being taken hostage by the Other, excludes the possibility of the same relation with another at the same time" (68–69).

Conclusion

1. Consider, for example, the following words of the historian W. E. H. Lecky: "Year by year what the old theologians had termed usury became more general. The creation

of national debts made it the very pillar of the political system. Every great enterprise that was undertaken received its impulse from it, and the immense majority of the wealthy were concerned in it" (258).

2. See Morley; and Bellew.

3. Ruskin further reveals this intimacy in a letter of 8 January 1878 to Henry Willett, who had sent him a copy of Blaxton's book. Ruskin wrote, "Anything more entirely delicious than this book you've sent me cannot be! It ends the matter—its wit and truths are flawless. I think I shall issue an entire reprint" (236–37). It is in a letter of 9 September 1879 to F. A. Malleson that Ruskin describes *The English Usurer* as "one I would not lose for its weight in gold" (298).

4. For further evidence that Ruskin tended to think of usury in terms of interest rather than in terms of risk and certainty, see Ruskin, *Ariadne Florentina* 438–40; and Ruskin, "Usury: A Reply and Rejoinder" 421, 423–25. Casillo points to specific moments in *Fors Clavigera* when Ruskin draws upon the Aristotelian formulation, but Casillo acknowledges as well the importance of Leviticus and Deuteronomy in Ruskin's views concerning interest. For further consideration of Ruskin's development of ideas concerning usury, see Anthony 83–86. Anthony regards Aristotle's formulation as the basis for Ruskin's rejection of interest, but it is clear that Ruskin's antipathy towards it in *Fors Clavigera* has its origins in Old Testament prohibitions on interest.

5. Ruskin's ostentatious presentation of his own self as of an older style runs throughout his writings and is particularly evident in letter 7 of *Fors Clavigera*, in which he cuts ties with the First International and declares himself to be of a deeper red than even the Parisian revolutionaries (esp. 117–25). Eagles rightly emphasizes the impact and influence of Ruskin's charity and benevolence (in his life and writing) but only in closing suggests how much greater an impact Ruskin might have had if he had not written "like an Old Testament prophet" (269).

6. See also "Ruskin on Usury."

7. Derrida would consider the ethic of Luke that underwrote early modern antifinance as problematic, as "an economy that integrates the renunciation of a calculable remuneration," insofar as it supposes, at a higher level, a rectifying and remunerating deity by which the gift is paid back to the giver. God will "pay back" your gift of the gift, but thus cancel out the very status of the gift as gift (which seeks no remuneration or payback) (*Gift of Death* 107). Here, however, Derrida would have done well to consider the gulf between his time, in which economism taints or potentially taints all relations, and the moment before the economic was conceivable as such. Focused upon the pervasive and corrupting economism of his present, Derrida maps that economism onto the whole of history and thereby reproduces the secularist hypothesis that religious belief, particularly Christian providentialist belief of the strand seen in anti-usury discourse, was always *really* just mystification that concealed or held within it an economic intention, imperative, or set of imperatives.

Bibliography

Addison, Joseph. *Spectator* 3. Mackie 188–91.

Allestree, Richard. *The Art of Patience and Balm of Gilead under All Afflictions.* London, 1694.

Ames, Richard. *Lawyerus bootatus & spurratus, or, The long vacation, a poem, by a student of Lincolns-Inn.* London, 1691.

Ames, William. *The Marrow of Sacred Divinity, Drawne Out of the Holy Scriptures.* London, 1642.

Anker, Michael. *The Ethics of Uncertainty: Aporetic Openings.* New York: Atropos, 2009.

Anthony, P. D. *John Ruskin's Labour: A Study of Ruskin's Social Theory.* Cambridge: Cambridge UP, 1983.

Appleby, Joyce. *Economic Thought and Ideology in Seventeenth-Century England.* Princeton, NJ: Princeton UP, 1978.

Aquinas, Thomas. "Question 78. Of the Sin of Usury, which is Committed in Loans." *Summa Theologica,* pt. 2. Trans. Fathers of the English Dominican Province. New York: Benziger, 1918. 329–41.

Aristotle. *Politics. The Complete Works of Aristotle.* Trans. Benjamin Jowett. Ed. Jonathan Barnes. Vol. 2. Princeton, NJ: Princeton UP, 1984. 1986–2129.

Arrighi, Giovanni. *The Long Twentieth Century: Money, Power, and the Origins of our Times.* London: Verso, 2010.

Asad, Talal. *Formations of the Secular: Christianity, Islam, Modernity.* Stanford, CA: Stanford UP, 2003.

Aubin, Penelope. *The Strange Adventures of the Count de Vinevil and his Family.* London, 1728.

Aurelius, Marcus. *The Emperor Marcus Antoninus, his conversation with himself. Together with the preliminary discourse of the learned Gataker.* Trans. Jeremy Collier. London, 1702.

Aveling, James Hobson. *The Chamberlens and the Midwifery Forceps.* London: Churchill, 1882.

Backscheider, Paula. *Daniel Defoe: His Life.* Baltimore: Johns Hopkins UP, 1989.

Bacon, Francis. *The Essays.* Ed. John Pitcher. London: Penguin, 1986.

Baird, Ileana, and Christina Ionescu. *Eighteenth-Century Thing Theory in a Global Context: From Consumerism to Celebrity Culture.* Burlington, VT: Ashgate, 2013.

Baker, Jennifer J. *Securing the Commonwealth: Debt, Speculation, and Writing in the Making of the Early American Republic.* Baltimore: Johns Hopkins UP, 2005.

Barnett, S. J. *The Enlightenment and Religion: The Myths of Modernity.* Manchester: Manchester UP, 2003.

Barney, Richard A. *Plots of Enlightenment: Education and the Novel in Eighteenth-Century England.* Stanford, CA: Stanford UP, 1999.

Barnfield, Richard. *The Encomion of Lady Pecunia; or, The Praise of Money. Richard Barnfield: The Complete Poems.* Ed. George Klawitter. Selinsgrove, PA: Susquehanna UP, 1990. 149–60.

Bartolomeo, Joseph F. "Restoration and Eighteenth-Century Fiction." *A Companion to Satire: Ancient and Modern.* Ed. Ruben Quintero. Malden: Blackwell, 2007. 257–75.

Bataille, Georges. *The Accursed Share: An Essay on General Economy.* Trans. Robert Hurtley. Vol. 1. New York: Zone, 1991.

———. "The Notion of Expenditure." *The Bataille Reader.* Ed. Fred Botting and Scott Wilson. Oxford: Blackwell, 1997. 167–81.

Battestin, Martin. *The Providence of Wit: Aspects of Form in Augustan Literature and the Arts.* Charlottesville: U of Virginia P, 1989.

Battestin, Martin, and Ruth C. Battestin. *Henry Fielding: A Life.* London: Routledge, 1989.

Baudrillard, Jean. *For a Critique of the Political Economy of the Sign.* Trans. Charles Levin. Saint Louis: Telos, 1981.

Baxter, Richard. *Directions and Perswasions to a Sound Conversion for Prevention of that Deceit and Damnation of Souls, and of those Scandals, Heresies, and Desperate Apostasies that Are the Consequents of a Counterfeit, or Superficial Change.* London, 1658.

———. *Saints Everlasting Rest.* London, 1650.

———. *Saints Everlasting Rest.* Abr. Benjamin Fawcett. 1758. *Christian Classics Ethereal Library.* http://www.ccel.org/ccel/baxter/saints_rest.i.html.

Bellamy, Liz. *Commerce, Morality, and the Eighteenth-Century Novel.* Cambridge: Cambridge UP, 2005.

———. "It-Narrators and Circulation: Defining a Subgenre." Blackwell 117–46.

Bellew, J. C. M., ed. *Poets' Corner: A Manual for Students in English Poetry.* London: Routledge, 1868.

Bentham, Jeremy. *Defence of Usury; Shewing the Impolicy of the Present Legal Restraints on Pecuniary Bargains in a Series of Letters to a Friend. To Which is Added a Letter to Adam Smith, Esq.; LL.D. on the Discouragements opposed by the above Restraints to the Progress of Inventive Industry.* 1818. http://www.econlib.org/library/Bentham/bnthUs2.html.

Berardi, Franco. *The Uprising: On Poetry and Finance.* Los Angeles: Semiotext(e), 2012.

Bigg, George. "From the Rev. George Bigg, D.D., Brighton College." *The Lord's Prayer and the Church: Letters to the Clergy by John Ruskin, D.C.L. with Replies from Clergy and Laity, and an Epilogue by Mr. Ruskin.* Ed. F. A. Malleson. London, 1880. 129–43.

Blackstone, William. *Commentaries upon the Laws of England*. Vol. 2. Chicago: U of Chicago P, 1979.

Blackwell, Mark, ed. *The Secret Life of Things: Animals, Objects, and It-Narratives in Eighteenth-Century England*. Cranbury, NJ: Associated UP, 2007.

Blaxton, John. *The English Usurer*. London, 1634.

Bogel, Fredric. *The Difference Satire Makes: Rhetoric and Reading from Jonson to Byron*. Ithaca, NY: Cornell UP, 2011.

Bolton, Robert. *A Short and Private Discourse betweene M. Bolton and one M.S. concerning Usury*. London, 1637.

Braddick, Michael. *The Nerves of State: Taxation and the Financing of the English State, 1558–1714*. Manchester: Manchester UP, 1996.

Brandt, Walther I. Introduction. *Trade and Usury*. Luther, *Luther's Works*, vol. 45. 233–43.

Brantlinger, Patrick. *Fictions of State: Culture and Credit in Britain, 1694–1994*. Ithaca, NY: Cornell UP, 1996.

Bremer, Francis J. "Knewstub, John (1544–1624)." *Oxford Dictionary of National Biography*. Ed. H. C. G. Matthew and Brian Harrison. Oxford: Oxford UP, 2004. Online ed. Ed. Lawrence Goldman. http://www.oxforddnb.com/view/article/15713.

Brewer, John. *Sinews of Power: War, Money and the English State, 1688–1783*. New York: Knopf, 1989.

Brod, Manfred. "Jones, David (1662/3–1724)." *Oxford Dictionary of National Biography*. Ed. H. C. G. Matthew and Brian Harrison. Oxford: Oxford UP, 2004. Online ed. Ed. Lawrence Goldman. http://www.oxforddnb.com/view/article/14989.

Brooke, J. M. S., and A. W. C. Hallen. *Transcript of the Registers of the United Parishes of S. Mary Woolnoth and S. Mary Woolchurch haw, in the City of London, From their Commencement 1538 to 1760. To which is prefixed A Short Account of Both Parishes, List of Rectors and Churchwards, Chantries, &c. Together with some interesting Extracts from the Churchwardens' Accounts*. London: Bowles, 1886.

Brown, Laura. *Ends of Empire: Women and Ideology in Early Eighteenth-Century English Literature*. Ithaca, NY: Cornell UP, 1993.

———. *Fables of Modernity*. Ithaca, NY: Cornell UP, 2003.

Brown, Thomas. *A Collection of Miscellany Poems, Letters, &c. by Mr. Brown, &c*. London, 1699.

———. "A Comical View of the *Transactions* that will happen in the Cities of *London* and *Westminster*." *A Legacy for the Ladies: Or, characters of the Women of the Age*. London, 1705. 109–92.

Brown, Vivienne. *Adam Smith's Discourse: Canonicity, Commerce, and Conscience*. Oxford: Routledge, 1994.

Bunyan, John. *Grace Abounding to the Chief of Sinners and the Pilgrim's Progress from this World to that which is to come*. Ed. Roger Sharrock. London: Oxford UP, 1966.

Burnet, Gilbert. *Bishop Burnet's History of his Own Time . . . From the Restoration of King Charles II to the Settlement of King William and Queen Mary at the Revolution*. Vol. 1. London, 1724.

Burton, William. *An Account of the Life and Writings of Herman Boerhaave*. London, 1746.

Calamy, Edmund. *The Prudence of the Serpent and the Innocence of the Dove*. London, 1713.

Calvin, John. *Commentary on the Book of Psalms*. Trans. James Anderson. Grand Rapids, MI: Christian Classics Ethereal Library, 1845.

Carruthers, Bruce. *City of Capital: Politics and Markets in the English Financial Revolution*. Princeton, NJ: Princeton UP, 1996.

Casillo, Robert. "Parasitism and Capital Punishment in Ruskin's Fors Clavigera." *Victorian Studies* 29.4 (Summer 1986): 537–67.

Cawdry, Robert. *A Table Alphabeticall Containing and Teaching the True Writing and Understanding of Hard Usual English Wordes*. London, 1609.

Chamberlen, Mr. *News from Hell: or, A Match for the Directors; A Satire*. London, 1721.

Chamillart, Michel. *The Present State of Europe: or, The Historical and Political Monthly Mercury* 20.2 (Feb. 1709): 67. *Eighteenth Century Journals Portal*. 2 Nov. 2012.

Chancellor, Edward. *Devil Take the Hindmost: A History of Financial Speculation*. New York: Farrar, Strauss, & Giroux, 1999.

Chapman, Alison. "Marking Time: Astrology, Almanacs, and English Protestantism." *Renaissance Quarterly* 60.4 (2007): 1257–90.

Clark, Dorothy K. "A Restoration Goldsmith-Banking House: The Vine on Lombard Street." *Essays in Modern English History in Honor of Wilbur Cortez Abbott*. Port Washington, NY: Kennikat, 1971. 3–47.

Clark, Gregory. "The Political Foundations of Modern Economic Growth: England, 1540–1800." *Journal of Interdisciplinary History* 26.4 (Spring 1996): 563–88.

Codr, Dwight. "'Various Adventures and Strange Turns of Fortune': John Law and Finance in Popular Culture." Rotenberg-Schwartz and Czechowski, *Global Economies* 175–96.

Collins, Anthony. *A Discourse of free-thinking, occasion'd by the rise and growth of a sect call'd Free-Thinkers*. London, 1713.

A Common Law Treatise of Usury, and Usurious Contracts: Wherein is set forth, The Nature of Usury, and what Contracts are said Usurious in our LAW. London, 1710.

Cooper, Thompson. "Huddleston, John (1636–1700)." Rev. Ruth Jordan. *Oxford Dictionary of National Biography*. Ed. H. C. G. Matthew and Brian Harrison. Oxford: Oxford UP, 2004. Online ed. Ed. Lawrence Goldman. http://www.oxforddnb .com/view/article/7837.

Cory, David. *Puss Junior and Robinson Crusoe*. New York: Grosset & Dunlap, 1922.

Craig, John. "Mosse, Miles (1559–1615)." *Oxford Dictionary of National Biography*. Oxford: Oxford UP, 2004. Online ed. Ed. Lawrence Goldman. http://www.oxforddnb .com/view/article/19406.

Crane, R. S. "The Concept of Plot and the Plot of *Tom Jones*." *Critics and Criticism: Abridged Edition*. Ed. Crane. Chicago: U of Chicago P, 1957.

Critchley, Simon. *Infinitely Demanding: Ethics of Commitment, Politics of Resistance*. London: Verso, 2012.

Cross, Wilbur Lucius. *The History of Henry Fielding*. Vol. 2. New Haven, CT: Yale UP, 1918.

Crouch, Samuel. *A Discourse upon Usury: or, Lending Money for Increase (Occasioned by Mr. David Jones's late Farewel Sermon)*. London, 1692.

Cruikshank, Robert. *Lessons of Thrift. Published for general benefit by a member of the Save-All Club*. London, 1820.

Culpepper, Thomas. *A Tract Against Usurie: Presented to the High Court of Parliament*. London, 1621.

Cunningham, William. *The Growth of English Industry and Commerce in Modern Times*. Cambridge: Cambridge UP, 1907.

Dalrymple, Sir John. *Memoirs of Great Britain and Ireland. From the Dissolution of the Last Parliament of Charles II until the Sea-Battle off La Hogue*. London, 1771.

Damrosch, Leopold, Jr. *God's Plot and Man's Stories: Studies in the Fictional Imagination from Milton to Fielding*. Chicago: U of Chicago P, 1985.

Daston, Lorraine. *Classical Probability and the Enlightenment*. Princeton, NJ: Princeton UP, 1995.

Davenant, Charles. *Discourses on the Publick Revenues and on the Trade of England. In Two Parts*. London, 1698.

de Britain, William. *Humane Prudence, Or the Art by which a Man May Raise Himself and his Fortune to Grandeur*. 1680. 9th ed. London, 1702.

Defoe, Daniel. *Anatomy of Exchange Alley*. London, 1719.

———. *Caledonia, A Poem, &c.* Edinburgh, 1706.

———. *A Compleat System of Magick*. London, 1729.

———. *The Complete English Tradesman, in familiar letters*. Vol. 1. London, 1726.

———. *The Director*. Defoe, *Works* 207–96.

———. *An Essay upon Literature*. London, 1726.

———. *An Essay upon Loans*. Defoe, *Works* 63–76.

———. *An Essay upon Projects*. 1697. Ed. Joyce Kennedy, Michael Seidel, and Maximillian Novak. New York: AMS, 1999.

———. *An Essay upon Public Credit*. Defoe, *Works* 49–61.

———. *The Family Instructor, in Three Parts*. 2nd ed. London, 1715.

———. *A General History of Discoveries and Improvements*. London, 1725–26.

———. [Sir Malcontent Chagrin]. "Individual Foibles, National Benefits." *Mist's Journal*, 7 Feb. 1719. Rpt. in *Daniel Defoe: His Life, and Recently Discovered Writings*. Ed. William Lee. Vol. 2. London: Hotten, 1869.

———. *A Plan of the English Commerce*. London, 1728.

———. *The Protestant Jesuit Unmask't*. London, 1704.

———. *Review of the State of the English Nation. Defoe's Review*. Ed. Arthur Wellesley Secord. 3.5:17–20. New York: Columbia UP for the Facsimile Text Society, 1938.

———. *Robinson Crusoe*. 1719. Ed. John Richetti. London: Penguin, 2001.

———. *A Tour Thro' the Whole Island of Great Britain*. London, 1742.

———. *The Villainy of Stock-Jobbers Detected*. London, 1701.

———. *The Works of Daniel Defoe: The Political and Economic Writings of Daniel Defoe.* Vol. 6, *Finance.* Ed. John McVeagh. London: Pickering & Chatto, 2000.

de Goede, Marieke. "Mastering 'Lady Credit.'" *International Feminist Journal of Politics* 2:1 (Spring 2000): 58–81.

———. *Virtue, Fortune, and Faith: A Genealogy of Finance.* Minneapolis: U of Minnesota P, 2005.

Derrida, Jacques. *Acts of Religion.* Ed. Gil Anidjar. London: Routledge, 2002.

———. *The Gift of Death.* Trans. David Wills. Chicago: U of Chicago P, 1995.

———. *Given Time: I. Counterfeit Money.* Trans. Peggy Kamuf. Chicago: U of Chicago P, 1992.

———. *Writing and Difference.* Trans. Alan Bass. Chicago: U of Chicago P, 1980.

de Vries, Jan. *The Industrious Revolution: Consumer Behavior and the Household Economy, 1650–Present.* New York: Cambridge UP, 2008.

Dickson, P. G. M. *The Financial Revolution in England: A Study in the Development of Public Credit, 1688–1756.* London: Macmillan, 1967.

Dorman, Joseph. *Folly: A Poem.* London, 1737.

Douglass, William. *A Summary, Historical and Political, of the first planting, progressive improvements, and present state of the British Settlements in North-America.* Vol. 2. London, 1760.

Dugaw, Dianne. "'All the Riches that we Boast Consist in Scraps of Paper': English Ballad Tradition and Emergent Capitalism in the Eighteenth Century." *Folklore Historian* 14 (1997): 23–30.

Dunnigan, S. M. "Ker, Patrick (*fl.* 1684–1691)." *Oxford Dictionary of National Biography.* Oxford: Oxford UP, 2004. Online ed. Ed. Lawrence Goldman. http://www .oxforddnb.com/view/article/15455.

Dunton, John. *Athenian Mercury* 6.11 (5 Mar. 1692): 97–98.

———. *Athenian Mercury* 6.18 (26 Mar. 1692): 103–4.

———. *The Hazard of a Death-Bed Repentance, further argued, from the late remorse of W—— late D—— of D—— with serious reflections on his adulterous life.* London, 1708.

Eagles, Stuart. *After Ruskin: The Social and Political Legacies of a Victorian Prophet, 1870–1920.* Oxford: Oxford UP, 2011.

Eagleton, Terry. *The Ideology of the Aesthetic.* Cambridge: Basil Blackwell, 1990.

Edwards, Jonathan. *The Works of President Edwards.* Vol 1. New York: Carter & Brothers, 1881.

Eliot, T. S. *The Wasteland. The Wasteland and Other Poems.* Ed. Joseph Black et al. Peterborough, ON: Broadview, 2011. 63–83.

Elton, Oliver. *A Survey of English Literature: 1730–1780.* London: Arnold, 1959.

Empson, William. "Tom Jones." *Twentieth-Century Interpretations of Tom Jones.* Ed. Martin Battestin. Englewood Cliffs, NJ: Prentice-Hall, 1968. 33–55.

Essay on the Necessity of Equal Taxes. London, 1702.

Exchange-Alley: or, the Stock-Jobber turn'd Gentleman; with the Humours of Modern Projectors. A Tragi-Comical Farce. London, 1720.

Fenton, Roger. *A Treatise of Usurie Divided into Three Books.* London, 1611.

Fielding, Henry. *Amelia.* Ed. Martin C. Battestin. Middletown, CT: Wesleyan UP, 1983.

———. *The Champion.* 1739. *The Complete Works of Henry Fielding, Esq. Miscellaneous Writings in Three Volumes.* Vol. 2. London: Heineman, 1903. 87–90.

———. *The History of Tom Jones, a Foundling.* Ed. R. P. C. Mutter. London: Penguin, 1985.

———. "Inquiry into the Causes of the Late Increase of Robbers." *The Works of Henry Fielding, Esq: A Voyage to Lisbon, Legal Papers and Poems.* Ed. Leslie Steven. London: Smith, Elder, 1882. 179–86.

———. *Joseph Andrews.* Ed. Paul A. Scanlon. Peterborough, ON: Broadview, 2001.

———. *The Life of Jonathan Wild the Great.* Ed. Hugh Amory. Oxford: Oxford UP, 2003.

———. *The Lottery: A Farce.* 2nd ed. London, 1732.

———. *The Modern Husband.* Fielding, *Plays.*

———. *Plays.* Vol. 2, *1731–1734.* Ed. Thomas Lockwood. Oxford: Clarendon, 2007.

———. *The True Patriot and Related Writings.* Ed. W. B. Coley. Middletown, CT: Wesleyan UP, 1987.

"Finance, n." *OED Online.* 2014. Web. 8 Jan. 2015.

Fliegelman, Jay. *Prodigals and Pilgrims: The American Revolution against Patriarchal Authority, 1750–1800.* Cambridge: Cambridge UP, 1982.

Folkenflik, Robert. "*Robinson Crusoe* and the Semiotic Crisis." *Defoe's Footprints: Essays in Honour of Maximillian Novak.* Ed. Robert M. Maniquis and Carl Fisher. Toronto: U of Toronto P, 2009. 98–125.

Foucault, Michel. *The Order of Things: An Archaeology of the Human Sciences.* New York: Vintage, 1973.

Fowler, Thomas. *Bacon's Novum Organum.* Oxford: Clarendon, 1878.

Franklin, Benjamin. "Advice to a Young Tradesman." *The Political Thought of Benjamin Franklin.* Ed. Ralph Ketcham. Indianapolis: Hackett, 2003. 51–54.

Fratianni, Michele, and Franco Spinelli. "Working Paper 112: Did Genoa and Venice Kick a Financial Revolution in the Quattrocento?" 2005. http://ebusiness.oenb.at/en/img/wp112_tcm16-38081.pdf.

Freud, Sigmund. "Dostoyevsky and Parricide." *Writings on Art and Literature.* Foreword Neil Hertz. Stanford, CA: Stanford UP, 1997. 234–55. Reproduced from *The Standard Edition of the Complete Psychological Works of Sigmund Freud.* Ed. James Strachey. London: Hogarth, 1953–74. 21:177–96.

A Full Account of the Rise, Progress, and Advantages OF Dr. Asheton's Proposal (As now Improved and Managed by the Worshipful Company of Mercers, London) for the Benefit of Widows of Clergymen and Others; By Settling Jointures and Annuities at the Rate of Thirty per Cent. London, 1700.

Galloway, Andrew. *The Penn Commentary on Piers Plowman.* Vol. 1. Philadelphia: U of Pennsylvania P, 2006.

Garon, Sheldon. *Beyond Our Means: Why America Spends While the World Saves.* Princeton, NJ: Princeton UP, 2012.

Garver, Eugene. *Machiavelli and the History of Prudence*. Madison: U of Wisconsin P, 1987.

Gauci, Perry. *Regulating the British Economy, 1660–1850*. Farnham, UK: Ashgate, 2011.

Gay, John. *Trivia: Or, The Art of Walking the Streets of London*. 1716. London, 1730.

George, Charles. "English Calvinist Opinion on Usury, 1600–1640." *Journal of the History of Ideas* 18.4 (Oct. 1957): 455–74.

Giuseppi, John. *The Bank of England: A History from Its Foundation in 1694*. Chicago: Regnery, 1966.

Godwin, George. *The Churches of London: A History and Description of the Ecclesiastical Edifices of the Metropolis*. Vol. 2. London, 1839.

Goggin, L. P. "Development of Techniques in Fielding's Comedies." *PMLA* 67.5 (Sept. 1952): 769–81.

Gordon, James. *The Character of a generous prince drawn from the great lines of heroick fortitude*. London, 1703.

Gordon, Scott Paul. *The Power of the Passive Self in English Literature, 1640–1770*. Cambridge: Cambridge UP, 2002.

Gordon, Thomas. *The Humourist: Being Essays Upon Several Subjects*. Vol. 2. London, 1720.

Gouge, William. *A Guide to Goe to God: or, An explanation of the perfect patterne of prayer, the Lords prayer*. London, 1636.

Grapard, Ulla, and Gillian Hewitson, eds. *Robinson Crusoe's Economic Man: A Construction and Deconstruction*. Oxford: Routledge, 2011.

Grassby, Richard. *The Business Community of Seventeenth-Century England*. Cambridge: Cambridge UP, 1995.

Gregg, Stephen. *Defoe's Writings and Manliness: Contrary Men*. Farnham, UK: Ashgate, 2009.

Halpern, Richard. *Shakespeare's Perfume: Sodomy and Sublimity in the Sonnets, Wilde, Freud, and Lacan*. Philadelphia: U of Pennsylvania P, 2002.

Hariman, Robert. Preface. *Prudence: Classical Virtue, Postmodern Practice*. Ed. Hariman. University Park: Pennsylvania State UP, 2003. vii–ix.

———. "Theory without Modernity." *Prudence: Classical Virtue, Postmodern Practice*. Ed. Hariman. University Park: Pennsylvania State UP, 2003. 1–32.

Harris, Jonathan Gil. *Sick Economies: Drama, Mercantilism, and Disease in Shakespeare's England*. Philadelphia: U of Pennsylvania P, 2004.

Hatfield, Glenn W. "The Serpent and the Dove: Fielding's Irony and the Prudence Theme of *Tom Jones*." *Modern Philology* 65.1 (Aug. 1967): 17–32.

Hawkes, David. *Idols of the Marketplace: Idolatry and Commodity Fetishism in English Literature, 1580–1680*. New York: Palgrave, 2001.

Haywood, Eliza, and Henry Fielding. *Anti-Pamela and Shamela*. Ed. Catherine Ingrassia. Peterborough, ON: Broadview, 2004.

Hearne, Thomas. *Remarks and Collections of Thomas Hearne*. Vol. 7. Oxford: Clarendon, 1906.

"Hearth Tax: City of London 1666: St Mary Woolnoth." *London Hearth Tax: City of London and Middlesex, 1666*. British History Online. 2011. Web. 15 Feb. 2013.

Hill, Christopher. *Puritanism and Revolution: Studies in Interpretation of the English Revolution of the 17th Century*. New York: Schocken, 1964.

Hill, John. *The Adventures of Mr. George Edwards, A Creole*. London, 1751.

Hirschman, Albert O. *The Passions and the Interests: Political Arguments for Capitalism before Its Triumph*. 12th anniv. ed. Princeton, NJ: Princeton UP, 1997.

The History of the Proceedings of the House of Lords. Vol. 4 [1727–36]. London, 1742.

Hoadly, Benjamin. *The Fears and Sentiments of All True Britains; With Respect to National Credit, Interest, and Religion*. London, 1710.

Hoeller, Hildegard. *From Gift to Commodity: Capitalism and Sacrifice in Nineteenth-Century American Fiction*. Durham: U of New Hampshire P, 2012. Project Muse. 9 Feb. 2014.

Holloway, William. *The History and Antiquities of the Ancient Town and Port of Rye, in the County of Sussex*. London, 1847. 333–34.

Hornby, Charles. *A Caveat against the Whiggs, in a Short Historical View of Their Transactions*. London, 1711.

Horneck, Anthony. *The Great Law of Consideration*. London, 1704.

Horsefield, J. K. *British Monetary Experiments, 1650–1710*. London: Bell & Son, 1960.

"House of Commons Journal Volume 10: 18 January 1692." *Journal of the House of Commons: Volume 10: 1688–1693*. London: His Majesty's Stationery Office, 1802. 630–32. British History Online. http://www.british-history.ac.uk/report.aspx?compid=29196&strquery=.

Hudson, Nicholas. "Tom Jones." Rawson, *Cambridge Companion to Henry Fielding* 80–93.

Hume, Robert D. *Henry Fielding and the London Theatre, 1728–1737*. Oxford: Clarendon, 1988.

———. "Marital Discord in English Comedy from Dryden to Fielding." *Modern Philology* 74.3 (Feb. 1977): 248–72.

Hunter, J. Paul. *The Reluctant Pilgrim: Defoe's Emblematic Method and Quest for Form in Robinson Crusoe*. Baltimore: Johns Hopkins UP, 1966.

Hunter, Michael, and Annabel Gregory. Introduction. Jeake, *Astrological Diary* 1–81.

Hunter, Michael, Giles Mandelbrote, Richard Ovenden, and Nigel Smith. Introduction. *A Radical's Books: The Library Catalogue of Samuel Jeake of Rye, 1623–90*. Ed. Hunter, Mandelbrote, Ovenden, and Smith. Woodbridge, Suffolk, UK: Brewer, 1999. xvii–xxiv.

Hymer, Stephen. "Robinson Crusoe and the Secret of Primitive Accumulation." 1971. Grapard and Hewitson 42–61.

Ingrassia, Catherine. *Authorship, Commerce, and Gender in Early Eighteenth-Century England: A Culture of Paper Credit*. Cambridge: Cambridge UP, 1998.

Innocense clear'd: or a short defence of Mr. Jones's farewel-sermon. In answer to a late scandalous and scurrilous pamphlet, entituled the Lombard-street lecturer's farewel-sermon answered, &c. London, 1692.

Jeake, Samuel. *An Astrological Diary of the Seventeenth Century: Samuel Jeake of Rye, 1652–1699.* Ed. and introd. Michael Hunter and Annabel Gregory. Oxford: Oxford UP, 1988.

Jelinger, Christopher. *The Usurer Cast.* London, 1676.

———. *Usury Stated Overthrown: or, Usuries Champions with their Auxiliaries, shamefully Disarmed and Beaten: By an Answer to its chief Champion, which lately appeared in Print to defend it. And Godliness Epitomized.* London, 1679.

Jenkins, Eugenia Zuroski. "Defoe's Trinkets: Figuring Global Commerce in the Early Eighteenth Century." Rotenberg-Schwartz and Czechowski, *Global Economies* 197–214.

Jewel, John. "An Exposition upon the Two Epistles of the Apostle St. Paul to The Thessalonians." *Writings of John Jewell, Bishop of Salisbury.* Philadelphia: Presbyterian Board of Publication, 1843. 83–188.

Johnson, Samuel. *An Account of the Life of Mr. Richard Savage, Son of the Earl Rivers.* London, 1744.

———. *Dictionary of the English Language.* London, 1755.

Jones, David. *A Farewel-Sermon Preached to the United Parishes of St. Mary Woolnoth, & St. Mary Woolchurch-Haw.* London, 1703.

Jones, D. *The Secret History of White-Hall, from the Restoration of Charles II, down to the Abdication of the Late K. James.* Vol. 1. London, 1717.

Jones, Norman. *God and the Moneylenders: Usury and Law in Early Modern England.* Oxford: Basil Blackwell, 1989.

———. "Usury." *Economic History Services.* http://eh.net/encyclopedia/article/jones.usury.

Jowers, Peter. "Risk, Sensibility, Ethics and Justice in the Later Levinas." *Trust, Risk and Uncertainty.* Ed. Sean Watson and Anthony Moran. Houndmills, Basingstoke, Hants: Palgrave Macmillan, 2005. 47–72.

Kadane, Matthew. *The Watchful Clothier: The Life of an Eighteenth-Century Protestant Capitalist.* New Haven, CT: Yale UP, 2013.

Kaufmann, M. "Mr. Ruskin as a Practical Teacher." *Scottish Review* (London) 24 (July & Oct. 1894): 21–44.

Kelleher, Paul. "'The Glorious Lust of Doing Good': *Tom Jones* and the Virtues of Sexuality." *NOVEL: A Forum on Fiction* 38.2/3 (Spring–Summer 2005): 165–92.

Kern, William S. "Robinson Crusoe and the Economists." Grapard and Hewitson 62–74.

Kerridge, Eric. *Usury, Interest, and the Reformation.* Aldershot, UK: Ashgate, 2002.

Keymer, Thomas. "Fielding's Machiavellian Moment." *Henry Fielding (1707–1754): Novelist, Playwright, Journalist, Magistrate.* Ed. Claude Rawson. Newark: U of Delaware P, 2008. 58–90.

Killigrew, Sir William. *Mid-Night and Daily Thoughts in Prose and Verse.* London, 1694.

Knight, Charles. "Fielding's Afterlife." Rawson, *Cambridge Companion to Henry Fielding* 175–89.

Konczal, Mike. "Robert Kuttner on the Aftermath of Debt Bubbles and Restructuring Debts." *Rortybomb.* 6 June 2011. Web. 21 Mar. 2013.

Korda, Natasha. "Dame Usury: Gender, Credit, and (Ac)counting in the Sonnets and *The Merchant of Venice.*" *Shakespeare Quarterly* 60.2 (Summer 2009): 129–53.

Kramnick, Isaac. *Bolingbroke and His Circle: The Politics of Nostalgia in the Age of Walpole.* Cambridge, MA: Harvard UP, 1968.

Lamb, Jonathan. *The Things Things Say.* Princeton, NJ: Princeton UP, 2011.

Landreth, David. *The Face of Mammon: The Matter of Money in English Renaissance Literature.* Oxford: Oxford UP, 2012.

Langholm, Odd. *The Aristotelian Analysis of Usury.* Bergen, Norway: Universitetsforlaget, 1984.

Laqueur, Thomas. *Making Sex: Body and Gender from the Greeks to Freud.* Cambridge, UP: Harvard UP, 1992.

Laurence, Anne, Josephine Maltby, and Janette Rutterford, eds. *Women and Their Money, 1700–1950: Essays on Women and Finance.* London: Routledge, 2009.

Lawson, William John. *The History of Banking.* London: Bentley, 1850.

Lazzarato, Maurizio. *The Making of the Indebted Man.* Trans. Joshua David Jordan. Los Angeles: Semiotext(e), 2012.

Lecky, William Edward Hartpole. *The History of the Rise and Influence of the Spirit of Rationalism in Europe.* Vol. 2. New York: Appleton, 1870.

Levinas, Emmanuel. *Otherwise than Being or Beyond Essence.* Trans. Alphonso Lingis. The Hague: Martinus Nijhoff, 1981.

Locke, John. *Two Treatises of Government.* Ed. Peter Laslett. Cambridge: Cambridge UP, 2004.

Lockwood, Thomas. "*The Lottery:* Introduction." Fielding, *Plays* 129–45.

———. "*The Modern Husband:* Introduction." Fielding, *Plays* 181–207.

Lodge, Thomas. *An Alarum Against Usurers. Containing Tried Experiences Against Worldly Abuses.* London, 1584.

The Lombard-Street Lecturer's Late Farewell Sermon, Answer'd: or, the Welsh Levite Toss'd De Novo. London, 1692.

Luther, Martin. *Luther's Works.* Vol. 45. Ed. Walther I. Brandt. Philadelphia: Muhlenberg, 1962.

———. *Trade and Usury.* Luther, *Luther's Works*, vol. 45. 245–310.

———. "Trade and Usury." Trans. W. H. Carruth. *Open Court* 9.1 (Jan. 1897): 16–34.

Luttrell, Narcissus. *A Brief Historical Relation of State Affairs: From September 1678 to April 1714.* Vol. 4. Oxford: Oxford UP, 1857.

Macaulay, Thomas Babington. *The History of England.* 1848–61. Ed. Hugh Trevor-Roper. London: Penguin, 1986.

———. *The Works of Lord Macaulay.* Ed. Lady Trevelyan. Vol. 4. London: Longmans, Green, 1875.

Mackay, Charles. *Extraordinary Popular Delusions and the Madness of Crowds.* 1841. New York: Three Rivers, 1980.

Mackie, Erin, ed. *The Commerce of Everyday Life: Selections from The Tatler and The Spectator.* Boston: Bedford/St. Martin's, 1998.

Macpherson, C. B. *The Political Theory of Possessive Individualism: Hobbes to Locke.* New York: Oxford UP, 1962.

Macpherson, Sandra. *Harm's Way: Tragic Responsibility and the Novel Form.* Baltimore: Johns Hopkins UP, 2010.

Mäkikalli, Aino. *From Eternity to Time: Conceptions of Time in Daniel Defoe's Novels.* Bern: Peter Lang, 2007.

Malynes, Gerrard de. *Saint George for England, Allegorically Described.* London, 1601.

Mandeville, Bernard. *Fable of the Bees: or, Private Vices, Publick Benefits.* London, 1714.

Manningham, Thomas. *Of Religious Prudence. A Sermon Preach'd before the Queen at White-Hall, On Sunday, Sept. 17. 1693.* London, 1694.

Marion, Jean-Luc. *The Reason of the Gift.* Trans. Stephen E. Lewis. Charlottesville: U of Virginia P, 2011.

A Master-Key to the Rich Ladies Treasury, or, The Widower and Batchelor Directory. London, 1742.

Mazur, Joseph. *What's Luck Got to Do With It?: The History, Mathematics, and Psychology Behind the Gambler's Illusion.* Princeton, NJ: Princeton UP, 2010.

McCloskey, Deirdre. "Avarice, Prudence, and the Bourgeois Virtues." *Having: Property and Possession in Religious and Social Life.* Ed. William Schweiker and Charles Matthews. Grand Rapids, MI: Eerdmans, 2004. 312–36.

McInelly, Brett. "Expanding Empire, Expanding Selves: Colonialism, the Novel, and Robinson Crusoe." *Studies in the Novel* 35.1 (Spring 2003): 1–21.

McKeon, Michael. "Fielding and the Instrumentality of Belief: *Joseph Andrews.*" Rivero, *Critical Essays* 57–68.

———. *The Origins of the English Novel, 1600–1740.* Baltimore: Johns Hopkins UP, 1987.

———. *The Secret History of Domesticity: Public, Private, and the Division of Knowledge.* Baltimore: Johns Hopkins UP, 2005.

Means, Howard. *Money and Power: The History of Business.* New York: Wiley, 2001.

"Meed, n." *OED Online.* 2014. Web. 15 Oct. 2014.

Memoirs relating to the impeachment of Thomas, Earl of Danby (now Duke of Leeds) in the year 1678. London, 1710.

Meron, Theodore. *Bloody Constraint: War and Chivalry in Shakespeare.* Oxford: Oxford UP, 1998.

Mitchell, Robert. *Sympathy and the State in the Romantic Era: Systems, State Finance, and the Shadows of Futurity.* New York: Routledge, 2007.

Moisan, Thomas. "'Which Is the Merchant Here, and Which the Jew?': Subversion and Recuperation in *The Merchant of Venice.*" *Shakespeare Reproduced: The Text in History and Ideology.* Ed. Jean E. Howard and Marion F. O'Connor. New York: Methuen, 1987. 188–206.

Molesworth, Jesse. *Chance and the Eighteenth-Century Novel: Realism, Probability, Magic.* Cambridge: Cambridge UP, 2010.

Moore, Matthew. "Religious leaders blame bankers' greed for financial crisis." *Telegraph.*
26 Dec. 2008.

Moore, Sean. *Swift, the Book, and the Irish Financial Revolution.* Baltimore: Johns Hopkins UP, 2010.

Morley, Henry, ed. *Shorter English Poems.* London: Cassell Petter & Galpin, 1876.

Morton, Rev. Charles. *Debt's Discharge, or some considerations on Romans 13:8.* London, 1684.

Mosse, Miles. *The Arraignment and Conviction of Usurie. That Is, The iniquitie, and unlawfulness of usurie, displayed in sixe Sermons, preached at Saint Edmunds burie in Suffolk.* London, 1595.

Motteux, Peter Anthony. *The Novelty. Every Act a Play.* London, 1697.

Mr. David Jones's Vindication Against the Athenian Mercury Concerning Usury. London, 1692.

Mulcaire, Terry. "Public Credit; Or, the Feminization of Virtue in the Marketplace." *PMLA* 114.5 (Oct. 1999): 1029–42.

Muldrew, Craig. *The Economy of Obligation: The Culture of Credit and Social Relations in Early Modern England.* New York: St. Martin's, 1998.

Murphy, Anne. "Dealing with Uncertainty: Managing Personal Investment in the Early English National Debt." *History* 91.302 (Apr. 2006): 200–217.

———. "Lotteries in the 1690s: Investment or Gamble?" *Financial History Review* 12.2 (2005): 227–46.

Neal, Larry. *The Rise of Financial Capitalism: International Capital Markets in the Age of Reason.* Cambridge: Cambridge UP, 1990.

Needham, Joseph. "Laud, the Levellers, and the Virtuosi." *Christianity and Social Revolution.* Ed. John Lewis, Karl Polanyi, and Donald K. Kitchin. London: Gollancz, 1935. 163–79.

Nelson, Ben. *The Idea of Usury: From Tribal Brotherhood to Universal Otherhood.* Chicago: U of Chicago P, 1969.

Newell, Margaret Ellen. *From Dependency to Independence.* Ithaca, NY: Cornell UP, 1998.

Nicholson, Colin. *Writing and the Rise of Finance: Capital Satires of the Early Eighteenth Century.* Cambridge: Cambridge UP, 1994.

Noonan, John T., Jr. *The Scholastic Analysis of Usury.* Cambridge, MA: Harvard UP, 1957.

Noorthouck, John, "Langbourn Ward." *A New History of London: Including Westminster and Southwark.* London, 1773. *British History Online.* http://www.british-history.ac.uk/report.aspx?compid=46766.

Norris, John. *Practical discourses upon several divine subjects.* London, 1691.

North, Douglass. *Structure and Change in Economic History.* New York: Norton, 1981.

North, Douglass, and Barry R. Weingast. "Constitutions and Commitment: The Evolution of Institutions Governing Public Choice in Seventeenth-Century England." *Journal of Economic History* 49.4 (Dec. 1989): 803–32.

Novak, Maximillian E., ed. *The Age of Projects.* Toronto: U of Toronto P, 2008.

———. *Daniel Defoe: Master of Fictions*. Oxford: Oxford UP, 2001.

———. "Defoe as an Innovator of Fictional Form." Richetti, *Cambridge Companion to the Eighteenth-Century Novel* 41–71.

———. Introduction. Novak, *Age of Projects*. 3–28.

O'Brien, P. K., and P. A. Hunt. "The Rise of a Fiscal State in England, 1485–1815." *Historical Research* 66 (1993): 129–76.

O'Donovan, Joan Lockwood. "The Theological Economics of Medieval Usury Theory." *Studies in Christian Ethics* 14 (2001): 48–64.

"Of Prudence, and its Profit." *Aristotle's secret of secrets contracted; being the sum of his advice to Alexander the Great, about the preservation of health and government.* London, 1702.

Oldham, James. *English Common Law in the Age of Mansfield*. Chapel Hill: U of North Carolina P, 2004.

Oldmixon, John. *The Secret History of Europe. Part III. Containing, A Review of the Reign of King Charles II from the Year 1670 to 1678.* London, 1712.

The Oxford Study Bible. Ed. M. Jack Suggs, Katherine D. Sakenfeld, and James R. Mueller. New York: Oxford UP, 1992.

Partridge, Eric. *Shakespeare's Bawdy*. London: Routledge, 2001.

Persky, Joseph. "From Usury to Interest." *Journal of Economic Perspectives* 21.1 (Winter 2007): 227–36.

Pesciarelli, Enzo. "Aspects of the Influence of Francis Hutcheson on Adam Smith." *History of Political Economy* 31.3 (1999): 525–45.

Pettit, Alexander. "What the Drama Does in Fielding's *Jonathan Wild*." Rivero, *Critical Essays* 21–34.

Phillips, Edward. *The New World of English Words, or, A General Dictionary Containing the Interpretations of Such Hard Words as Are Derived from Other Languages.* London, 1658.

Phillips, Nicola Jane. *Women in Business, 1700–1850*. Woodbridge, Suffolk, UK: Boydell, 2006.

Philopenes [John Huddleston]. *Usury Explain'd; or, Conscience Quieted in the Case of Putting out Mony at Interest*. London, 1695.

Pincus, Steven C. A. "A Revolution in Political Economy?" Novak, *Age of Projects* 115–40.

———. *1688: The First Modern Revolution*. New Haven, CT: Yale UP, 2009.

Pocock, J. G. A. *The Machiavellian Moment: Florentine Political Thought and the Atlantic Republican Tradition*. Princeton, NJ: Princeton UP, 1975.

———. "Post-Puritan England and the Problem of the Enlightenment." *Culture and Politics from Puritanism to the Enlightenment*. Ed. Perez Zagorin. Berkeley: U of California P, 1980. 91–111.

The Poetical Calendar. Containing a collection of scarce and valuable pieces of poetry. Vol. 10. London, 1763.

Poovey, Mary. *Genres of the Credit Economy: Mediating Value in Eighteenth- and Nineteenth-Century Britain*. Chicago: U of Chicago P, 2008.

Pope, Alexander. *Epistle III: To Bathurst*. Pope, *Poetry and Prose* 176–88.

———. *An Epistle to Allen Lord Bathurst. The Major Works*. Ed. Pat Rogers. Oxford: Oxford UP, 2008. 250–64.

———. *The Poetry and Prose of Alexander Pope*. Ed. Aubrey Williams. Boston: Houghton Mifflin, 1969.

Potter, Tiffany. *Honest Sins: Georgian Libertinism and the Plays and Novels of Henry Fielding*. Montreal: McGill-Queen's UP, 1999.

Preda, Alex. *Framing Finance: The Boundaries of Markets and Modern Capitalism*. Chicago: U of Chicago P, 2009.

The Present State of Europe: or, The Historical and Political Monthly Mercury 20.2 (Feb. 1709). Web. 2 Nov. 2012.

Preus, J. Samuel. "Secularizing Divination: Spiritual Biography and the Invention of the Novel." *Journal of the American Academy of Religion* 59.3 (Autumn 1991): 441–66.

Price, Jacob M. "Heathcote, Sir Gilbert, first baronet (1652–1733)." *Oxford Dictionary of National Biography*. Ed. H. C. G. Matthew and Brian Harrison. Oxford: Oxford UP, 2004. Online ed. Ed. Lawrence Goldman. http://www.oxforddnb.com/view/article/12847.

"Prudence, n." *OED Online*. 2013. Web. 13 Feb. 2014.

Rabelais, François. *The fifth book of The Works of Francis Rabelais, M.D., containing the heroic deeds and sayings of the great Pantagruel to which is added the Pantagruelian prognostication*. Trans. P. Motteux. London, 1694.

Randall, David. "The Prudential Public Sphere." *Philosophy and Rhetoric* 44.3 (2011): 205–26.

Rawson, Claude, ed. *The Cambridge Companion to Henry Fielding*. Cambridge: Cambridge UP, 2007.

———. "Henry Fielding." Richetti, *Cambridge Companion to the Eighteenth-Century Novel* 120–52.

Reilly, Patrick. *Tom Jones: Adventure and Providence*. Boston: Twayne, 1991.

Reinking, Conradus [Patrick Ker]. *Politikos megas: the grand politician or The secret art of state-policy discovered. In evident demonstrations of unparalleled prudence . . . by the most remarkable witts of former ages*. London, 1691.

"Return, n." *OED Online*. 2013. http://www.oed.com/

"Review of Gerard Noodt, *De Fœnere et Usuris*." *The History of the Works of the Learned or, An Impartial Account of Books Lately Printed in all Parts of Europe. With a Particular Relation of the State of Learning in Each Country*. Vol. 1. London, 1699. 85–88. *Eighteenth Century Journals Portal*. 5 Oct. 2012.

Ribble, Frederick G. "Aristotle and the 'Prudence' Theme of *Tom Jones*." *Eighteenth-Century Studies* 15.1 (Autumn 1981): 26–47.

Richard, Jessica. *The Romance of Gambling in the Eighteenth-Century British Novel*. Houndmills, Basingstoke, Hants: Palgrave Macmillan, 2011.

Richetti, John, ed. *The Cambridge Companion to the Eighteenth-Century Novel*. Cambridge: Cambridge UP, 1996.

———. *Popular Fiction before Richardson: Narrative Patterns, 1700–1739*. Oxford: Clarendon, 1969.

Rivero, Albert J., ed. *Critical Essays on Henry Fielding*. London: Hall, 1998.

———. "The Politics of the Playhouse: *Pasquin* and *The Historical Register for the Year 1736.*" Rivero, *Critical Essays* 10–34.

Robbins, Jeremy. "Prudence and the Compass of Deceit." *Bulletin of Spanish Studies* 82.8 (2005): 97–130.

Rosengarten, Richard A. *Henry Fielding and the Narration of Providence: Divine Design and the Incursions of Evil*. New York: Palgrave, 2000.

Roseveare, Henry. *The Financial Revolution, 1660–1760*. New York: Longman, 1991.

Rotenberg-Schwartz, Michael, and Tara Czechowski, eds. *Global Economies, Cultural Currencies of the Eighteenth Century*. New York: AMS, 2012.

Rothschild, Emma. *Economic Sentiments: Adam Smith, Condorcet and the Enlightenment*. Cambridge, MA: Harvard UP, 2001.

Rowell, David, and Luke B. Connelley. "A History of the Term 'Moral Hazard.'" *Journal of Risk and Insurance* 79.4 (2012): 1051–75.

Roy, Douglas. *Taxation in Britain since 1660*. Houndmills, Basingstoke, Hants: Macmillan, 1999.

Ruskin, John. *Ariadne Florentina*. Ruskin, *Works* 22:292–490.

———. *Fors Clavigera: Letters to the Workmen and Labourers of Great Britain*. Vol. 2. Ruskin, *Works*, vol. 28.

———. *The Letters of John Ruskin. Volume 2: 1870–1889*. Ed. E. T. Cook and Alexander Wedderburn. London: George Allen, 1909. Ruskin, *Works*, vol. 37.

———. Letter to Henry Willett. 8 Jan. 1878. Ruskin, *Letters* 236–37.

———. Letter to Rev. F. A. Malleson. 9 Sept. 1879. Ruskin, *Letters* 298.

———. *Præterita: Outlines of Scenes and Thoughts Perhaps Worthy of Memory in My Past Life*. Vol. 1. Sunnyside, Orpington, Kent: George Allen, 1886.

———. *"Unto This Last" and Other Writings*. Ed. Clive Wilmer. London: Penguin, 1985. 159–228.

———. "Usury: A Reply and Rejoinder." 1880. Ruskin, *Works* 34:398–425.

———. *The Works of John Ruskin*. Ed. E. T. Cook and Alexander Wedderburn. 39 vols. London: George Allen, 1903–12.

"Ruskin on Usury." *Morning Light: A New-Church Weekly Journal* 112.3 (21 Feb. 1880): 74–75.

Sanderson, Robert. "Sermon IV: In St. Paul's Church, London 4 November, 1621." *Ad Populum. The Works of Robert Sanderson, D.D.* Vol. 3. Oxford: Oxford UP, 1854. 91–144.

———. *Ten Sermons Preached*. London, 1627.

Schabas, Margaret. *The Natural Origins of Economics*. Chicago: U of Chicago P, 2005.

Schama, Simon. *The Embarrassment of Riches: An Interpretation of Dutch Culture in the Golden Age*. Berkeley: U of California P, 1988.

Schmidgen, Wolfram. *Eighteenth-Century Fiction and the Law of Property*. Cambridge: Cambridge UP, 2002.

Scott, W. R. *The Constitution and Finance of English, Scottish and Irish Joint-Stock Companies to 1720*. Vol. 1. Cambridge: Cambridge UP, 1911.

Seager, Nicholas. "Prudence and Plagiarism in the 1740 Continuation of Defoe's *Roxana*." *The Library: Transactions of the Bibliographical Society* 10.4 (Dec. 2009): 357–71.

See and Seem Blind: Or, A Critical Dissertation on the Publick Diversions, &c. June 1732.

Seidel, Kevin. "*Robinson Crusoe* as Defoe's Theory of Fiction." *Novel: A Forum on Fiction* 44:2 (Summer 2011): 165–85.

Sen, Amartya. *On Ethics and Economics.* Oxford: Basil Blackwell, 1987.

Shakespeare, William. *The Merchant of Venice.* Ed. Leah S. Marcus. New York: Norton, 2006.

Sharpe, Kevin, and Steven Zwicker. "Introduction: Refiguring Revolutions." *Refiguring Revolutions: Aesthetics and Politics from the English Revolution to the Romantic Revolution.* Ed. Sharpe and Zwicker. Berkeley: U of California P, 1998. 1–21.

Shaw, Samuel. *The True Christians Test, or, Discovery of the Love and Lovers of the World.* London, 1682.

Sherlock, William. *The Charity of Lending without Usury and The True Notion of Usury briefly stated. In a Sermon Preach'd before the Right Honourable The Lord Mayor, at St. Bridget's Church, on Tuesday in Easter-Week.* London, 1692.

Sherman, Sandra. *Finance and Fictionality in the Early Eighteenth Century: Accounting for Defoe.* Cambridge: Cambridge UP, 1996.

Shesgreen, Sean. *Engravings by Hogarth.* New York: Dover, 1973.

Sill, Geoffrey. *The Cure of the Passions and the Origins of the English Novel.* Cambridge: Cambridge UP, 2001.

Sinclair, Sir John. *The History of the Public Revenue of the British Empire.* New York: Kelly, 1966.

Skinner, Gillian. *Sensibility and Economics in the Novel, 1740–1800: The Price of a Tear.* Houndmills, Basingstoke, Hants: Macmillan, 1999.

Smith, Adam. *An Inquiry in the Nature and Causes of the Wealth of Nations.* Ed. R. H. Campbell, A. S. Skinner, and W. B. Todd. 2 vols. Indianapolis: Liberty Fund, 1981.

———. *The Theory of Moral Sentiments.* Ed. D. D. Raphael and A. L. Macfie. Indianapolis: Liberty Fund, 1982.

Smith, Nathaniel. *Observations on East India Shipping; being a comparative view between the freights of 1773, and those of the seven preceding years.* London, 1774.

Smollett, Tobias. *Travels through France and Italy. Containing Observations on Character, Customs, Religion, Government, Police, Commerce, Arts, and Antiquities.* Vol. 2. Dublin, 1772.

Stafford, Fiona. *The Last of the Race: The Growth of a Myth from Milton to Darwin.* Oxford: Oxford UP, 1994.

Starr, G. A. *Defoe and Spiritual Autobiography.* Princeton, NJ: Princeton UP, 1965.

Stewart, Dugald. *Lectures on Political Economy.* Vol. 2 of *Collected Works of Dugald Stewart.* Edinburgh: Constable, 1856.

Sullivan, Ceri. *The Rhetoric of Credit: Merchants in Early Modern Writing.* London: Associated UP, 2002.

Sylla, Richard. "Origins of the New York Stock Exchange." *The Origins of Value: The*

Financial Innovations that Created Modern Capital Markets. Ed. William N. Goetz-
mann and K. Geert Rouwenhorst. Oxford: Oxford UP, 2005. 299–312.

Taeusch, C. F. "Business Ethics." *International Journal of Ethics* 42.3 (Apr. 1932): 273–88.

Tawney, R. H. *Religion and the Rise of Capitalism: A Historical Study.* Gloucester, MA:
Peter Smith, 1962.

Taylor, Charles. *A Secular Age.* Cambridge, MA: Harvard UP, 2007.

Tenison, Thomas. "Letter, unsigned." Sept. 1727. MS 2716, f222. Archbishops' Papers.
Lambeth Palace Library. London.

Thompson, James. *Models of Value: Eighteenth-Century Political Economy and the Novel.*
Durham, NC: Duke UP, 1996.

Thornton, William. *The Counterpoise, Being Thoughts on a Militia and a Standing Army.*
London, 1753.

Todeschini, Giacomo. "Usury in the Christian Middle Ages: A Reconsideration of the
Historiographical Tradition (1949–2010)." *Religion and Religious Institutions in the
European Economy: 1000–1800.* Ed. Francesco Ammannati. Florence: Firenze UP,
2012. 119–30. Academia.edu. 1 Oct. 2014.

Trevelyan, George Otto. *The Early History of Charles James Fox.* London: Longmans,
Green, 1881.

Troup, Frances B. "Biographical Sketch of the Rev. Christopher Jelinger, M.A." *Report
and Transactions of the Devonshire Association* 32 (1900): 249–70.

Turner, Thomas. *The Joyful News of the Opening of the Exchequer to the Gold-Smiths of
Lombard-street, and their Creditors.* London, 1677.

Valeri, Mark. *Heavenly Merchandize: How Religion Shaped Commerce in Puritan America.*
Princeton, NJ: Princeton UP, 2010.

———. "William Petty in Boston: Political Economy, Religion, and Money in Provincial
New England." *Early American Studies: An Interdisciplinary Journal* 8.3 (Fall 2010):
549–80.

Vanbrugh, Sir John. *A Short Vindication of The Relapse and The Provok'd Wife from
Immorality and Prophaneness.* London, 1698.

Varey, Simon. *Henry Fielding.* New York: Cambridge UP, 1986.

Wallace, Dewey D., Jr. "Morton, Charles (*bap.* 1627, *d.* 1698)." *Oxford Dictionary of
National Biography.* Oxford: Oxford UP, 2004. Online ed. Ed. Lawrence Goldman.
http://www.oxforddnb.com/view/article/19360.

Ward, Edward. *A Hue and Cry after a Man-Midwife Who Has Lately Delivered the
Land-Bank of their Money.* London, 1699.

———. *The London-Spy Compleat. In Eighteen Parts.* London, 1700.

———. "The Lotteries." Mackie 251–55.

———. *The Rambling Rakes, or, London Libertines, by the author of The Step to the Bath.*
London, 1700.

Watt, Ian. *The Rise of the Novel: Studies in Defoe, Richardson, and Fielding.* 2nd American
ed. Berkeley: U of California P, 2001.

Weber, Max. *The Protestant Ethic and the Spirit of Capitalism.* Trans. Talcott Parsons.
London: Routledge, 2002.

Webster, Noah. *An American Dictionary of the English Language.* New York: Converse, 1828.

———. *A Collection of Essays and Fugitiv Writings.* Boston, 1790.

Weed, David M. "Sexual Positions: Men of Pleasure, Economy, and Dignity in Boswell's *London Journal.*" *Eighteenth-Century Studies* 31.2 (1997–98): 215–34.

Wennerlind, Carl. *Casualties of Credit: The English Financial Revolution, 1620–1720.* Cambridge, MA: Harvard UP, 2011.

Westberg, Daniel. *Right Practical Reason: Aristotle, Action, and Prudence in Aquinas.* Oxford: Clarendon, 1994.

"What Is Usury?" *Saturday Review of Politics, Literature, Science, and Art,* 7 Feb. 1880, 178–79.

White, George. *An Account of the Trade to the East-Indies.* London, 1691.

White, Hayden. *Tropics of Discourse: Essays in Cultural Criticism.* Baltimore: Johns Hopkins UP, 1997.

White, Michael V. "Reading and Rewriting: The Production of an Economic *Robinson Crusoe.*" Grapard and Hewitson 15–41.

Whyte, Lawrence. "To Mrs. Mary and Elizabeth Burgh." *Poems on Various Subjects, Serious and Diverting.* Dublin, 1740. 185–89.

Williams, Raymond. *Marxism and Literature.* Oxford: Oxford UP, 1977.

Wilputte, Earla A. "Wife Pandering in Three Eighteenth-Century Plays." *Studies in English Literature, 1500–1900* 38.3 (Summer 1998): 447–64.

Woods, Charles B. "Notes on Three of Fielding's Plays." *PMLA* 52.2 (June 1937): 359–73.

Worden, Skip. *Godliness and Greed: Shifting Christian Thought on Profit and Wealth.* Lanham, MD: Lexington, 2010.

Wykes, Michael. "Devaluing the Scholastics: Calvin's Ethics of Usury." *Calvin Theological Journal* 38 (2003): 27–51.

Index